Bonhoeffer

as

Youth Worker

Andrew Root

Baker Academic
a division of Baker Publishing Group
Grand Rapids, Michigan

Published by Baker Academic
a division of Baker Publishing Group
P.O. Box 6287, Grand Rapids, MI 49516-6287
www.bakeracademic.com

Printed in the United States of America

Library of Congress Cataloging-in-Publication Data
Root, Andrew, 1974–
    Bonhoeffer as youth worker : a theological vision for discipleship and life
together / Andrew Root.
        pages cm
    Includes bibliographical references and index.
    ISBN 978-0-8010-4905-7 (pbk.)
    1. Bonhoeffer, Dietrich, 1906–1945. 2. Church work with youth. I. Title.
BX4827.B57R66 2014
259′.23092—dc23   2014011051

14   15   16   17   18   19   20   7   6   5   4   3   2

In keeping with biblical principles of creation stewardship, Baker Publishing Group advocates the responsible use of our natural resources. As a member of the Green Press Initiative, our company uses recycled paper when possible. The text paper of this book is composed in part of post-consumer waste.

To Owen,
who is so much like the ten-year-old
who lost Mr. Wolf

Contents

Part 2 A Youth Worker's Guide to *Discipleship* and *Life Together*

Preface

B ooks are always written for someone. Usually the best books are
written for the author. Especially theological books, I believe, need
to be written for the author by the author. The reader is blessed by
participating in the ministry of the theologian who is brave enough
to wrestle with God for faith as he or she writes. The very classic
theological texts of the Christian tradition like Athanasius's *On the
Incarnation*, Augustine's *Confessions*, Luther's *Freedom of the Christian*, and even Barth's *Epistle to the Romans* seem to be written first
and foremost for the author.

This book you hold promises none of the impact of those listed
above. Yet this book too was written first and foremost for me. This
book comes out of great joy. It allowed me to sketch out something
that I had seen in the life of Bonhoeffer that no other Bonhoeffer
thinker had directly addressed. In this project I devoted the time and
concentration to dive headlong into the history of Bonhoeffer, a story
that has intrigued me for nearly two decades. It also allowed me to
show something about Bonhoeffer's life that I deeply hope is a blessing to many ministers out in the day-to-day struggle of standing with
and for young people.

So it is true that books are for the author, but they must also be
let out into the world to become books for others as well. This book
is first for the youth worker, the minister to youth. It is a book that
explores how Dietrich Bonhoeffer—the great theological mind of the
twentieth century that lived his faith all the way to death—was a youth

minister himself. As a matter of fact, this book shows that there is nearly no time between 1925 and 1939 (the core of Bonhoeffer's life) that he was not doing either children's or youth ministry. My great hope is that this book is a gift to youth workers, showing them that their calling stands on the broad shoulders of Bonhoeffer. In these pages they will not only see Dietrich's own youth work, but I hope they will also be inspired as I seek to tease out the ramifications of Bonhoeffer's thought for their own ministry today.

So while this book is first for the youth worker, it is also for Bonhoeffer scholars. While for youth ministers I offer the encouragement of revealing Bonhoeffer as one that goes before them, to Bonhoeffer scholars I hope to reveal a lacuna in Bonhoeffer discourse. There has been no thorough examination of Dietrich Bonhoeffer's youth work, and often conversations about it have been presented in order to make other points. For instance, discussion of his Sunday school leadership in Harlem has not engendered conversations about why this young man always chose youth ministry over other forms of ministry. I offer this book as just such a study of the centrality of Bonhoeffer's youth work.

When books move from being for the author to being for others, there are usually intermediaries, or even midwives, that help this move to occur, checking on the health of the project to make sure it is fit for the world. I have been blessed with such people in relation to this project. Dirk Lange, my colleague at Luther Seminary, was so kind to give time from his sabbatical to read through this project. Dan Adams, an American pastor ministering in South Africa, also took the time from writing his own thesis on Bonhoeffer to read this project. I've been blessed in the last seven years to travel often and to meet so many faithful ministers of the gospel across the world. Dan was one of these people, and his insight as a budding Bonhoeffer scholar and youth minister was rich. I would also like to thank Bob Hosack at Baker, who saw the vision for this book. Robert Hand at Baker also provided significant help in making this project more readable. Thanks also to Erik Leafblad for the hard work on the index. But finally, my biggest thanks goes to Kara Root, who is *always* the first to read anything I write and provide insight on argument, style, and direction. I first studied Bonhoeffer in seminary with Kara, so it only makes sense that in this full-length book, her fingerprints would be all over it.

1

Youth Ministry and Bonhoeffer

Finding a Forefather

The room was packed with youth workers, and I knew their presence had nothing to do with me. I was brand new in the youth-ministry presenting world, and, for the most part, these youth workers had no idea who I was. I had already done an earlier breakout session at this big conference, on a topic directly related to youth ministry, like "Caring for Hurting Teenagers" or something similar. During that session, my room, ready to receive hundreds, saw only a trickle of twenty or so skeptical participants walk in, spreading themselves from one end to the next as if it were a competition to always keep a dozen chairs between them. The largest collective stayed near the door, comforted that if things went lame they could make it down the hall to another presentation before long.

I was expecting pretty much the same for this second breakout session, and my inner forecaster expected the drought of participants to not only continue but worsen. After all, the first presentation had been more directly on the practice of youth ministry, on the *practical*.

And if there was anything that the youth workers at this conference wanted, it was the know-how of the practical.

As I readied my computer for this second presentation, shifting cords and moving keynote slides, a trickle of youth workers already began to enter the room. Soon the trickle became a steady stream that surged to become a flood. Now youth worker after youth worker sought seats before they disappeared into the humanity of one another, sliding by each other to grab a chair in the middle of rows. All these practical, thirsty-for-know-how-and-new-ideas youth workers were cramming themselves together, coming to hear something promising no practicality at all; they had no idea who I was or how this topic would help them. Nevertheless they came—and only because my title read, "Dietrich Bonhoeffer and Youth Ministry."

As I concluded my fifty minutes of rambling, youth worker after youth worker lined up to talk to me. Yet almost none had a question; rather, they stood to give a confession, saying to me, "Hey, thanks; Bonhoeffer is my hero," or "I came because I just find Bonhoeffer so interesting." I stood for nearly an hour hearing one after another confess how this German man had impacted them. Many explained in shameful candor that they actually knew little about Bonhoeffer, but that the little they knew drew them in deeply and impacted them significantly.

Bonhoeffer and Youth Ministry

It was clear that day that youth workers were not unlike so many others who find intrigue and inspiration from Dietrich Bonhoeffer. Bonhoeffer ranks high on nearly every list of influential Christians; and across very distinct groups (whether liberal or conservative, mainline or evangelical, youth worker or senior pastor),[1] nearly all include Bonhoeffer in either their formal or informal pantheon of impactful leaders.

Yet it just may be that youth workers have a particular (and so often unexplored) connection with Bonhoeffer. Youth workers, as my experience highlights, have an admiration for Bonhoeffer, but hearing their confessions that day, none articulated (or seemed to know)

1. Stephen Haynes discusses this list in his interesting *The Bonhoeffer Phenomenon: Portraits of a Protestant Saint* (Minneapolis: Fortress, 2004).

how Bonhoeffer was connected to them through a shared calling to minister to young people. It seems, in fact, that most Bonhoeffer lovers (not to mention scholars) have forgotten or overlooked the amount and depth of youth ministry that encompassed his life and work. It may be even fair to say (as I'll try to show below) that a central way to understand Bonhoeffer is as a pastor to youth and/or as a talented thinker who constructed some of the most creative theological perspectives of the early twentieth century with young people on his mind. Youth workers, like so many others, feel drawn to Bonhoeffer, but few have seen the links that connect them to Bonhoeffer, feeling he's just a theologian they like rather than a forefather to their very calling. This forefather may stand at the beginning of a slowly evolving movement in youth ministry itself.

A Forefather to a Movement

It can be argued that youth ministry is a post–World War II North American phenomenon.[2] This, then, would make it quite strange to call its forefather a German man who was killed in 1945. Actually, as we'll see in the chapters below, Dietrich Bonhoeffer more than likely would have been strongly against many of the forms American youth ministry has taken since its inception. Bonhoeffer, after all, was against overly exuberant ministerial endeavors like the Oxford Movement[3] and had certain disdain for the entrepreneurial spirit of American religion and its desire to always be *doing* without thinking (and confessing) the faith.[4] Dietrich Bonhoeffer, in intellectual pursuit

2. Of course there were many youth-oriented or youth-directed ministers prior to the middle of the twentieth century, but youth ministry as the professional phenomenon that it is today can be seen as beginning to take shape post–World War II in North America. For more on this history, see Andrew Root, *Revisiting Relational Youth Ministry* (Downers Grove, IL: InterVarsity, 2007); Mark Senter, *The Coming Revolution in Youth Ministry* (Wheaton: Victor Books, 1992); and Thomas Bergler, *The Juvenilization of American Christianity* (Grand Rapids: Eerdmans, 2012).

3. Bonhoeffer came into contact with the English Oxford Movement during his time at Finkenwalde. It was assumed that this English ministry and Bonhoeffer's own seminary community overlapped. But Bonhoeffer saw none, having harsh words to say about their exuberant displays of spirituality.

4. See, for example, his piece *Protestantism without Reformation* (Dietrich Bonhoeffer Works, 15:438), as well as the many letters to Max Diestel back in Germany in 1930–31 about his experience of the American church. Bonhoeffer was no fan.

and personal disposition, was far from the stereotypical image we have of the contemporary youth worker.

So it would not be right in any way to call Dietrich Bonhoeffer the forefather of North American–like youth ministry. But it would also be a great oversight not to see how central ministry to youth was for Bonhoeffer. Therefore, when I call Bonhoeffer a forefather to a movement, I mean to disconnect youth ministry from its post–World War II North American phenomenon and link Bonhoeffer with what Kenda Creasy Dean and I have called "the theological turn in youth ministry" (something we see as more global and reflective than post–World War II North American youth ministry).[5]

Dean and I have noticed, and sought to foster, a slowly evolving movement of youth workers that have taken what we've called a theological turn. These are youth workers who, in response to their previous ministry or the larger ethos of American youth ministry's "industrial complex," have sought to move into the theological. They have turned to the theological not for the sake of the academic or the intellectual but for the sake of the ministerial. They believe that turning theological can give them frameworks and direction in doing ministry with and for young people.

These are youth workers who have shifted from seeing youth ministry as a technical pursuit that seeks the functional ends of solving a problem, like getting young people religiously committed, entertained, or morally and spiritually safe. Instead, they see youth ministry as a concrete locale to reflect upon and participate in the action of God.[6] They have turned theological as a way of directing the very shape of their ministries.

Or we could say it this way: American youth ministry, since its inception in the mid-twentieth century, has been engendered with a technological mind-set; North American youth ministry has been a *technology*. It is no surprise that the age of the technological—the age in which American society was gripped by a consumptive drive for the

5. See Andrew Root and Kenda Creasy Dean, *The Theological Turn in Youth Ministry* (Downers Grove, IL: InterVarsity, 2011).

6. See also my series A Theological Journey through Youth Ministry; the four titles are *Taking Theology to Youth Ministry* (Grand Rapids: Zondervan, 2012); *Taking the Cross to Youth Ministry* (Grand Rapids: Zondervan, 2012); *Unpacking Scripture in Youth Ministry* (Grand Rapids: Zondervan, 2013); and *Unlocking Eschatology and Mission in Youth Ministry* (Grand Rapids: Zondervan, 2013).

new and better (that only a technological society could provide)—was the age of contemporary American youth ministry's beginnings.

Technology is science used for functional ends, to achieve or solve some problem that will result in increased capital.[7] Youth ministry was created as a technology, needed to solve the problem of adolescent religious apathy, and thus it existed for functional growth, as all technologies do. Youth ministry was created to increase capital by solving the technical problem for which it was created. This functional problem was low religious commitment (kids didn't like church) and immoral behavior (kids were doing drugs, having sex, and not reading their Bibles). As a technology created to functionally solve these problems, youth ministry could only be judged by its increased capital; if *more* kids were coming to church or youth group on Sunday and Wednesday, and if more kids were sober and sexually pure, youth ministry was successful—it was meeting the functional end it was created for. And as a technology, its good (its reason to exist at all) was only for accomplishing its functional end by expanding the desired capital.

This technological ethos has begun to feel like a noose around the neck of many youth workers. Tied up in this technological ethos, it feels as if their ministry is always in search of the next big program, model, or idea. In other words, it's looking for the next big technological breakthrough that will finally help them exponentially increase their capital (yielding a big youth group filled with virgins). Some youth workers have begun to wonder if there is not more to ministry, or if ministry is even something different altogether than managing technologies to increase religious capital. They are wondering about God, and God's action in youth ministry, or whether such deep thoughts and reflection are sucked dry by youth ministry's technological addictions. It is those that have taken the brave step away from the technological and sought the action of God in their ministries with youth that have taken *the theological turn*.

I was shocked at the attendance of my Bonhoeffer presentation at the conference because the topic (and, as I hope to show, Bonhoeffer himself) stood opposed to the binding of (youth) ministry to the

---

7. This capital could be social, cultural, or much more. But most often this capital is economic. Innovation often happens or is sponsored because of the money it might make, because of the increases it might bring.

technological. In fact, it may be in part this very different starting point of Bonhoeffer's that attracts so many to him. We hear something different in Bonhoeffer, something that moves us away from our addiction to ministry technology, something that turns us to place our ministries on the revelation of God.

Turning to the Forefather

Dean and I have noticed and sought to perpetuate a turn of youth ministry from the *technological* to the *theological*. We have tried to encourage youth workers to see youth ministry not for solving a functional problem that, when resolved, will increase capital (the technological), but instead to see youth ministry as a locale to encounter the revelation of God next to the humanity of young people themselves (the theological). Youth ministry, we believe, seeks to reflect deeply on the action of God in and through the lives of young people who are both within and outside the church.

But I need to be precise and say that the turn to the theological is not, and is different from, a turn to *theology*.[8] To turn to theology is to turn solely to doctrines and traditions, believing that if you can get such information into young people's heads that you've met your goal. A turn to theology would risk a retreat away from the concrete and lived experience of young people.[9] Rather, we call this a *theological* turn because it seeks to explore the very concrete[10] and

8. This is similar to an argument Mark Lewis Taylor makes. Though my thoughts and his are very different in many ways, I find his distinction between theology and the theological helpful here. See *The Theological and the Political: On the Weight of the World* (Minneapolis: Fortress, 2011).

9. Here Bonhoeffer, in his own words, points toward the theological: "Theology is the interpretation of the confession from particular viewpoints and the ongoing testing of the confession against the scriptures. Faith arises from the preaching of the word of God alone. It does not need theology, but true preaching needs the confession and theology. Faith, which arises from preaching, in turn seeks its confirmation in scripture and the confessions and thus itself does theology" (*Conspiracy and Imprisonment: 1940–1945*, Dietrich Bonhoeffer Works [Minneapolis: Fortress, 2006], 16:494).

10. Ernst Feil says, "Bonhoeffer sought God as the *concretissimum*; to him God was both concrete reality and the mystery that is close to us. In God there is true reality which transcends what is alleged to be reality understood positivistically" (*The Theology of Dietrich Bonhoeffer* [Philadelphia: Fortress, 1985], 39).

lived experience young people have as the location for encounter with God.[11]

A youth ministry that turns to *theology* seeks to move young people into forms of formal knowledge (to assimilate to the doctrinal). A youth ministry bound in the *technological* seeks to increase numbers and behavior. A youth ministry that turns to the *theological* seeks to share in the concrete and lived experience of young people as the very place to share in the act and being of God.[12]

For those of us seeking to live into the theological turn in youth ministry, I seek in the pages of this project to show Dietrich Bonhoeffer as our forefather. It would be impossible to make Bonhoeffer the forefather of technological North American youth ministry. Not only will his history and context not allow for it, but his very thought and commitments stand in opposition to it. In the same way, it would be hard to make Bonhoeffer a forefather to the turn to *theology* in youth ministry. Bonhoeffer was, without doubt, conversant with doctrine and confessions, even teaching them to his confirmation students. But in the end, the very shape of Bonhoeffer's ministry to young people reveals that his desire was not for getting information into their heads but for sharing in their lives as a way of mutually experiencing the very revelation of God in Jesus Christ.

It is this theological attention, this focus on God's act in our concrete lives, that I believe makes Bonhoeffer so intriguing to so many, and it is the fact that he himself lived and died seeking to follow Jesus Christ in the concrete and lived that draws roomfuls of people to come hear his story.[13]

11. With this as its commitment the theological may no doubt, as my work has, turn to the doctrinal. I'm deeply *for* doctrine. However, following Bonhoeffer, we must be moved into discourse with the doctrinal *through* the concrete and lived. To cut off the concrete and lived is to fall into the trap of "theology" as I'm using it here.

12. This theological focus I have also called *Christopraxis*. *Christopraxis* is a perspective that has its origins in the thought of Ray Anderson, who came to this perspective through a deep reading of Dietrich Bonhoeffer. Yet this theological focus also has strong resonance with more recent missional theology. It is Dean's attention to missional theology, as well as our mutually being impacted by practical theological perspectives, that moves us to see the theological as we do.

13. David Hopper explains further the importance of the concrete:

In his Chicago lectures of 1961, [Eberhard] Bethge made this motif of "concreteness" the subject of his opening discussion of Bonhoeffer's thought. He made

Dietrich Bonhoeffer, I will argue then, is the forefather to those taking the *theological* turn in youth ministry. For those of us seeking to make such a turn, I hope to show how we stand on the shoulders of Bonhoeffer, and how we might claim him and learn from him as we turn theological in youth ministry. Dietrich Bonhoeffer is the forefather to the theological turn because he incomparably weaves together youth work, attention to concrete experience, and commitment to the revelatory nature of God's continued action in the world through Jesus Christ. In these pages, then, Bonhoeffer will be our teacher. We will explore the richness of his theological projects, seeing from his life and writings what we might learn for our own contemporary theological turn.

Therefore, to start this journey, we must begin where all conversations about Bonhoeffer must: with his biography. Nearly every Bonhoeffer book published has been unable to resist a chapter or two on biography. This project hopes not simply to be pulled in by the intrigue of Bonhoeffer's story (though it is quite intriguing) but to mine his narrative and tell a piece of Bonhoeffer's story that has been so often overlooked or underplayed: Bonhoeffer's very work as a minister to youth. Therefore, in part 1 I will seek to tell the story of Dietrich Bonhoeffer, the youth worker; in part 2 I'll explore two of Bonhoeffer's most important writings—*Discipleship* and *Life Together*—for their relevance to youth ministry today.

---

two points in this connection: first, that for Bonhoeffer concreteness was an "attribute of revelation itself," and secondly, that the message of the church to the world had to also be concrete. In regard to the first point, Bethge asserted that in the early writings and continuing throughout the later, "Incarnation is . . . at the heart of Bonhoeffer's theology. There cannot be any speculation about a God before or outside this concreteness. The incarnated God is the only one we know. We cannot even think of concreteness as an addition God put on later to his being. All we know, and this is breathtaking, is that the incarnated concreteness IS the attribute as far as we can think." (*A Dissent on Bonhoeffer* [Philadelphia: Westminster, 1975], 64)

Part
1

The History of Dietrich Bonhoeffer, the Youth Worker

2

Dietrich Bonhoeffer, the Youth Worker

I made a bold statement at the end of chapter 1 that I now need to justify. I have asserted that *Dietrich Bonhoeffer is the first theological youth worker*. This statement is slightly hyperbolic, though I'm ready to stand behind it. It is hyperbolic because to say "first" is quite hard to prove. There clearly have been other pastors or theologians in the history of the church (and particularly outside Protestantism) that could be argued to predate Bonhoeffer as theologians of youth work or youth ministry, though I do think it could be very difficult to connect a figure earlier than the twentieth century with doing so. This would be difficult because our modern conceptions of childhood and, most particularly, adolescence were not nearly as present and defined as they were in Bonhoeffer's own time and after.

Yet the point of this chapter is not to debate primacy; I admit that it is hard to prove the "first" in my statement. But while the "first-ness" is hard to prove, the "theological" element of my statement is beyond debate. It would be difficult to see Bonhoeffer in any other light than a theological one. He is, after all, the author of intricate theological books like *Act and Being*, significant christological lectures, and essays on ethics. And these are not simply works of theology, but, as almost all Bonhoeffer interpreters would agree, theological (as I defined it in the last chapter). Bonhoeffer was, from first to last, seeking to think about God's act in and through the concrete and lived. There are few, I would imagine, who would challenge the "theological" in my assertion.

Yet what is at stake in this chapter is my statement that *Dietrich Bonhoeffer is . . . [a] youth worker*. The goal of part 1 of this book is to show this point historically. But I hope to do more with part 1 than just show that Bonhoeffer did youth work. I will also make a case that Bonhoeffer's theological work was impacted by his ministry to youth, showing that his youth work (youth ministry) was central to him and formative for his conceptions of ministry.

"The Bonhoeffer Phenomenon"

Any biographical work on Dietrich Bonhoeffer comes with a danger, which is to read Bonhoeffer's biography as simply supporting one's own commitments. Dietrich Bonhoeffer has often become the mascot of many divergent groups, all claiming him as their saint.

It is quite unusual to have such rich historical material on a person (there is no shortage of long scholarly biographies on Bonhoeffer) and yet find such divergent interpretations of him. Stephen Haynes has called this reality the "Bonhoeffer Phenomenon."[1] Haynes explains that the Bonhoeffer phenomenon revolves around what I saw in my youth worker presentation in chapter 1: an overwhelming love for Bonhoeffer that is too often combined with a lack of understanding of the very biography of Bonhoeffer (the scholarly biographies are rarely read).

But who was Bonhoeffer really? What commitments shaped his thought and ministry? Part 1 not only seeks to reveal Bonhoeffer as a youth worker but also hopes to inform youth workers of who Dietrich Bonhoeffer was, helping them into the story and shape of his life.

1. See Haynes, *Bonhoeffer Phenomenon*.

The Revolutionaries

Haynes explains more in depth how three divergent groups have claimed Bonhoeffer, making a part of his biography central to justify a theological or ministerial position of their own. The first group to do this Haynes calls "the revolutionaries." It was actually this group that ushered Bonhoeffer from obscurity to fame. Bonhoeffer, for the most part, died as an unknown young pastor and theologian. He had written some books and impressed many (including Karl Barth) with his potential. But "in potential" is tragically how he died, swallowed by the war before he could make a true impact.

Nevertheless, two decades after his tragic death, his impact came; it erupted with the publication of Bonhoeffer's Tegel prison letters (*Letters and Papers from Prison* in English). These letters were seized by a number of English-speaking revolutionary theologians in the 1960s who were exploring an atheistic Christianity. They pounced on certain phrases and thoughts in Bonhoeffer to support their own position. Most particularly, Bonhoeffer's conception of "religionless Christianity" caught their attention, making Bonhoeffer the face of radical (anti-)Christianity. Haynes states, "For radicals Bonhoeffer is a 'seer'—a man born out of time who perceived the future with uncanny prescience."[2]

As Haynes explains further, Bonhoeffer's prison experience became central to who he was for the revolutionaries.[3] They out-and-out ignored or spoke against the earlier confessional and theological articulations of Bonhoeffer, claiming that the Bonhoeffer in prison made a radical shift, moving beyond all that had come before, even the tight-knit conservative family he grew up in. All attention to orthodoxy,

---

2. Ibid., 29.

3. It was Bishop Robinson and his book *Honest to God* (London: SCM, 1963) that not only made Bonhoeffer's name more fully known in the English-speaking world but also set forth the radical interpretation of Bonhoeffer. While, for the most part, this position has been seen to be problematic by Bonhoeffer scholars (most see it as a failure to take into account the full breadth and scope of Bonhoeffer's life and thought), it remains a position. For instance, a few postmodern theologians and philosophers of religion continue to return to a revolutionary Bonhoeffer. Perhaps the most popular of these is Peter Rollins, who so deeply misreads Bonhoeffer along these lines that he admits disdain for the earlier historical and intellectual elements of Bonhoeffer's thought.

community, and the revelation of Jesus Christ was conveniently deleted by those in the revolutionary interpretation.

This historical/theological interpretation would have been the default perspective on Bonhoeffer if Bonhoeffer's own surviving student and closest friend had not railed against it. Eberhard Bethge, the addressee of most of the letters from prison, stood against the radical Bonhoeffer interpretation, exhorting that Bonhoeffer could not be read as a 1960s death-of-God theologian (or today as a radical postmodern theologian).[4] Bethge claimed there was no break (though there was development) in the thought and life of Bonhoeffer.

The Liberals

Haynes explains that a new group of Bonhoeffer interpreters evolved through direct conversation with Bethge—Haynes calls these interpreters "the liberals." This group was enamored with Bonhoeffer's attention to social justice, exploring particularly Bonhoeffer's resistance to National Socialism and his advocacy for the Jews. But, Haynes explains, these historical realities are not the central biographical lens through which they see Bonhoeffer. They instead draw on the themes of resistance, advocacy, and the call for justice, centered on Bonhoeffer's experience in New York City, and particularly in Harlem in 1930–31. These mainly American liberal theologians see the historical key to unlocking a true vision of Bonhoeffer as his experience in America with pre–civil rights African Americans.[5] And there

4. Haynes writes, "Van Hoogstraten compares Bonhoeffer's anti-metaphysical pronouncements in *Letters and Papers from Prison* with the postmodern critique of metaphysics by Richard Rorty and Gianni Vattimo" (*Bonhoeffer Phenomenon*, 25). He continues, "In a manner strikingly akin to postmodern thinkers, Thiemann maintains, Bonhoeffer sketches a theology that is 'non-metaphysical and non-foundational, in solidarity with the powerless and suffering, and committed to righteous action in perilous and uncertain situations'" (ibid., 26).

5. "For three decades Bonhoeffer's reception among religious and social liberals has foregrounded his identity as the grandfather of liberation theology" (ibid., 46). Haynes continues,

> According to Melano, Bonhoeffer's education in contextualized theology continued at Union Theological Seminary, where fellow student Frank Fisher took Bonhoeffer to Harlem and introduced him to "the outcasts, the marginalized and pariahs of American society." Professor C. C. Webber's course "Church and Community" familiarized Bonhoeffer with the church's role in confronting

is no doubt that this experience had a lifelong impact on Bonhoeffer. Never again did Bonhoeffer do ministry without the Negro spiritual; he played the records he bought in New York for his confirmation class and then his young students at the illegal Confessing Church seminary in Finkenwalde. Bonhoeffer, it seems clear, used the Negro spiritual to help his own students move into the theological, dwelling in the deep pathos of the spiritual as a way to seek for God in the concrete and lived.

It is impossible to see Bonhoeffer outside some strain of liberalism. He did, after all, take his PhD at Berlin, the bastion of liberal thought.[6] He did, after all, attend Union Theological Seminary. And he was a dear family friend of church historian and fellow Berliner Adolf von Harnack, a giant of liberal thought (Bonhoeffer not only took the train with Harnack weekly from Grunewald to the university but was given the honor of eulogizing the great theologian at his national funeral).

Yet Bonhoeffer also took distinctive steps away from liberalism. For instance, in 1926 Bonhoeffer became enamored with the thought of Karl Barth, the theologian railing against Bonhoeffer's very teachers in Berlin and against the bankruptcy of liberal theological thought.[7]

"the problems of labor, civil rights, and juvenile criminality." Harry F. Ward, whose "untraditional approach to Christian Ethics was tinged with socialism," also left his mark. In New York, in other words, Bonhoeffer learned to see the world "from below." Melano notes that upon returning to Germany Bonhoeffer taught a confirmation class among a "restless proletariat" in the working-class district of Wedding, keeping "direct contact with the people, including the communists and the socialists." These experiences provided the raw material that would be refined in Bonhoeffer's theological writings. (ibid., 49)

6. "But if the University of Berlin was in a state of decline when Bonhoeffer matriculated, it is also true that too much emphasis in the study of Bonhoeffer has been placed upon his reaction against his teachers and too little on the great influence they exerted upon him" (John Phillips, *Christ for Us in the Theology of Dietrich Bonhoeffer* [New York: Harper & Row, 1967], 34).

7. Haynes elaborates,

However, significant ironies are involved in making Bonhoeffer the sort of religious liberal familiar to twenty-first-century Christians. First, while it is not surprising that North American liberals want to cast him as an exemplar of progressive religiosity, Bonhoeffer's own experience made him severely critical of American theology. Bonhoeffer was immersed in American liberal Protestantism during his yearlong sojourn in New York, and he was unimpressed. The humanistic language, the privileging of the social gospel, the "philosophical and organizational secularization of Christianity," the lack of concern for

Bonhoeffer was receiving from his cousin Hans-Christoph von Hase some of Barth's earliest lectures. Von Hase had gone to Göttingen to study medicine but was converted to the study of theology after one Barth lecture. Now, taking every lecture Barth gave, von Hase would handwrite, word for word (something not uncommon for German students at the time), each lecture and mail it to his cousin in Berlin.

Even in New York in the classrooms of Union, Bonhoeffer was standing against liberalism. He spoke so vigorously for Barth (whom few knew at the time) in New York that the great Reinhold Niebuhr (whom Bonhoeffer took classes from at Union) would mistake Bonhoeffer for decades as a Barthian acolyte. Bonhoeffer was disturbed and shocked when in these classes he spoke of sin and all the liberal Union students laughed, finding his confessional language so backward as to be ridiculed.

Even after Bonhoeffer's time in New York City, even after teaching Sunday school to the Harlem youth at Abyssinian Baptist Church (which we will return to below), Bonhoeffer's intrigue with Barth and his prophetic message against liberalism only deepened. Immediately upon Bonhoeffer's return to Europe from New York in the summer of 1931, he went to Bonn to hear and dialogue with Barth (all set up by his fellow European companion at Union, the Swiss national Erwin Sutz, who had studied with Barth).

The Conservatives

The Bonhoeffer phenomenon is deepened, as Haynes explains it, not only because of Bonhoeffer's adaptation by revolutionary and liberal theologians but, most shockingly, by conservative evangelicals, especially in the last few decades.[8] As the revolutionaries are intrigued

---

doctrine, and the "unbearable" sermons built around quotes from William James all contributed to Bonhoeffer's dismissal of liberal Protestantism as vapid humanism. (*Bonhoeffer Phenomenon*, 59)

8. Haynes states:

The most scientific evidence for Bonhoeffer's warm reception among evangelicals comes from surveys of evangelical opinion. At the end of the last decade, the editors of *Christian History* magazine (published by Christianity Today, Inc.) asked readers and historians to list the five most influential Christians of the twentieth century, as well as the five well-known Christians who had been most influential for them personally. When the results were published in the

by "religionless Christianity" and liberals by justice for the oppressed, so the conservatives embrace with firm grip the ideas in *Discipleship*.[9] It is the directness of the call into risk for faith that captures their imagination, Haynes believes.[10]

And these ideas are centered on the biographical last days of Bonhoeffer and his death at Flossenbürg as a martyr for his faith. Bonhoeffer is a hero for conservatives because he not only *spoke* boldly of following Jesus but also *did so*   into the hands of his executor. Haynes explains that it is these last days and words that become the central biographical lens that frames their interpretation of Bonhoeffer. It has led even the likes of James Dobson to herald his love for Bonhoeffer.[11]

---

magazine's winter 2000 edition, Bonhoeffer ranked tenth among both scholars and readers on the "most influential" list, and fifth on the most "personally influential" lists of both groups. Bonhoeffer was not only the highest-ranked theologian, but was one of only six figures who finished in the top ten in all four categories (the others being Billy Graham, C. S. Lewis, Mother Teresa, Martin Luther King Jr., and Francis Schaeffer—all preachers, activists, or apologists). (ibid., 69)

9. When this book was originally translated into English, it took the title *The Cost of Discipleship*. However, more recent translations have returned to the title that more closely connects with Bonhoeffer's original: *Discipleship*.

10. Haynes makes an interesting point here: "The major figures of twentieth-century European theology—Bonhoeffer's rough contemporaries Paul Tillich, Rudolf Bultmann, and Karl Barth—are typically regarded by American evangelicals as something less than 'true' believers whose theologies are all the more dangerous for their apparent orthodoxy. Yet today, when it is difficult to find a positive mention of any of these men in evangelical publications, Bonhoeffer (who had much in common with them and was a product of the same church and university systems) is honored by a broad array of evangelical authors, publications, and institutions" (*Bonhoeffer Phenomenon*, 69).

11. Haynes reports,

The most influential evangelical leader to identify Bonhoeffer as a paradigm for Christian cultural engagement is James C. Dobson, founder and president of Focus on the Family. In a series of articles published between 1999 and 2002, Dobson offered Bonhoeffer's life as a case study in Christian activism at a time when the evangelical obligation to shape society was being called into question. In a *Christianity Today* article titled "The New Cost of Discipleship," Dobson responded to the charge that Christians have wasted their time opposing abortion, homosexual marriage, pornography, and the assault on traditional values. Citing Bonhoeffer's failed activism, Dobson asked: "Since when did being outnumbered and under powered justify silence in response to evil?" Bonhoeffer took a stand against the Nazi regime and paid with his life. Would those endorsing Christian isolationism suggest that he should have accommodated Hitler's henchmen because he had no chance of winning? (ibid., 74)

It is Bonhoeffer's devotion and commitment to faith against a hostile, anti-Christian society that draws conservative evangelicals to embrace him as a hero, for they, too, feel the need to commit to a faith they perceive to be under attack by a corrupt (anti-Christian) society. Haynes states, "For evangelicals, discipleship . . . connotes the countercultural demands of Christian faith, which beckon believers to choose the narrow path of authentic Christian living over the broad way of participation in culture-defining institutions."[12]

My Lens

I'm sure that as you read my own account of Bonhoeffer below you'll see ways that I may, at times, look through one or more of these above lenses, though you will also notice that I find none of these three interpretive lenses conclusive (and at times find one or more distorting). For instance, I will lean heavily on the biographical work of Eberhard Bethge. I'm not shy in stating that in my mind Bethge's thousand-page biography is unmatched, and it only takes a little looking to see how it has been an ur-source for so many other pieces. Yet my following of Bethge's historical account will not force me into wearing a liberal interpretive lens. Bethge himself would be uncomfortable with a solely liberal interpretation of Bonhoeffer.[13]

The many different biographies have a tendency to interpret Bonhoeffer in generally one of these three ways. But while it is impossible to draw from a Bonhoeffer biography and not be pulled into this or that interpretation, I will seek to avoid foreclosure on any one interpretation (for example, I'll draw from Schlingensiepen as much as Bethge) so that I might be free to make my own (new) case for interpreting Bonhoeffer.

My own lens for interpreting Bonhoeffer will focus on what is often glossed over in other historical accounts, whether those historical

12. Ibid., 78.
13. In the same vein, you will see *no* reference to Eric Metaxas's Bonhoeffer biography, which I find so flawed and earnest to paint Bonhoeffer as a conservative (not possessing the openness of Bethge's work) that I cannot follow him in any way, for to do so would be to foreclose on one of the above interpretations.

accounts have their origin in the revolutionary, liberal, or conservative interpretations of Bonhoeffer. These glossed-over experiences
are Bonhoeffer's shockingly consistent ministry to and with young
people. These experiences begin in 1925, when Bonhoeffer was but
nineteen years old, and continue until the outbreak of the war in
1939. Through nearly all the central biographical events and periods
that are used by other interpretive lenses, it was ministry to youth
that was consistent to Bonhoeffer's direct ministry experience. For
example, as the liberal lens makes central Bonhoeffer's time in New
York, it often fails to attend to Bonhoeffer's teaching Sunday school
in Harlem. And where the conservative interpretation hones in on
Discipleship, it fails to take into account Bonhoeffer's confirmation
class in Wedding and ecumenical youth work while in London. The
revolutionary interpretation overlooks how even in prison Bonhoeffer's thoughts turn to his confirmands, fellow younger prisoners, and
former students called to the front and dying.

Therefore, the pages that will follow seek to present not a revolutionary, liberal, or conservative Bonhoeffer but a youth worker Bonhoeffer, a Bonhoeffer busy with many things, yes—things like speaking
for the oppressed, shouting for his church to obey and confess, and
reimagining Christianity for a world come of age—but in and through
all these endeavors, I hope to show, a Bonhoeffer doing youth ministry
and doing it *theologically*.

---

(3)

The Origins of the
Youth Worker

To begin making this case for interpreting Bonhoeffer as a youth worker, we must commence at the beginning. It appears conclusive that Dietrich Bonhoeffer was uniquely talented for youth ministry. Multiple sources across distinct times in his life report that he was superb with children, and not only able to connect with them but to take them on deep theological journeys. To understand the origins of this gift (if the mystery of any gift can be understood) is to recognize the family that Bonhoeffer grew up in and his place within it.

Origins

The Germany that Dietrich Bonhoeffer was born into in 1906 was an idyllic Germany. A German history of war and conflict seemed remembered only in history books, and the hell of the two world wars was not yet on the horizon. The last decades of the nineteenth century in the *Deutsches Reich* was a time of prosperity, peace, poetry, and philosophy; it was a time of cultural depth and advance. Bonhoeffer was born into a family thriving in such a setting.

Dietrich Bonhoeffer's mother, Paula von Hase, was the child of the noble von Hase family; their nobility was won through their church engagements. Both her father and grandfather (Dietrich's grandfather and great-grandfather) were professors of theology; Dietrich's great-grandfather, church historian Karl-August von Hase, was the more prestigious of the two. Dietrich's grandfather, Karl-Elfred von Hase, was a professor of practical theology, who in his career was also the court preacher to King Wilhelm II.

Though Paula possessed the blood of noble churchmen, she married a man possessing neither noble blood nor a propensity for the church. Karl Bonhoeffer, Dietrich's father, came from the upper-middle class, and it was in the upper-middle class that all the prosperity, poetry, and philosophy was being produced. It was a time of noble (aristocratic) decline and middle-class escalation in prestige and power. And no locale was open to the middle class more so than the university. Karl Bonhoeffer became one of Germany's leading psychiatric voices—a stern, direct, scientific man who, both personally and theoretically, stood in opposition to the thought and procedures of Sigmund Freud.[1]

Karl Bonhoeffer took great pride in having no noble blood and being a self-made, scientific, middle-class man through and through, and as such he had no need or patience for the church. The church in his mind was either for aristocrats like Paula's family, who were living in the privilege of the old, or for those of the underclass. But for a self-made, scientific man, the church and its God were superfluous.

German Youth Movement

Yet this national ethos of prosperity and peace bound in the middle class did not come without some tension, and this tension was borne on the backs of young people. Living within the distinct middle-class ethos of the time, a number of middle-class German youth felt disconnected and aimless, experiencing both a sense of societal

---

1. For more see Clifford Green's "Two Bonhoeffers on Psychoanalysis," in A. J. Klassen, *A Bonhoeffer Legacy: Essays in Understanding* (Grand Rapids: Eerdmans, 1981).

purposelessness and an emotional rigidity from (particularly) their fathers. It appears that nearly all youth movements are born in the middle class (whether the 1960s American hippy youth movement, the late-nineteenth-century German youth movement, or the young people of the Arab Spring with their Twitter accounts). It actually may be that the shadows of the so-called middle-class utopia always cast heavily on children, particularly in their adolescence. And this is so because the middle class is the proprietor and perpetuator of the category of childhood; living within the economic advantage of not needing children to work (or serve as marriage pawns for continued nobility) leads to a conception of childhood innocence. The child is hidden from the world behind the structural walls of family and education. Middle-class parents take on a heavy burden of seeing it as their core vocation to protect and advance their children. But this projecting and advancing appears to always come with tension as the innocent middle-class child turns into the alien middle-class adolescent.[2]

The sheltered middle-class adolescent reaches for adventure and often does so by opposing some of the very structures that hold up the middle-class ethos and shelter the adolescent from the scorching sun of reality. The adults call her mad, alien, and overloaded with hormones, not really because she is[3] but because she does the

2. I'm glossing over a very important topic—the historical arrival of the category of adolescence—that would simply take me too far afield in this project. As I have articulated in my other writing, I tend to hold that, at least in America, adolescence is a late, post–World War II creation. However, in Germany this may not be the case. In Germany adolescence may have arrived in the late nineteenth century. Clearly, in some ways and in some cultural locales the same could be argued for North America. It might be that the arrival of the German middle class in the late nineteenth century brought forth adolescence there. This expansive middle-class ethos was not present in America until after World War II, thus why I see it as so late a concept in America.

3. Though this is debated. Some have pointed to adolescent brain science as fact that adolescents are overwhelmed with the hormonal or incapable of adult decision making. I do not doubt that the science reads this way and that MRIs can show such brain activity. However, I do not subscribe to biological determinism and instead hold that cultural and societal realities can impact the biological. So it could be that young people are overflowing with hormones and that their neural loops are this or that, but these biological actualities may be the result of cultural practice and ideology—just as we contend that early menstruation is due to cultural/societal realities.

seemingly crazy act of attacking the middle-class ethos (with rebellion or romanticism) that gives her all her privilege to be angsty or nostalgic in the first place.

It was not so much rebellion that fueled the German youth movement (as it did in the American youth movement of the 1960s); rather, it was romanticism.[4] In the last decades of the nineteenth century, at the very time Karl and Paula Bonhoeffer were courting, marrying, and bringing their own children into the world, the middle-class youth of Germany were "rambling" (wandering).

A youth movement called *Wandervogel* sprang from the discontent of the very middle-class communities within which Karl and Paula were living.[5] The *Wandervogel* was a form of protest, but a protest without political ambition. As Walter Laqueur says in his book *Young Germany*, "The German youth movement was an unpolitical form of opposition to a civilization that had little to offer the young generation, a protest against its lack of vitality, warmth, emotion, and ideals."[6] Laqueur continues, "The young people of the *Wandervogel* and the groups that succeeded it were for the most part sons and daughters of professional people, middle or higher government officials, or people of similar status in the world of industry and commerce, i.e., the middle classes proper."[7] These middle-class young people felt aimless, and felt little emotional warmth as their middle-class parents pushed and protected them to achieve and succeed in the middle-class ethos of Germany.

Karl Bonhoeffer was unmistakably one of these middle-class fathers. Firm and cold, he provided all that his children needed materially

4. Walter Laqueur explains: "The Wandervogel chose the other form of protest against society—romanticism. Their return to nature was romantic, as were their attempts to get away from a materialistic civilization, their stress on the simple life, their rediscovery of old folk songs and folklore, their adoption of medieval names and customs. Romanticism probably has a closer hold on Germany than on any other country. There have been classical schools in every culture, but nowhere has romanticism been so deeply rooted as in German literature, music, art, and the general Zeitgeist" (*Young Germany: A History of the German Youth Movement* [New Brunswick, NJ: Transaction Publishers, 2001], 6).

5. "This Free Youth Movement started, and remained, as an exclusively bourgeois phenomenon and, despite many efforts, failed to strike any roots in the German working class" (ibid., xxii).

6. Ibid., 4.

7. Ibid., 13.

and intellectually, but was rarely open to them emotionally. Dietrich's youngest sister, Susanne, tells the story of being but a child herself and accompanying her father to the hospital for his psychological rounds with sick children. Susanne watched as her father softly and lovingly took these strange children on his knee, speaking softy as he touched them gently. Susanne reports that upon seeing this she loved her father more than ever, but loved him painfully, for never had he touched and held her with the warmth and gentleness he had for these children. Never had she experienced this tender Karl herself; it was only outside the home and outside his role as "father" that he was free to be emotionally available. He could be such as doctor, but not as father.[8]

What Susanne speaks of is not so much a deficiency in Karl himself but the very expectations and practices (the habitus) of middle-class parenting in German society at this time. It was such experiences, even years before Karl and Paula had children of their own, that led the youth of the German middle class to "ramble." And ramble they did; the *Wandervogel* was a recovery of a kind of medieval European experience, a time of itinerant wandering scholars and artists. So, latching on romantically to this bygone age, middle-class youth came together to re-create it. The *Wandervogel* youth movement revolved around walking. A group of adolescents, led by an older adolescent, would simply gather in their middle-class neighborhood and then together wander the countrysides of the continent, embracing the ideals of adventure as they gave each other the emotional support they lacked in their privileged but cold homes.

The youth hostels that remain in Europe are the relic left by the *Wandervogel*. The rambling youth would march and sing from neighborhood through the forest to a youth hostel, stay the night, and then awaken and ramble their way to the next hostel. To this day, most of the hostels of Europe are called "youth" hostels, though they have no distinct connection to youth. The "youth" remains in the name as an unintended witness to the German youth movement, for the hostel phenomenon was created for the rambling of the *Wandervogel*.

8. Renate Wind makes this point strongly in her book *Dietrich Bonhoeffer: A Spoke in the Wheel* (Grand Rapids: Eerdmans, 2000).

Laqueur explains that the movement was never extraordinarily large, maybe sixty thousand at its max, and never (until the inclusion of the Hitler Youth) drew working-class young people. Nevertheless, it had its impact on German society, becoming a kind of cultural stable within it, most especially during the decades of Bonhoeffer's own youth. The *Wandervogel* youth movement and then its second derivative, the *Bunde*, coming on the scene after World War I, located the issue of young people (the crisis of youth) central to the societal consciousness of Germany during the time of Bonhoeffer's maturation. Much like how the hippy youth movement in America in the late 1960s pushed the state of our youth onto the nation's consciousness, in part engendering in America the investment of local churches in youth ministry, so too in Germany the ethos in which Bonhoeffer came of age was one of concern for or interest in youth.[9]

None of the Bonhoeffer children ever became officially engaged in the youth movement. Not ironically, the only one to have any direct interaction with the youth movement was Dietrich, who in the years after World War I joined the Boy Scouts, part of the *Bunde* youth movement.[10] As Bethge says, "The Youth Movement reappeared on

9. Reinhart Staats adds some texture:
   Bonhoeffer's engagement with children and young people during these years was part of a larger process of socialization in Germany at the time that, for many of the children of solid, middle-class families, began in the German youth movement. Indeed, this background often resonates in Bonhoeffer's own dialogue with young people. The guiding moral slogan of Walter Flex's 1917 book *Der Wanderer zwischen beiden Welten*, which had become the guidebook for idealistic hikers and nature lovers among the postwar youth and for Bonhoeffer as well, was: "Remain pure means remaining a child, even after you become a man." In this context, Bonhoeffer's "Notes for a Young Man" also give the impression of a conversation with himself: "Remaining pure means remaining a child, even after you have become a man." This impression is especially strong when Bonhoeffer interprets the travels of the young man in a theological sense as expressed in his favorite verse, "Each day tells the other / my life is but a journey / to great and endless life"; this verse will accompany him the rest of his life. (afterword to Dietrich Bonhoeffer, *Barcelona, Berlin, New York: 1928–1931*, Dietrich Bonhoeffer Works [Minneapolis: Fortress, 2008], 10:606)

10. Laqueur explains the place of the Boy Scouts in the youth movement: "Several other youth organizations were founded in the decade before the First World War, but only one of them, the German variant of the Boy Scouts, subsequently became part of the youth movement. The others were either sports clubs or semi-military

the scene, partly with very ambiguous aims and motivations. Caught up in this wave, thirteen-year-old Dietrich joined the Boy Scouts."[11]

Where *Wandervogel* revolved around rambling—unkempt young people romantically singing songs as they walked arm in arm (not unlike a Coca-Cola commercial)—the *Bunde* consisted of more organized and ordered groups, often having a certain task, like scouts with its military ethos.[12] Where *Wandervogel* had only very moderate leadership, and this leadership came from older youth, the *Bunde* was often led by adults. Bonhoeffer, in his own later adolescence, joined the scouts only to quit after a short time, confessing that he wasn't wired to take orders from anyone and was sick of all the marching (plus, his older brothers teased him relentlessly for his involvement).

Yet the *Bunde* experience—the experience of youth groups—made its impact on Bonhoeffer. In his young adulthood (even in the last years of his adolescence) he began a number of such groups within the congregational ministries he was called to.[13] It was not uncommon

---

patriotic groups of no specific interest to the present survey, and only to be mentioned in passing" (*Young Germany*, 72).

11. Eberhard Bethge, *Dietrich Bonhoeffer: A Biography* (Minneapolis: Fortress, 2000), 31.

12. "Whereas the ideal figure of the Wandervogel had been the itinerant Scholar, an anarchist if not a democrat, the aristocratic tendencies of the Bunde were reflected, not only in the exemplary image of the knight who sets himself a rule of conduct in deliberate contrast to that of the multitude. But also in a strict hierarchy within the Bunde" (Laqueur, *Young Germany*, 135).

13. Staats connects the period of the youth movement with Bonhoeffer's youth work in Barcelona and New York:

> Although this proximity to the German Youth Movement is certainly not everywhere as evident within the larger corpus of Bonhoeffer's work, until 1931 he was still very much a child of his own German social history in this regard. The Bonhoeffer household, of course, was not really very profoundly affected by the characteristic features of organized youth associations. Members of the family could certainly poke fun at the uniforms, banners, camps, and indeed at the entire emotionalism. Yet even the Bonhoeffer children had gone hiking with one another, relatives, and friends, and had engaged in the accompanying youth rituals of spending the night in some farmer's barn or in youth hostels. Such memories probably provided the background to Bonhoeffer's initial disappointment in Barcelona when he remarked that "the era of the youth movement in Germany passed by without leaving a trace here." In America, too, he immediately sought out activities with young people and enthusiastically recalled his own, decidedly German memories, especially of one particular summer evening singing folk songs around a campfire "with

for both Protestant and Catholic churches to have their own *Bunde* groups, like American churches four decades later, attending to the reverberating buzz of the youth movement in the larger society. Just as American youth ministry (as the initiative of the local congregations) can be seen, at least in part, as having its origin in the rebellious youth movement of the late 1960s, so Bonhoeffer's own youth ministry had its origins in the romantic youth movement of the 1920s.[14]

Yet like so much else in Germany, the German youth movement would have its demise in the Third Reich. The Nazis had a way of either strangling things dead or enveloping them into their own agenda. The youth movement met not so much a violent end as a co-opted one. The Hitler Youth would become the Third Reich's own youth movement that, along with the churches, was taken into the National Socialist agenda once the Nazis were in power. The Hitler Youth was the Nazi strategy of possessing for itself the energy and attention youth received in Germany at this time. Yet, uniquely, the Nazis were able to turn the middle-class youth movement's nonpolitical concerns uber-political, by co-opting and using working-class animosity. After World War II and the splitting of Germany, the *Wandervogel* and *Bunde* youth movements became a relic buried under the rubble of a Europe lost to a sky that rained bombs.

The Bonhoeffer Family

The Bonhoeffer children may never have been drawn deeply into the German youth movement because, though Karl lacked emotional availability, he unquestionably gave all his children (daughters as well as sons) a sense of purpose. The Bonhoeffer children were never susceptible to middle-class aimlessness, for they knew themselves to be leaders and shapers of Berlin, if not the whole of German society. None of Karl and Paula's children lacked confidence, and Dietrich

---

a group of young people from our German youth movement." (afterword to Bonhoeffer, *Barcelona, Berlin, New York*, 607)

14. "The Protestant and Catholic youth groups were strongly influenced by the Bunde in the twenties and were frequently indistinguishable from them, except by the stress put on religious motives in their cultural activities" (Laqueur, *Young Germany*, 163).

is a shining example. Dietrich's confidence bordered on arrogance, a reality he saw in himself and regretted after 1932—a dangerous character flaw he sought to keep in check for the rest of his life.[15]

Karl and Paula brought eight children into their ordered and intellectually elite upper-middle-class family; the arrival of these eight children stretched over ten years, giving the family a kind of two-stage sense of the older and younger ones. Dietrich was of the younger. He entered the Bonhoeffer family as the fourth son and sixth child, arriving just minutes before his twin sister, Sabin. Dietrich's older brothers Karl-Friedrich and Klaus were cut from the same cloth as their father. They were firm, scientifically minded young men who had little time or concern for the church. As a matter of fact, none of the Bonhoeffer children went to church, and it was not until Dietrich decided to be a theologian that he began to attend regularly.

But this doesn't mean there was no sense of religious formation in the Bonhoeffer home. Karl and his older sons were outspoken agnostics, but Paula had a deep spirituality that she sought to pass along to her children. Not only did she often read them Bible stories but the children's nanny was always a woman of faith who also taught piety and Scripture to the children.[16] As a matter of fact, Paula Bonhoeffer took charge of not just the religious instruction but all of the children's education. In her own way she revolted against the middle-class ethos that engendered the youth movement; as a woman from a noble family she had distance enough from the middle-class ethos of Germany to be critical of it. Paula spoke out against it by saying that a German youth "got his back broken twice in life, once at school and then in the army."[17] Paula would have none of

15. This is at least in part what Bonhoeffer means when he says he did his work in a very unchristian way. See Bethge, *Bonhoeffer*, 204.

16. The primary nanny, who was there the longest, was Maria Horn. Her sister also nannied for them. Bethge explains: "Maria Horn, the beloved family governess from 1906 to 1923, was an adherent of the Moravian Brethren, but she did not have much religious influence over the children. Because of her attractive and imperturbable personality she was like a member of the family, but it was her personality that was appreciated; expressions of her piety were merely tolerated" (*Dietrich Bonhoeffer*, 35).

17. Leonore Siegele-Wenschkewitz, "Die Ehre der Frau, dem Manne zu dienen: Zum Frauenbild Dietrich Bonhoeffers," in *Wie Theologen Frauen sehen—von der Macht der Bilder*, ed. Jost and Kuberg (Freiburg: Herder Verlag, 1993), 105.

this for her own children; she wanted to foster their creativity and independent thinking. As a kind of silent deal for keeping the children away from church, Karl allowed Paula to educate the children herself, at home, until they were ready to enter gymnasium (high school).

This resulted in making the Bonhoeffer home a self-enclosed world. Their house was large (both before 1912, in Breslau, and then after, when Karl moved the family to Berlin to take the chair of psychiatry at Humboldt University), with a study for Karl that the children were forbidden to enter; but around every other corner were always others to be with, to join in playing games and putting on plays. The house was always filled with not only siblings but also the siblings' friends; especially the older children always had playmates from similar upper-middle-class families over to visit. And the house itself not only had the children's live-in nanny (governess) within its walls but also a full-time cook and chauffeur. And as if that wasn't enough, Karl often entertained colleagues from the university in his home, welcoming some of Germany's greatest minds to the world of this close-knit family.[18] The family home was a place where childhood was nurtured, but nurtured in the dense air of intellectual advantage.

The Siblings

All the Bonhoeffer children benefited from this environment. The oldest, Karl-Friedrich, became a world-renowned physicist, and Klaus became a lawyer. Dietrich would always feel close to them, but like almost every younger brother, a spirit of competitiveness also fueled their relationship, especially for Dietrich. For not only was he the youngest brother, he was a great deal younger, just a small child in their own adolescence and a budding adolescent as they entered

18. Phillips states who was present: "The wooded Berlin suburb of Grunewald offered a cultural and intellectual environment for Bonhoeffer's upbringing. Hans Delbruck and Adolf von Harnack were neighbours, and Ernst Troeltsch was a frequent visitor to the Bonhoeffer household. There were many memorable evening discussions between Ferdinand Tonnies, Max and Alfred Weber, and Dietrich's elder brothers" (*Christ for Us*, 14).

adulthood and married.[19] Dietrich hovered around the edges of his older brothers' lives, treated with respect by them but always as the younger one. This experience of being always treated as young in his family, of having his familial identity as one of the young ones (as the only boy of the younger half of the family), solidified in Dietrich a kind of sensitivity to the experience of fellow young ones, of children. Dietrich's role in his own family system was as the gifted, adventurous young one; this was how the family viewed him, even into his thirties. This was a role that he, for the most part, would never shed. Unlike all of his other siblings, Dietrich remained single, even living at his parents' home throughout most of his life.

The two oldest daughters, Ursula and Christine, married important men in their own right. Ursula married lawyer Rudiger Schleicher, and Christine married a playmate of Klaus's named Hans von Dohnanyi. Dohnanyi became a high-ranking government official, and it was eventually Dohnanyi who not only filled in the Bonhoeffer family on the barbarism of the Nazis but made way for Dietrich to enter the Abwehr (the German intelligence agency of which Dohnanyi was a high-ranking member) and become a double-agent spy.

These two men officially entered into the family in Dietrich's own adolescence.[20] Both of these men gave great attention to young Dietrich, debating issues with him and taking him places. It may be that the origins of Dietrich's own giftedness with young people rests with these two men and their attention to him. Both Schleicher and Dohnanyi listened intently to Dietrich, respected his opinion, asked him many questions, and, even at a young age, treated him like a young friend. These relationships became a kind of model for Dietrich in his own youth ministry. Schleicher and Dohnanyi loved to enter into deep conversation with Dietrich about issues of the day or his own hopes and struggles; Dietrich was known for doing the same with his confirmands, even starting youth groups to have such conversations.

19. This is not true for Klaus, who would not marry until after Dietrich's university days. But Karl-Friedrich and Ursula would, and it is to this that I'm referring.

20. I stand by the above statement, but I should be clear. Christine did not marry Hans until 1925. Dietrich was nineteen at the time. Yet it is fair to say that Hans had a significant impact on Dietrich even before he wed Christine. Karl-Friedrich actually married Hans's sister Grete, so Hans was engaged with the Bonhoeffer family from the time of Dietrich's adolescence, taking an interest in him.

But it wasn't only this attention in conversation that shaped young Dietrich's relationships with Schleicher and Dohnanyi; these brothers-in-law also invited Dietrich to plays, operas, and other cultural outings in Berlin. This, too, became a major staple of Dietrich's own youth ministry, as he paid out of his own pocket for the young people with whom he was ministering to join him in hearing an orchestra or enjoying the countryside.

Dietrich's very location within the family gave him the unique opportunities to have adults take interest in him, mentoring him. It was both these relationships and his role as young (as always a young one) in his family that I believe directed his own interests and forged his gifts in youth ministry.

But there may be more that solidified this sensitivity toward young people for Dietrich, this sensitivity that was born from his own childhood experience. Not only was Dietrich seen always as a young one within his family system but also, as one of the young ones, he was the leader of the young ones. So along with the privilege of the upper-middle-class intellectual family with its multiple older-sibling mentors, within his environment Dietrich was still able to flex muscles of leadership. Both his twin sister, Sabin, and his youngest sister, Susanne, report that Dietrich was their hero, always protecting and leading them as these young ones were shuttled away from the activities of the older children and parents, spending many hours alone playing, dreaming, and contemplating. It was Dietrich who was the leader of these games and existential journeys.

Young Dietrich led his sisters in prayer, played church with them, created secret codes for them to communicate, and led them into times of contemplating death. These three young ones were often alone to wrestle together with the mysterious questions of childhood—the mysteries of transcendence, connection, and loss—and Dietrich was their guide into such contemplation.[21] So not only was

21. This long quote provides a feel of Dietrich's childhood experience with his sisters:

This text refers us directly back to Bonhoeffer's early childhood, about which his twin sister Sabine recounts: "From eight to ten years old Dietrich and I slept in the same room and when we were in bed at night we used to have earnest discussions about death and eternal life. The war of 1914 had broken out, and we heard of the deaths of our older cousins and some of our classmates'

Dietrich always seen as young in the family system and embraced by his brothers-in-law, being taught the intrinsic value of childhood, but with his younger sisters he was taken into the depth and mystery with which children must wrestle, mysteries like death and attachment. With his younger sisters, Dietrich explored these mysteries, pretending—even wishing—that he would die, imagining with them what it would be like at his funeral.

And these questions may have sat near the surface for Dietrich not only because he was attached to a close-knit family and allowed to embrace his childhood but also because his own being was bound to Sabine's as her twin. This wrestling with attachment and yet difference seemed to engender questions that Dietrich would wrestle with his whole life. It is interesting to think that the very social orientation of his theology, the deep place of relationship and community ("Christ as existing as church-community," the thesis of his first theological work, *Sanctorum Communio*), had its origins in his childhood experience of being a twin, of grappling with the mysteries of existence as a child with his younger sisters, and of always being respected and heard in friendship by the husbands of his older sisters.

---

fathers. And so in the evenings, after prayers and hymn singing, in which our mother always took part when she was in the house, we used to lie awake for a long time and try to imagine what it must be like to be dead and to have entered eternal life. We used to make special efforts . . . to think only of the word eternity and not admit any other thought to our minds. This eternity seemed to us very long and uncanny. . . . We staunchly kept up this self-imposed exercise for a long time. . . . All this was an absolute secret between us twins." (Bonhoeffer, *Barcelona, Berlin, New York*, 594)

4

The Fracture of the Idyllic

The Death of Walter and the Adolescence of Dietrich Bonhoeffer

The idyllic state of both the Bonhoeffer family and Germany as a whole would be punctured in 1914 as the kaiser announced war. With these words the national ethos of peace and prosperity was lost. But this loss came with little societal regret; rather, the German populace celebrated the announcement, as if the peace and prosperity had become all too boring and war promised some excitement to break the monotony of middle-class poetry, philosophy, and productivity. Eleven-year-old Christine Bonhoeffer, upon hearing the news of war, ran into her home overwhelmed with excitement as if a movie star had arrived in her neighborhood. As she ran to her mother, shouting in excitement for the war, Paula boxed her ears, asserting war should never be celebrated.

Soon all of Germany would understand why, as hell came to earth and swallowed so many of Europe's young men. But as the war began, there was only excitement. Even eight-year-old Dietrich became caught up in it, following the troop movements on the front with pins on a map and news clippings from the paper.

The hell of war would touch everyone, even the Bonhoeffers. All three of the oldest Bonhoeffer sons entered the military and went to the front; the oldest two, Karl-Friedrich and Walter, went first. If Karl-Friedrich and Klaus took after their father, then it was Walter (who in age rested between Karl-Friedrich and Klaus) who belonged to his mother. Walter was sensitive and artistic, in many ways his mother's favorite. As the two older boys departed, the Bonhoeffer family had known only success and happiness and had no reason to worry that such a state would not continue. But it would not, as Walter met his demise, penning a final letter to his parents as he died from injuries, telling them not to worry as he relayed information of his battalion's advance with his last breaths.

Yet Walter's letter was no comfort to Karl and Paula but a bitter, poisonous pill. Paula, particularly, was broken, howling the deepest wounds of loss as she grieved her vanished boy. The perfect upper-middle-class house had to receive into its walls the screams of the god-forsaken pain of a mother for her dead child. Twelve-year-old Dietrich, right on the cusp of his own adolescence, could only listen, witnessing his mother's keening and his father's silent agony. As Schlingensiepen says, "Twelve-year-old Dietrich could never forget his mother's wild suffering."[1] It would mark his childhood and adolescence.

Both parents could barely stand up under the loss and grief. Paula could not stand being haunted by the house, so in her frantic agony she left and stayed with a neighbor for nearly a year, bedridden and in anguish, grieving the loss of her Walter away from Karl and the children. Karl retreated into his study, to stew in his pain, finding no will to write in the family journal for years to come. The journal was a testimonial to the family's growth, but now the soil in which the family was planted was soaked with Walter's blood.

Dietrich was left to contemplate Walter's loss with only his sisters, turning over and over in his head what this meant. The impact of such an experience in childhood cannot be underestimated. This was, by all accounts, the first great tragedy for the family, and in turn, the first of Dietrich's young life. Such an experience lived on within him, and

---

1. Ferdinand Schlingensiepen, *Dietrich Bonhoeffer 1906–1945: Martyr, Thinker, Man of Resistance* (Edinburgh: T&T Clark, 2010), 13.

having this experience as a child may have further given him sensitivity to the personhood and mystery of children and youth. The depth of this experience on Dietrich's own person can be substantiated by the fact that after Walter's death Dietrich was given Walter's confirmation Bible as his own. And it was this Bible, with Walter's name still inscribed in it, that Dietrich used for the rest of his life,[2] picking it up to teach his confirmation students, preach a sermon, or write about the Sermon on the Mount for his book *Discipleship.* This Bible not only reminded him always of his brother but no doubt must have also continually taken him back to his own childhood and the heavy experience of enduring the rupture in his family.

And this may be true for many of us also; we find ourselves in youth or children's ministry not because we are immature, unable to escape some Peter Pan Syndrome, but, I would bet, because many of us have had deep childhood experiences that we cannot shake, that make us aware of the depth and mystery of childhood itself. It is this depth and mystery that draws us to minister to young people, to stand beside them and hear their questions and thoughts, knowing that young people may be touching a deep reality where the divine and human collide. It was just such an experience that happened to me as a child that continues to draw me into ministry and theological contemplation with and for young people.[3]

Adolescence

There was no great rebellion to report in Dietrich Bonhoeffer's own adolescence—no crime spree or parties or dramatic girlfriend breakups;

2. "The death of his brother Walter and his mother's desperate grief left an indelible mark on the child Dietrich Bonhoeffer. At his confirmation three years later, she gave him the Bible that Walter had received at his confirmation in 1914. Bonhoeffer used it throughout his life for his personal meditations and in worship. The figure of his brother and the way in which he died were in Dietrich's mind years later, when he talked to his students about the problem of preaching reverently on Memorial Day, even though he personally had long since turned to thoughts of pacifism" (Bethge, *Dietrich Bonhoeffer*, 28).

3. I have written about my own such experience in *The Promise of Despair* (Nashville: Abingdon, 2010) and *Christopraxis* (Minneapolis: Fortress, 2014). There I discuss how, at four years old, my best friend—my first friend—Benjamin, died of cancer.

and there were no fighting matches with his parents, I'm sure. Karl and Paula ran too tight a ship to allow for any disrespect, and the ethos of the time would not allow it.

Yet to claim a total absence of rebellion in the adolescence of Dietrich would not be quite true. Actually, Dietrich made a major and controversial act of adolescent rebellion, an act that gave him the space to create an identity for himself outside the orbit of his high-achieving brothers and brothers-in-law, and even outside the forceful magnetic pull of his father's personality. This great rebellion came over and against his father.

The great rebellion of Dietrich Bonhoeffer's adolescence was to become a theologian. Bethge says, "He became a theologian to out dupe them all," explaining that of the many other fields a Bonhoeffer could enter, nearly all had already been conquered by his brothers or brothers-in-law.[4] Theology was one they never considered. It was a wide-open space that Dietrich could enter and make a way for himself. He would become himself, freeing himself from the shadow of brothers and father by giving himself to the study of theology. So, toward the end of his gymnasium days, he registered for Hebrew and then announced to his class that he would indeed become a theologian.

This announcement came with the disapproval of his father and the shaking of heads for wasted potential by his brothers. Of course, it wasn't absurdly radical; Dietrich's maternal grandfather and great-grandfather had been theologians. But still, Karl found it a waste, and Karl-Friedrich and Klaus tried to persuade him into another field, reminding him that the church was too backward to be worth his time. With the hubris of adolescent passion, Dietrich's retort to his brothers' disapproval was that if the church was backward then *he* would reform it!

4. Bethge uses this phrase as a heading of one of his sections in the biography *Bonhoeffer*. Wind describes the talent of Dietrich's brothers and brothers-in-law and Dietrich's need to find some area they had not already conquered: "Karl Bonhoeffer, the renowned psychiatrist; Karl-Friedrich, the professor of physics; and Klaus Bonhoeffer, the legal representative of the German airline Lufthansa. So too were Dietrich's brothers-in-law Rudiger Schleicher and Hans von Dohnanyi, counselor in the Transport Ministry and the personal assistant to Franz Gurtner, Minister of Justice, the only minister whom the Nazis took over from the Weimar Republic, to give a pretense of the independent administration of justice" (*Dietrich Bonhoeffer*, 80).

Karl Bonhoeffer was not happy with the decision of his son, but bit his lip and allowed Dietrich to pursue his desires. It may be that Karl's silence was won by Paula. It seems clear that in the aftermath of Walter's death, Dietrich was given to his mother as a replacement for the son she so loved and lost. If she was to come back from her grief and continue as they had before Walter's death, then Karl must allow Dietrich to embrace the artistic and religious side that Paula so admired (and yet that so annoyed Karl).[5] After all, the other two boys were so much like Karl, but Dietrich, she was determined, must be affirmed for taking after her.

Of course, this decision to study theology did not come out of the blue. Dietrich's uncle, Paula's brother Hans von Hase, was a pastor and had been encouraging Dietrich to consider theology, offering suggestions and prods over their holidays together. Hans von Hase had

5. Kenneth Earl Morris provides rich insight into this experience of the loss of Walter for the Bonhoeffer family and Dietrich particularly. He says,

> Specifically, a kind of family "bargain" seems to have been struck between the religious and irreligious factions—that is, between the mother and the father. This "bargain" was to be a kind of solution to the pain of Walter's death. Its substance was that young Dietrich would be allowed to continue his religious pursuits and so to offer himself to his mother as a kind of replacement for Walter while, at the same time, possibly overcoming the limitations of Walter's memory by engaging in the one endeavor which promised a way out of death: religion. Karl Bonhoeffer, himself struck down by the senselessness of his son's death, would agree to look the other way as Dietrich and Paula formed a religious alliance. And Paula Bonhoeffer, overcome by an undeserved though understandable mother's guilt over Walter's death, would maintain over Dietrich the kind of influence she had relinquished with her elder sons. (*Bonhoeffer's Ethics of Discipleship: A Study in Social Psychology, Political Thought, and Religion* [University Park: The Pennsylvania State University Press, 1986], 82)

Morris continues:

> This is what Dietrich was given as a gift, the Bible that had belonged to Walter. The giving of such a gift undoubtedly has elements of a parental injunction that through his faith, Dietrich would somehow be able to "make up" for Walter's death and the parental guilt surrounding it. But for such a gift to have its desired effect, of course, it must be received in something close to the spirit in which it was given. Thus it most surely was, for it was Walter's Bible that Bonhoeffer used for his personal meditations throughout his life. In all—for he also wore a ring bearing the Bonhoeffer coat of arms—Bonhoeffer's religious pilgrimage appears to have been firmly anchored in the spirit of his family, and this spirit reached its sharpest focus when Walter died and Dietrich was choosing his vocation. (ibid., 85)

become the family's personal pastor; as they did not attend church, it was Paula's brother and the children's uncle who took care of any pastoral needs (like baptisms or weddings). It seems logical that von Hase's encouragement was fueled by Paula's wishes. Yet Dietrich still sought a way to bring together both the maternal and paternal sides of himself. Dietrich followed more the maternal path of his history, yet remained his father's son by choosing to study theology as an academic, imagining a life as a lecturer, like his father, in a university.

Student Days

Like his older brothers and sisters, Dietrich started his student days at Tübingen, the school of his father. Dietrich moved in with his paternal grandmother, Julia Bonhoeffer, away from the Berlin home but still within the family. All the sons would study at Tübingen,[6] but Dietrich was the only one to follow his father's footsteps further by joining his old fraternity, the Hedge Hogs. The older boys wanted nothing to do with it, but Dietrich joined, perhaps as a way of compensating for his distinct break with Karl to study theology.

Though Dietrich was a full member of the fraternity, he continued to live with his grandmother. Julia Bonhoeffer was a great support for Dietrich both in those early student days away from home and beyond. Later in life Julia always encouraged (even funded) Dietrich's international travels and pushed him to actualize his dream (which in the end was never met) of going to India and studying with Gandhi.

Julia Bonhoeffer was a strong, fearless woman, the perfect house-mate for a young man trying to find his own voice outside the orbit of brothers and father. Later it was Julia who would take the Bonhoeffer family's first defiant stand against the Nazis. In 1938, after age had forced her to leave her Tübingen home for Karl and Paula's big house in Berlin, she walked through the chaos of the Kristallnacht (the night the Nazis vandalized Jewish shops and ostracized Jewish shop owners) to her favorite store owned by a Jew, refusing to bend to Nazi intimidation.

6. Christine also studied at Tübingen.

Under Julia's care Dietrich excelled at Tübingen, confirming his theological destiny. Yet her care could not keep Dietrich from an ice-skating accident that concussed him enough to send his parents to Tübingen to look in on him. For whatever reason, after this accident Karl and Paula encouraged Dietrich to take a semester abroad and clear his head, offering to pay for Dietrich and Klaus to study in Rome. Maybe Karl felt some guilt for opposing Dietrich's theological wishes, his injuries reminding him of what was important. Or maybe Karl figured a little travel, particularly with Klaus, would finally clear Dietrich's head from all these theological desires—maybe the concussion had rattled theology loose from his ambitions.

Yet Dietrich's life would be forever transformed, and in a theological direction, by his time in Rome. Within days he had fallen in love with the city, mesmerized by the worshipers as they journeyed to the Vatican. Two fuses inside him lit as he took in the glory of the edifices of the ancient city. With a spark, a fuse lit that led him to his theological project, to explore the concrete *theological* life of the church. How was it that Jesus Christ was present in the church as a concrete social reality? Sitting in the Roman sun with the Vatican stretched before him, these questions became intoxicating.

But this same experience seemed to spark another fuse as well. Dietrich's Roman experience opened the possibility that maybe the child who never went to church was being called to the pastorate. Both the professor's lectern and preacher's pulpit were equal fuses inside him. And though they seemed opposed, they weaved themselves tightly together around Dietrich's concern for the concrete social orientation of the church. But though woven together, they were nevertheless awkwardly so, for the young Dietrich sought an advanced theological degree while also seeking ordination in a church he had little contact with. Bethge explains,

> Bonhoeffer's path to theology began . . . in a "secular" atmosphere. First came the "call," in his youthful vanity, to do something special in life. Then he plunged with intellectual curiosity into theology as a branch of knowledge. Only later did the church enter his field of vision. Unlike theologians who came from families that were active in the church and theology, and discovered the existence of the "world"

only later, Bonhoeffer embarked on his journey and eventually discovered the church.[7]

Extending his time in Italy as long as possible, Dietrich decided to return home to Berlin to take a doctorate at his father's university, taking up residence again in his family bedroom. The University of Berlin at this time possessed the greatest theological faculty in the world. Liberalism still held the day (though the Barthian revolt had started). And Berlin was the birthplace of liberal theology, which got its start in the bosom of the theological faculty's founder, Friedrich Schleiermacher, before it moved in succession to Albert Ritchel and in Dietrich's own day to the Bonhoeffer family's neighbor and friend, Adolf von Harnack.

Yet standing in this great liberal tradition, Bonhoeffer refused to be anyone's devotee. He loved Harnack, took a number of seminars with him, and found him not only a wonderful teacher but also a wise and caring mentor. Harnack pushed hard for the nineteen-year-old prodigy to study church history with him. But Bonhoeffer refused, fearing that if Harnack was his teacher that he would be too bound to him and unable to think for himself. So instead Bonhoeffer chose Reinhold Seeberg as his mentor and systematics as his area of study.[8] He was drawn to Seeberg because of the teacher's interest in the social, and Bonhoeffer wanted to attend to not just the theology of the creedal or doctrinal conception of the church but its very concrete, lived, and social reality (the *theological*, as I define it above). Bonhoeffer found some affinity with Seeberg around these issues, but then made a distinct move away from his advisor by pulling this concrete

7. Bethge, *Dietrich Bonhoeffer*, 44.

8. I'm biased here, but I think there is some evidence that if Bonhoeffer had survived the war, his interests may have turned from systematic theology to practical theology. Bethge explains Dietrich's great interest in practical theology even in his student days: "Bonhoeffer enthusiastically participated in the practical theological seminars, presenting more papers than were required. He strove to gain more experience in his natural gift for dealing with people, especially children. Dialectical theology taught him new things as well, since its origins were in practical ministry, which it regarded as the crown of the theological existence. Unlike many of his fellow students, he did not regard his work with Friedrich Mahling (professor of practical theology since 1909) as secondary. He wrote his catecheses quickly and with enjoyment" (ibid., 88).

social orientation of the church into conversation with the thought of Karl Barth.

These three years of doctoral work were the conclusion, one could argue, of Dietrich Bonhoeffer's own adolescence. He started his degree at age nineteen and completed and defended it at twenty-one. And it was during this period, during his writing on the church, that the young Bonhoeffer finally entered the church, really, for the first time.

---

(5)

From a Youth to
Doing Youth Ministry

The Theological in Sanctorum Communio

S till standing between a destiny at the professor's lectern or the
pastor's pulpit, Dietrich Bonhoeffer took steps to begin ordination
in the United Prussian Church.[1] But he was quite young, years away
from meeting the ordination qualifying age of twenty-five. And he had
limited church experience. So while he spent his days writing theological prose about the revelation of Jesus Christ in the concrete life
of the church, he was encouraged by local church leadership to spend
his weekends in the church. "At the end of 1925, about the same time
Bonhoeffer began work on his dissertation, he began working with

---

1. This was a denomination of Lutheran and Reformed churches. Bonhoeffer has
been claimed as a Lutheran; this no doubt is correct, for he was deeply impacted
by Karl Holl and his new research on Luther. Therefore, Luther finds his way into
much of Bonhoeffer's work. And Bonhoeffer clearly sees himself as a Lutheran, as
he reports back to Max Diestel about the Lutheran churches in America. But it is
interesting that the very church he was ordained into was a church that had brought
together both Lutheran and Reformed congregations. It then is little wonder that
the theology of the Reformed theologian Karl Barth would sound in tune to young
Bonhoeffer's ear.

a children's Sunday school group," Bethge writes. "Thus, just as he was embarking on the heavy reading load demanded by *Sanctorum Communio*, he was devoting himself to a group of children who required a considerable amount of his time, for he always prepared his lessons carefully and the children made clamorous demands on him."[2]

So 1925 is a significant year that is often overlooked in Bonhoeffer scholarship, for in 1925 Bonhoeffer began his first major theological project, which Karl Barth much later called a theological miracle. This project became his first book, *Sanctorum Communio*, and set the trajectory for much of the rest of Bonhoeffer's theological work. But it should not be missed that this first theological piece was begun at the same time that Bonhoeffer was doing children's/youth ministry. And this "doing" was not simply a distinct task on a to-do list but was closely connected to the heart of Bonhoeffer's calling, as he gave his all to both. In fact, especially with the early Bonhoeffer (pre-1939), it is hard to find a time where he did significant theological work outside his ministerial embeddedness in youth and children's ministry.

As Bonhoeffer wrote about the concrete church, he was doing concrete ministry with children. Themes like *Stellvertretung* (place-sharing), objective spirit, and open/closed relationality may very well have had their creative origins, or at least gained energy, in his children's/youth ministry experience. For as Bonhoeffer is reported as saying at this time, "When children expect something it is impossible to give only part of oneself to them."[3] *Sanctorum Communio* is a theological project that surrounds the giving of Christ to us in and through the communal life of giving ourselves to one another. So as Bonhoeffer was giving himself to children, he was exploring theologically how the church does such relational giving (place-sharing) in ways that uphold the distinct humanity of others. Place-sharing (*Stellvertretung*), from *Sanctorum Communio* to the prison letters, is a key theme in Bonhoeffer's work, and it may have its origins in his work in children's/youth ministry. As he was a deputy, an advocate, and a place-sharer for young people, he saw how Jesus Christ does the same for us.[4]

2. Bethge, *Dietrich Bonhoeffer*, 91.
3. Ibid., 92.
4. I have decided to translate this phrase as "place-sharing," believing it points to the ministerial (and christological) direction Bonhoeffer wishes. Clifford Green

As Bethge's quote in the first paragraph of this chapter says, this work was time-consuming, for Bonhoeffer's children's/youth ministry was no simple hoop to jump through. We are not completely sure how it was that Bonhoeffer got pulled into leading this Sunday school class in Grunewald, other than needing to become involved in some kind of church ministry. To meet that end Bonhoeffer was sent to his neighborhood church to glean the necessary experience. Like so many of us in youth ministry today, Bonhoeffer was sent to work with the young ones because he was young. For some of us, our own calling into youth ministry started because others felt youth or children's ministry was an appropriate place for us to cut our ministerial teeth, and for a number of us this happened in the congregation in which we grew up. This was true for Bonhoeffer; though he never really grew up in a church (since his family didn't go to church), the neighborhood church in which he was confirmed was where he did his first (youth) ministry. Yet, also like many of us, cutting his ministerial teeth in youth ministry at his home church, Bonhoeffer soon saw it not as a stepping-stone to "true" ministry but as a distinctly rich locale of ministry itself and something to which he must give his whole person. Bethge reports on how this practical ministry experience with children set the terms for Bonhoeffer's theological work, fusing his theological work with his ministry with young people.

> For Bonhoeffer, this first step in practical church work was much more than the fulfillment of a requirement for taking his examinations. It confronted him with a very personal issue: should practical work be the counterpoint to the theme of his theological existence—or should it be the other way around? After his uncommitted beginnings in Tübingen, it had become plain that there was a gulf between the two realms; but it was also clear that the existence of this gap should not be acknowledged. Thus he spiritedly wrote Widmann that the hardest theological

offers more on *Stellvertretung*: "To translate 'Stellvertreter' as 'deputy,' 'substitute,' or 'proxy,' would barely approach Bonhoeffer's meaning; the English terms have rather formal, legal connotations, and they suggest a secondary role. For Bonhoeffer, Christ the *Stellvertreter* is the initiator and reality of the new humanity. The person and action of Christ is 'vicarious' in that he does for human beings what they cannot possibly do for themselves" (*Bonhoeffer: A Theology of Sociality* [Grand Rapids: Eerdmans, 1999], 56).

pronouncements of Barth were worthless if they could not be explained thoroughly to the children in Grunewald [at this ministry site].[5]

Sanctorum Communio

So from 1925 to 1927 Bonhoeffer's life was mutually framed by children's ministry and the writing of *Sanctorum Communio*. The subtitle of *Sanctorum Communio* speaks of the project's objective; it reads, "A Theological Study of the Sociology of the Church." This project that the nineteen-year-old children's minister is after is grounded in the lived; it is the theological, for its focus is not on doctrine only but also the concrete lives of the community of faith. Bonhoeffer hopes to show how the sociological shape of the church has theological depth, that it is through the social life of the church that we encounter the living Christ, who comes to us (who exists) as church-community.[6] So, following Karl Barth, Bonhoeffer is seeking to articulate the ways in which people encounter the revelation of God. But, unlike Barth, he is placing that revelation in the experience of community.

It is more than a little ironic that the boy who never went to church asserts that it is in the church that people directly encounter the presence of the living Christ. There is little doubt that Bonhoeffer's experience in Rome triggered *Sanctorum Communio*, but I think it is also logical that the weekly ministry with children that seems to be so rewarding to Bonhoeffer continues to inspire and motivate the project through 1927. Rome may have been the push into the project, but children's/youth ministry is the sustaining force that moved Bonhoeffer to continue to see the church as the locale for experiencing the living Christ.

5. Bethge, *Dietrich Bonhoeffer*, 93.

6. Thomas Day speaks congenially of the weakness of the project. While it has so much merit, it does lack a true empirical locale. It is better to think of the book as a kind of theological (even philosophical) reflection on the concrete church-community. "The basic weakness of his argument is that, despite all insistence on the real, concrete church, he starts from a 'concept of the church' rather than from a church community. His considerations move primarily on the level of conceptual, clarification, warping the empirical evidence of the historical Christian churches and their self-understanding into the tight woof of the Hegelian renaissance's paradoxical logic" (*Dietrich Bonhoeffer on Christian Community and Common Sense* [New York: Edwin Mellen, 1982], 11).

Yet, to be clear, for Bonhoeffer it is not necessarily in the church (as institution) that we encounter the living Christ but in the church-community (*Gemeinde*). And the church-community is not constituted in institutional operations or even liturgical practices but in the shared life of persons—in relationship. And while Bonhoeffer may have had little exposure to the institutional church and its functional/liturgical processes, he had deep experiences of the shared life of persons. He knew this kind of community in and through the life of his family. His family had been a community of shared life through personhood. It had been a community where children were embraced in their personhood and given belonging.

It may be that *Sanctorum Communio* was the pushing forth of Bonhoeffer's concrete experience in his family into theological reflection, for just as he was experiencing the communion of personhood with children in ministry, so he was reminded of his family's embracing of his own personhood. It is the objective of the dissertation to explore this experience in and through theological language. This may be a slight exaggeration—but only slight—for after 1940 and during the time of the conspiracy to overthrow Hitler, Bonhoeffer's family again (as when he was young) became his most essential community, and a community that he believed was taking on responsibility as participation in the person of Christ.

Sanctorum Communio's great theological contribution is Bonhoeffer's ability to articulate how personhood (a personhood he experienced as a child in his family) is a deep theological reality. Bonhoeffer delves into an incarnational theology, showing that God takes the form of personhood in Jesus Christ, and it is now in and through the reality of personhood that we encounter the living Christ, who is person with and for the Father, by being person with and for humanity. Jesus is the Son of God that overcomes sin and death, making us all children of God.[7] Even today it is in and through the reality of personhood

7. Brian Gregor explains,

> Consequently, God is present as a mediator between the I and the You. God or the Holy Spirit joins the concrete You; only through God's active working does the other become a You to me from whom my I arises. The other person is only a "You" insofar as God brings it about. . . . The claim of the other rests in God alone; for this very reason, it remains the claim of the other. In saying this, however, Bonhoeffer does not want to suggest that the other is merely a

that we encounter Christ. And it is the church-community that takes Christ's form by being a community of persons in relationship. Clifford Green says it this way: "Revelation, that is, the person of Christ, exists in a social form: the church. Revelation is not an idea, a past historical happening, a doctrine or an entity. It is a person, and since person and community are inseparable, the revelation of Christ is present in a personal-communal form."[8]

Personhood can only be constituted in community for Bonhoeffer, for community takes the shape of something like a family, making each member a person, a distinct child, where each person is bound to but distinct from one another. Children in families are distinct individuals, valued in and of themselves; they are not to be swallowed in the collective. For even small children have distinct wills, and parents encounter this distinct will revealing their children as a distinct self. But, while they are distinct willing persons, children nevertheless have their being only in and through others, through the sharing of wills, through parents who relationally share in their person by being willing to embrace them and share in their lives.

Bonhoeffer shows that what it means to be a person, then, is to belong (is to have our very being) in and through others. There can be no such thing as a singular human, for we are persons who have our

---

proxy for God, or a stepping-stone to God. Instead, he insists on the integrity of the other, arguing that this need not strike up a rivalry in which God and the other vie for the affection of the I. God has given the other to me, and I am charged with her care. ("Bonhoeffer's 'Christian Social Philosophy': Conscience, Alterity, and the Moment of Ethical Responsibility," in Brian Gregor and Jens Zimmermann, *Bonhoeffer and Continental Thought: Cruciform Philosophy* [Bloomington: Indiana University Press, 2009], 206)

Green draws this out further:

God is not immanent in us, but is present to us in the social relationship. The transcendence of God means God's presence as "Other." . . . We do not deal with an invisible God in an invisible world of our wishful fantasies; God is met and heard only in the real world where human, personal wills encounter one another; God is to be sought in the real experience of historical, social, ethical existence. Furthermore . . . the purpose of the divine presence is precisely to renew the personal and corporate life of human sociality. Human personal being, then, derives ultimately from the personal being of God. If God has been philosophically described as absolute Geist, Bonhoeffer insists that God, as well as human beings, must be fundamental as Person. (*Bonhoeffer*, 36)

8. Green, *Bonhoeffer*, 53.

being in and through I-Thou relationships that make us so. Bonhoeffer says in *Sanctorum Communio* that "individuals exist only in relation to an 'other.' . . . For the individual to exist, 'others' must be there."[9]

So for Bonhoeffer, persons are fundamentally bound to others, but as such are distinctly themselves, just as parents are to children and children to their siblings, bound one to another as wills in communion. A person is not enmeshed and drowned in a relationship; their distinct will is honored, as it is in a family. The I-Thou relationality that constitutes persons honors the distinct will as a *barrier* of difference.[10] To be a person is to be bound one to another in and through our respect of the barrier between us. The other person is bound to us, but bound to us as a distinct other and respected as such.

This then means that persons are free;[11] they must be free from enmeshment, for personhood is a barrier between us that reminds us that we must not cross it, that we must honor the other person and act responsibly for the other in love. Bonhoeffer asserts that love is only possible through respect of the other's barrier, by honoring personhood as free.

But this freedom is not a freedom *from* but a freedom *for* the other,[12] a freedom much like the love of brothers and sisters—or like a children's minister to his or her Sunday school class. We have our personhood and find the living Christ when we enter others' lives, encountering their persons as wills that are a barrier, reaching out

9. Dietrich Bonhoeffer, *Sanctorum Communio: A Theological Study of the Sociology of the Church*, Dietrich Bonhoeffer Works (Minneapolis: Fortress, 1998), 1:51.

10. Green explains further the place of will and shows how it pushes into ethics, which I do not have the space to explore above. "A person's will constitutes a 'limit' for others, and participates in human 'reality' in encountering their wills. The essence of a person is to will in responsible decision in ethical relationships, and such decision manifests the historicity of human life. In short, the person is a social-ethical-historical being before God" (*Bonhoeffer*, 36).

11. Jürgen Moltmann explains: "Here, in a discussion of human freedom, [Bonhoeffer] shows what he means by the *analogia relationis*, a term he had coined himself. Man's likeness to the Creator consists in his freedom. But freedom is not something man has for himself or can find in himself. 'Freedom is a relationship and nothing else.' It is a relationship between two persons. To be free means 'being free for the other' because this other has bound me to him. Only in relationship with the other am I free" (Jürgen Moltmann and Jürgen Weissbach, *Two Studies in the Theology of Bonhoeffer* [New York: Charles Scribner's Sons, 1967], 54).

12. Bonhoeffer is drawing directly from Luther for this distinction in freedoms.

to them in a freedom that draws near to them (Bonhoeffer developed this more through the *analogia relationis* in his book *Creation and Fall*[13]).

There is no doubt that Bonhoeffer is drawing from the personalist thought of Eberhard Grisebach and Max Scheler, as well as the theology of Barth, as *Sanctorum Communio* takes its shape. And it seems logical that his own familial experience is energizing the constructive edges of his project. But it may also be his ministry experience in Grunewald as children's minister that is behind the coalescing of these concepts. The child can be seen most clearly as a person, for the child stands less obscured by Western individualism. The child reveals personhood, for the child cannot *be* without the belonging of others; a child is a distinct will in the world that is given personhood through the will of those who act in freedom to be for him. The child has his being in and through the acts of others who love and care for him. He shares in others' persons—his mother and father—and these other persons share in him, giving him personhood through acts of love and care.

Yet this relationship that the child is invited into (even elected into) exists in and through barrier, in and through encounter of distinct wills. It is dependent on parents being parents and children being children. Their distinct otherness must be respected, honored, and even obeyed. Both parent and child remain free, but their freedom is the freedom *for* each other.

This direction into the contemplation of children is more nascent in *Sanctorum Communio*, but it became more explicit in just over a year as Bonhoeffer begins to argue that being a child is not simply a stage of life but *the form of our eschatological being*. Bonhoeffer began these thoughts in a lecture in Barcelona and fleshed them out further at the end of his second book, *Act and Being* (which will be discussed more fully below).[14] Yet, while these thoughts are nascent, children and even Sunday school do find their way directly into *Sanctorum Communio*, showing, I believe, how Bonhoeffer's practice of children's/youth ministry was impacting his thought, leading us to

13. *Creation and Fall: A Theological Exposition on Genesis 1–3* (Minneapolis: Fortress, 1997).

14. *Act and Being*, trans. Martin H. Rumscheidt (Minneapolis: Fortress, 1996).

assume this ministry experience is at least part of the current inside him directing his thoughts.

Children and the Church

Bonhoeffer gives his first direct reference to children on page 90 of *Sanctorum Communio*[15] (maybe pointing to the importance of his own children's ministry in his theoretical development). Here Bonhoeffer is discussing "typology of social communities" and is drawing heavily on the classic sociological work of Ferdinand Tönnies and his contrast between the *Gemeinschaft* (the community) and the *Gesellschaft* (the society). Tönnies grieves that the Western world has lost the centrality of community in the escalation of societies of function and independence, and the fetishizing of productivity. Bonhoeffer follows Tönnies in seeing community as distinct from the society, seeking a church that takes the shape of *Gemeinschaft* over the *Gesellschaft*, for it is the *Gemeinschaft* that upholds and even creates personhood; the *Gemeinschaft* wears at least some of the stripes of the family.

To show this, Bonhoeffer points to the child. He explains that all communities are life-communities,[16] meaning that communities are constituted in concrete, lived acts of belonging, and this belonging happens through participation, through shared life. We enter a community by entering its life. "Thus," Bonhoeffer says, "even young children can sense it, for example, through an act of love, trust, or obedience." Bonhoeffer shows us that even young children are taken into the center of communities, not through rational consent but through persons acting with and for the child's person. One wonders if Bonhoeffer saw his own children's ministry in Grunewald as directing the children into the church-community's life-world.

Children for Bonhoeffer, then, are not future or even "young" members of our church communities; they are full members. For they find their way deep into our community as their persons experience love and trust, as their persons experience the life of the community. If

15. All references are to Bonhoeffer, *Sanctorum Communio*.
16. Here he is following Max Scheler.

our churches are more than religious societies, and instead are life-communities, children cannot be excluded or minimized, for as persons who are loved and who love, they find their way deep into communal existence, for they share in its life.

In our own day children's and youth ministers seem to be working so hard to include children in the church, debating issues like children in worship, because for decades or more children have been either directly or functionally moved to the periphery. Yet Bonhoeffer would remind us that such a move only shows that the church has sought to operate more as a society than as a life-community. We have organized ourselves around religious functions and productivity, seeking to build institutions. Against this backdrop, children have little to no value. Bonhoeffer says even more directly that "only a community [*Gemeinschaft*], not a society [*Gesellschaft*], is able to carry children."[17]

The ramifications of this are direct: a church that seeks to embrace its children in and through the revelation of Jesus Christ, a church with a truly rich children's ministry, is *not* the church with the flashiest children's ministry program. This may only reveal that the church is a society, seeking to use its children's program to productively gain members and strengthen its own place within the larger society. Rather, in Bonhoeffer's mind the church with a rich children's ministry is the church that is a community, where the life of young people is taken into the life of the community, where their person is shared in. Earlier in *Sanctorum Communio*, Bonhoeffer says directly, "Unlike the society, a *community can support young children*."[18] And the support that he is referring to is *not* the support of programs but of *Stellvertretung* (place-sharing), which happens only in the community of persons of will.

But this leads to a problem, because Bonhoeffer has claimed the centrality of will. We share in each other's life by encountering the other's person as barrier of will. Bonhoeffer says directly, "This [understanding of life-community] is not to introduce the genetic concept of community; rather, young children in a community are *a part of*

17. Bonhoeffer, *Sanctorum Communio*, 257.
18. Ibid., 90; Bonhoeffer's italics.

their parents' will until they can will for themselves—a thought that would be absurd in a society."[19]

Bonhoeffer throughout *Sanctorum Communio* asserts that all personhood is collective personhood. We have our personhood in relationship with others. We are distinct wills, though we have our personhood never individually but only through relationship with others. The small child wills within the family, within the dynamic of mother and father (object relations psychology has taught of this). Cries for food and comfort are ever reminders that even the infant wills, and as such is barrier (is other) to the mother and father. Yet, though the child is other, through the life-acts of love, care, and trust, child and mother become a collective person, weaving their lives together.

In larger communities (like the church) the will of the small child is absent, for the child lacks the language and direct agency that would confront the community with her will. But this should not make the child invisible or unimportant in the community, for the child's will enters the collective person of her parents. The child's will is represented through the *Stellvertretung* (the place-sharing) of her parents; she is deeply part of the community as her parents invite persons in the church to care for her and share in her.

Bonhoeffer calls such a perspective "absurd in a society" because a society has no sense of the collective person; it asserts that we are so distinctly individuals that a small child can only be seen as a *potential* (member, voter, consumer) and never as a *barrier* (a person) to encounter. This has huge ramifications for our own conception of children in our contemporary churches. Are children seen as potential members housed in children's ministry programs? Or are they seen as persons to encounter, even in their infancy, through the life, suffering, and yearning of their mother and father? It may be then that Bonhoeffer is pushing us to see children's ministry as, at least in part, a deep reaching out and caring for parents. Ministry is not only the running of games, crafts, and hand-motion songs but more so the embracing of the deepest fears, hopes, and questions of the young mother and father, for they, with their child, are a collective person. And these

19. Ibid.; Bonhoeffer's italics.

collective persons experience Jesus Christ as they are drawn into the life-community of the church.

The Place of Baptism and Sunday School

It is not until pages 240–41 (150 pages later) that children reappear in *Sanctorum Communio*. This passage was shortened when Bonhoeffer revised his dissertation for publication, but in 1926 or 1927, in the heart of his own children's ministry in Grunewald, Bonhoeffer could not help but draw the ideas he was constructing into his own practice of ministry. And he did so with potency.

This passage begins with a discussion of infant baptism. Picking up where we ended in the last section on children, Bonhoeffer must deal with how an act that happens outside the will—in this case of the child—can be a personal act that takes the child into the life of the community. If the children cannot will to be baptized, how can infant baptism be a personal act? And if the personal act is lost, how does infant baptism not become a functional operation—or magic incantation—of the church, a volunteer act that is done because parents and/or grandparents seemingly want to feel religious or safe? Baptism outside the personhood of the life-community of the church can so easily be seen as either a religious function that appeases religious "oughts" or that superstitiously keeps children safe. Either perspective lends itself toward individualism in a volunteer society that seeks to provide individuals what they want. And this undercuts baptism to its core. As Bonhoeffer says, "Infant baptism within an association [a volunteer society] is an internal contradiction."[20]

To explore infant baptism within the *Gemeinde* (church-community), Bonhoeffer returns to familial language. He asserts that after children are baptized, "the church-community as the community of saints [as the *sanctorum communio*] now carries its children like a mother, as its most sacred treasure."[21] And this is not just poetic language for Bonhoeffer; he truly means that the church must see the

20. Ibid., 257.
21. Ibid., 240. This passage is from footnote 345 and, as mentioned above, is only found in the dissertation version of the project.

child baptized as the child born into the community and treasure the child as such. The very form of the practical life of church-community becomes motherhood. It is through the mothering, the deep caring for the child, that she is taken into the life of the community. Baptism, Bonhoeffer believes, is the act in which the human encounters the divine, giving the whole church-community familial shape in its practical life.

There is often a critique of *Sanctorum Communio* for lacking empirical/practical help in living as *Gemeinde*, yet it is here that Bonhoeffer provides a vision. The practical life of the church-community is to carry the personhood of others; it is to take on the practice of motherhood.[22] The event of baptism, and the continued practice of motherhood, is the practical shape of the church-community, and this shape secures children as essential and places them not on the church's periphery but at its very center.

But this is possible only if the church is *Gemeinschaft*. As Bonhoeffer says, "[the church] can do this only by virtue of its 'communal life.'"[23] Only through the church's communal life can it treasure children, carrying them in its life of shared personhood. And this "carrying" is not the job of the children's or youth minister but of the whole community, for what carries children is the very shared life of the community itself. The child needs the personal life of the community, given to her through Jesus Christ, as she is baptized into his body.[24]

Infant baptism is only theologically legitimate, Bonhoeffer believes, if the church-community commits to carrying the child like a mother. For this community is a community of persons who are barriers of will. When the child is baptized, he is baptized because his parents

22. It is no wonder that Bonhoeffer has been accused by some of returning to Catholicism; church as mother finds a different, but nevertheless significant, presence in *Sanctorum Communio*.

23. *Sanctorum Communio*, 240.

24. John Godsey explains Bonhoeffer's position on baptism: "For Bonhoeffer, evangelical baptism is infant baptism. Since children do not yet have faith (not even as *fides directa*) and yet the sacrament demands faith, the objective spirit of the community assumes the role of the subject of the faith and through baptism receives the child into itself. Thus baptism, which, on the one hand, is an efficacious divine action in the gift of grace by which the child is placed in the community of Christ, also involves the demand that the child should remain in the Christian community" (*The Theology of Dietrich Bonhoeffer* [Philadelphia: Westminster, 1958], 49).

will it, and, as we saw above, this is theologically valid. But it is only theologically valid if, once baptized, the child is carried by the church-community, "since," as Bonhoeffer says, "the child is borne by the church-community according to God's will without knowing or consciously willing it."[25] To baptize the child and then have no sense or concern to carry the child is, in Bonhoeffer's mind, to abandon the child. No one wills to be either born or baptized; it is the result of the will of others. But once willed, the act (of birth or baptism) is so powerful that it brings a willing being into the world that never willed to be. But now being willed, the child receives his personhood only by being bound to others as a barrier of will. The child has no choice (or will) whether to be born or baptized, but now that he has been, he enters an environment where he can only be as one who meets his world through his own will that draws him to other persons.

To baptize and not carry the child is similar to a mother birthing a baby and then abandoning him; the child is discarded and never able to exercise his will to the one who birthed him. This one that birthed the child is only made mother once she has encountered the will of the child, tending to his cries by giving him her breast, or the many other acts of mothering. Infant baptism without carrying the child is the spiritual act of birthing the child without wishing to encounter his will—it is to baptize the child and then desert him. And whether spiritual or parental, to void the will of the other is to void his person. Bonhoeffer says directly, "Infant baptism ceases to be meaningful wherever the church can no longer envision 'carrying' the child, where it is internally broken, and where it is certain that baptism will be the first and last contact the child will have with it as a church-of-the-people."[26]

These are deeply prophetic words for North American churches and deeply difficult ones for a mobile culture like ours, where people switch churches often or simply decide to no longer go to church, but yet for some reason still want their children baptized. To combat these larger cultural forces of a competitive religious marketplace and growing secularization, our churches have been distracted from

25. Bonhoeffer, *Sanctorum Communio*, 241.
26. Ibid., 240.

"carrying" children. We have been tempted—and often succumb—to being not life-communities that "carry" children but programmed spaces of volunteer societies that attract them. We have sought programs, not communities, for our children to be housed, using these initiatives as ways of attracting individuals. The whole church then gives over its responsibility for "carrying" to the children's or youth ministries, which are too often initiatives disconnected from the life of the church. We hypocritically baptize the child in the sanctuary but then outsource the "carrying" to a program. If we wish to be honest, and to continue as volunteer societies of program initiatives, then we should allow the child to be baptized in the youth group or children's ministry, for it is almost solely in these spaces and through these people that the child will be "carried." The kind of "carrying" that Bonhoeffer calls for can only be done when children are drawn deeply into the life-world of a community, when children are known, heard, and prayed for. It is here in the life-world of a community that children encounter Christ existing as the church-community, as concrete persons encounter their will and embrace their young humanity by carrying them in joy and suffering.

It is around this need for the whole church-community to "carry" the child that Bonhoeffer draws his own ministry experience as Sunday school teacher in Grunewald into his thesis in *Sanctorum Communio*. Bonhoeffer's words are prophetic; he says, "The charge to carry the children must be a serious [warning] for the church-community with respect to its children's programs and Sunday school, and especially for confirmation classes. To understand baptism as an act of the church-community means challenging any Protestant use of the concept of the masses."[27]

As if warning himself and his own ministry, Bonhoeffer says boldly that the children's and youth ministry must serve as the "carrying" of children into the center of the life of church-community. Sunday school or confirmation cannot be a disconnected appendage of the church-community but must be a fully integrated ministry of the whole church-community. Bonhoeffer is not obliterating these spaces of Sunday school, confirmation, and more, but is challenging these

27. Ibid.

spaces to open themselves up to the full life of the community and to see their responsibility as carrying the child—but carrying the child *to* its mother, to the center of the life of the community.

The Shape of Bonhoeffer's Ministry

As the above discussion of *Sanctorum Communio* shows, Bonhoeffer's theological work was anything but simple or thin. Rather, the young man was pushing deep in theological and philosophical conceptions. But as Bethge says, he nevertheless wanted these deep theological thoughts to impact his ministry with the children. Again, Bethge reports Bonhoeffer as writing to Widmann that "the hardest theological pronouncements of Barth were worthless if they could not be explained thoroughly to the children in Grunewald."[28]

From 1925 to 1927 Bonhoeffer tried to do this. For these three years it was his ministerial responsibility to not only teach (preach to) the children but to also help others prepare their lessons. Bonhoeffer met every Friday night at Pastor Karl Meumann's home to craft the Sunday school lessons. On Sunday mornings Bonhoeffer led the catechism classes, becoming known for his energetic children's sermons, in which he never failed to tell stories with drama and flair, blending the Bible with analogies and imaginative hooks, such as "about the devil who stole a pot of red paint and painted the humble mushroom, bestowing upon it the poison of pride; about the old woman caught in a snowstorm outside a locked door (an Advent story); and he gave a dramatic account of the struggle for the people's confidence between the prophets Jeremiah and Hananiah. He had no qualms about taking liberties with the text."[29] These children's sermons were so important to Bonhoeffer that he never failed to write them out word for word. Bethge explains, "He made biblical stories as exciting as sagas or as appealing as fairy tales. He went to great trouble to hold the children's attention, which is why he so carefully wrote out in advance what he proposed to tell them."[30]

28. Bethge, *Dietrich Bonhoeffer*, 93.
29. Ibid., 92.
30. Ibid.

With Bonhoeffer's passion and attention, the classes ballooned, and soon Bonhoeffer needed some help, especially with the girls. So he convinced his youngest sister, Susanne, to join him in ministry. Susanne, of course, like Dietrich, had little experience in the church, though coincidentally (or not) she would end up marrying a theologian/pastor named Walter Dress. So Susanne took charge of the girls and Dietrich, the boys.

By 1927 enough children had outgrown the Sunday school to warrant the starting of a youth group. So Bonhoeffer began meeting with these adolescents on Thursday nights at his parents' home. The youth group lacked any funny skits or mixers and turned instead to heavy conversation. Bonhoeffer invited each of the young people to come with a topic, sometimes even a prepared introduction, and to offer it as entree into conversation. Bethge explains the feel and direction of the group.

> Since April 1927 Bonhoeffer had invited those who had outgrown Sunday school to [his family] home for a "reading and discussion evening." The program would have done credit to a college; it covered systematic, religious, ethical, denominational, political, and cultural topics. He gave a report on Catholicism, and the young people prepared short introductions to the evening discussions. They attended the opera and concerts together; before taking them to a performance of *Parsifal* Bonhoeffer gave them an introductory talk on the subject.[31]

If the shape of his children's ministry had been formed in the engaging environment of the Bonhoeffer family home and its openness to children's music, plays, and stories (coupled with Bonhoeffer's own deep childhood questions), then his ministry with adolescents was shaped by his own adolescent experience with his brothers-in-law and their respect for his thoughts and ideas. All the young people were mature and engaged; a number of them come from Jewish homes in the neighborhood and tragically, as Bethge reports, died in either concentration camps or the front during the war.[32]

31. Ibid., 95.
32. "Nearly all the members of this group later died in Hitler's war or his concentration camps; Goetz Grosch died in action on the front" (ibid.).

We can hear the spirit of this youth group in Bonhoeffer's own words from his Barcelona journal.

> On 18 January [1928] I held the last meeting of my Thursday group. A newcomer, Peter Rosenbaum, was there, a young man of unusual intelligence and sensitivity—he defended Luther's doctrine of the real presence! The young people had brought questions that we discussed. Finally, I asked what they thought of the fact that Christianity had conquered the world in comparison with many other religions; this led us to the question of the essence of Christianity, and we discussed revelation and religion, and the contrast and connection between them.[33]

By Christmas of 1927 both Bonhoeffer's dissertation and children's/youth ministry in Grunewald were nearly finished. The children's/youth ministry couldn't have ended more positively for Bonhoeffer. He had stumbled into youth work, but it became a central theme for the next decade of his life, as central as his interest in Karl Barth's theology and the social orientation of the church, and even more so than any political interests (the political did not become important to him until 1933). The pull between the lectern and pulpit was now even more complicated by his passion for and skill in youth ministry. Schlingensiepen states, "Bonhoeffer had a definite gift for working with children. . . . Bonhoeffer really loved this work and did not give it up."[34]

The tension between the lectern and pulpit could not be mitigated and needed to be equally explored, so to continue toward the pulpit Bonhoeffer agreed to take a yearlong internship in Barcelona. His voyage was not a departure from the lectern and academic life, however. Rather, he spent his time in the warm Spanish sun not only delving deeper into ministry (and as we'll see, youth ministry) but also revising *Sanctorum Communio* for publication.

As the final days came before his departure to Spain, the affirmation for his children's/youth ministry at Grunewald came pouring forth. The Thursday night group gave him a hearty good-bye and, as a gift of appreciation, Albert Schweitzer's book *On the Edge of the Primeval Forest*. Goetz Grosch took over the group after Bonhoeffer's

33. Ibid.
34. Schlingensiepen, *Dietrich Bonhoeffer 1906–1945*, 31.

departure and, in a strange twist of fate, seven years later became a
student of Bonhoeffer's at the underground Confessing Church seminary at Finkenwalde.[35]

The children said good-bye on the Sunday before Bonhoeffer's
train took him to Barcelona through Paris. At the Sunday service the
children prayed for him, blessing him as he went, thanking him for his
ministry. A statement from Bonhoeffer's journal relays how meaningful
this good-bye was to him; his statement communicates its importance
so deeply because of the humorous honesty of how church prayers
had so often left Bonhoeffer bored. Bonhoeffer's journal reads, "What
affected me most was saying good-bye to the church work. . . . Pastor
Meumann mentioned my name in his general prayer. For a long time
church prayer has been something that has left me cold but, when the
throng of children with whom I have spent two years prayed for me,
the effect was incomparably greater."[36]

This quote from Bonhoeffer shows how ministry to young people
may be transformative for ourselves as well. The young people are
witnesses to the depth of the life-world of the community, not only
because they are carried but also because they minister to their elders. Here the children were ministering to Bonhoeffer, their prayers
awakening his spiritual life, bringing the stale institutional prayers to
life as the shape of community.[37]

35. See Bethge, *Dietrich Bonhoeffer*, 95.
36. Wind, *Dietrich Bonhoeffer*, 39.
37. This insight was pointed out to me by the talented Dan Adams.

6

Tears for Mr. Wolf

Barcelona and After

Soon after finishing his children's/youth ministry in Grunewald, Bonhoeffer boarded a train and, really for the first time, left his family behind. It is thus logical to call this period of his life, when he was twenty-one years old, his entrance into adulthood. When Bonhoeffer had gone to Tübingen, he had lived with his grandmother, and even when he went to Rome, he was with his brother Klaus. As his train steamed toward the sun of Spain, it was the first time that he was truly on his own.

The impetus for the journey abroad came from both Bonhoeffer's desire to stretch his legs and see something new and as a strategic move of his ecclesial mentor, Max Diestel. Diestel was superintendent and oversaw Bonhoeffer's ordination process. Diestel and Bonhoeffer connected over many things, but at the center was their shared love for travel and experiences abroad.[1] Bonhoeffer's encounter with

---

1. Schlingensiepen explains how Max Diestel came to "discover" Bonhoeffer: That first sermon, with its portentous opening, was given by the 19-year-old theology student at the request of Superintendent Max Diestel, his supervisor, who needed a substitute for a pastor who had suddenly fallen ill in Stahnsdorf, on the south side of Berlin. Bonhoeffer asked his superintendent

Rome had ignited a desire to experience more of the world. And Diestel was deeply involved in the ecumenical movement, seeking friendship and partnerships between churches across the Western world. Diestel saw in this young man great potential, witnessing how the mind of a scholar and the heart of a pastor to youth came together uniquely in Bonhoeffer. Seeing also Bonhoeffer's passion to travel, Diestel couldn't help but take steps to mold Bonhoeffer for a future in the ecumenical movement.[2] But this may sound more calculating than it was; Diestel had plans for young Bonhoeffer, but knew regardless that it would serve him well to find himself outside the orbit of his important family and the pulls of Berlin. This all made an internship in Barcelona fitting.

Diestel took center stage in Bonhoeffer's life from this period until the heat of the church struggle in 1933. Diestel, more than anyone else, helped direct the next steps of Bonhoeffer's life. He is the addressee of many of Bonhoeffer's letters from Barcelona and then New York—many of Bonhoeffer's most insightful thoughts, particularly about America, were shared with Diestel. Diestel was a churchman more than an academic theologian, and it was Diestel's tending of Bonhoeffer that pushed Bonhoeffer further into imagining a life in the pastorate.

Bonhoeffer had always had older siblings and brothers-in-law taking an interest in him and helping direct him, but they never understood his theological or church interests. And at the university he had academic advisors, but he had taken distinct steps to keep them at arm's length, choosing, for example, to study with Seeberg instead of Harnack because of his confidence that he would never come under the charms of Seeberg. So Diestel became Bonhoeffer's first true mentor.

---

to discuss the draft of the sermon with him, and Diestel, who had a canny feel for people and their particular gifts, kept an eye on him from then on. It is not saying too much to call him the discoverer of Bonhoeffer, as he was the first to consider how the young man's career could be furthered, without telling him so or influencing him in any way. (*Dietrich Bonhoeffer 1906–1945*, 34)

2. Schlingensiepen says, "In his strong handwriting, Diestel wrote in the margin of the c.v.: 'I consider him to be a young man who is outstandingly gifted both in church praxis and in scholarly activities, a young man who can only broaden his experience through his anticipated activities in the United States. I recommend that things be made as easy for him as possible and that at the same time we keep him in mind for future practical work'" (ibid., 55).

He lacked the academic accomplishments that Bonhoeffer, even at twenty-one, possessed, but he had a vision of an important contribution Bonhoeffer could make.

Diestel was the first on a very short list of such mentors. Both a deep streak of arrogance and a fierce desire to think for himself kept this list ever short in Bonhoeffer's life; following Diestel, only Karl Barth and the English bishop of Chichester, George Bell, would be included—and neither of them until after 1931.

Bonhoeffer arrived in Barcelona and jumped right into his pastoral duties. His supervisor was Pastor Fritz Olbricht, a man who liked only food more than the sound of his own voice. Bonhoeffer liked him, but he lacked all the culture of a Berliner from Grunewald. And Bonhoeffer wasn't shy in relaying this to his parents in letters.

Olbricht was a German national, and the church Bonhoeffer served with Olbricht was a German-speaking congregation made up of businessmen, their families, and others who had migrated to Spain to find labor or fortune. Economically, the congregation was much more diverse than Bonhoeffer had experienced before. Bonhoeffer moved into a small, run-down room in a house managed by German sisters. Bonhoeffer conveyed to his parents that the bathroom met the standard of a third-class toilet on a train, something he could only imagine, for rarely if ever did he travel third class. But it was little bother to him. Like his mother he loved talking with people and hearing their stories, and, tucked away in this little house of tenant rooms, he had an abundance of stories and encounters with which to occupy himself.

Bonhoeffer's experience was similar to many other interns; things started strongly, hit bumps of jealousy and mistrust, and then recovered potency and ended well. Bonhoeffer was thankful that Olbricht gave him many opportunities and a great deal of freedom. Olbricht, too, was thankful that his young, elitist intern from Berlin was so capable, allowing him to leave the congregation to Bonhoeffer's care for generous stretches of time so he could holiday.

Bonhoeffer's ministry involved a great deal of preaching, and he enjoyed this very much; it allowed him to flex some of his academic muscles while giving full attention to ministry. It may have been because he was a new, young voice, but soon the lagging attendance at Sunday services spiked when Bonhoeffer was preaching. Olbricht was no career climber; he had taken the pastorate in Barcelona to get away from the intensity of Germany and relax into the Spanish laid-back culture. But he was not keen to be overshadowed by his twenty-two-year-old intern. Fearful that his parishioners would want more from him, Olbricht decided to no longer advertise who was preaching on Sunday, blunting the embarrassment of Bonhoeffer's popularity.[3]

Though Bonhoeffer enjoyed preaching, he could not escape his first love: youth ministry. Bonhoeffer made the following remark in a letter back to his ordination committee: "Since I had already become especially interested and engaged in youth work during my period of study in Berlin, it was a great pleasure for me that in Barcelona I could devote myself particularly to this branch of practical work as well."[4]

Olbricht had settled into the lowest common denominator of ministerial commitment, which meant that the Sunday school had been unattended to for years, leading to its diminished state of nearly no children participating. Bonhoeffer sought to rectify this, taking over the teaching. But his exuberance could not awaken the Sunday school; only three children showed up for his first session. Undeterred, Bonhoeffer decided to visit each child personally, inviting them to come to Sunday school. And come they did; within weeks the group was large and most of Bonhoeffer's time was spent teaching and being with them.[5]

The older boys, particularly, became Bonhoeffer's focus. He met to play sports with them and had them over to his tenant house for music. This was the first time, but not the last, that Bonhoeffer witnessed the material needs of the young people to whom he was ministering. Around Christmas he wrote to his father asking for extra money to buy some of the boys Christmas presents.

Bonhoeffer pushed his youth ministry out into local schools, asking to teach classes on religion in the primary school. Olbricht wasn't

3. Clifford Green says, "The pastor was Fritz Olbricht, and initially Bonhoeffer got on very well with him. But as the vicar's popularity increased, particularly with the young people and their parents, Olbricht became jealous and stopped announcing the preacher for the following Sunday" (editor's introduction to Bonhoeffer, *Barcelona, Berlin, New York*, 5).

4. Staats, afterword to ibid., 606.

5. Bethge explains: "He promptly visited the home of each child who attended. The next time thirty turned up, and attendance never dropped below that number" (*Dietrich Bonhoeffer*, 109).

happy with this new endeavor, fearing that when Bonhoeffer departed, it would leave him with more work than he wished. Yet Bonhoeffer found ways to reach out to many of the youth at the school by starting a discussion group.[6] "After a short time Bonhoeffer's room was regularly filled with a swarm of schoolboys," Bethge explains. Bonhoeffer "knew how to settle their school problems, help them with their work, and move angry teachers toward a more considerate opinion of them." Using the money from his father, "He gave one boy a bicycle and another a tent. His pupils gave him a tremendous Christmas, the first he had spent away from home."[7]

Maybe the most interesting incident of youth ministry for Bonhoeffer in Barcelona happened when a ten-year-old boy came to him on an errand and ended up in pastoral care. The boy was in tears because Mr. Wolf, his German Shepherd, had died, and the boy wanted to know if the dog would go to heaven. Many of us who have worked with children and youth have been confronted with this same question of the destiny of a dead beloved pet. Bonhoeffer relays the incident and his response in a letter to Walter Dress (his sister Susanne's soon-to-be husband). The letter (an unintended verbatim account of the experience) is filled with compassion, theological depth, and ministerial sensitivity. As Schlingensiepen explains, this story, which "only became known in 1999 when a cache of letters that Bonhoeffer had written in 1928 to Walter Dress, his youngest sister's fiancé, was discovered—reveals just how unusual was Bonhoeffer's gift for

6. See ibid., 110.
7. Ibid. Schlingensiepen explains this further:
    Bonhoeffer didn't have such an easy time with his proposal to introduce religious instruction into the upper classes at the German school. The teachers and Pastor Olbricht were immediately worried about what would happen to this when Bonhoeffer left. Olbricht didn't want to take on this instruction on top of his other duties. But as soon as he arrived with his fashionable round hat, the "vicar" from Berlin had already created a sensation among the older pupils, and proved to be such a magnet that they took to visiting him at his pension. His room there was large enough to accommodate them, and weekly discussion evenings were soon under way. Bonhoeffer again began calling on the parents right away, and since he also helped to resolve difficulties at school, more than once putting in a good word with a teacher for one of his young visitors, he soon became very popular in the German colony. (*Dietrich Bonhoeffer 1906–1945*, 43)

dealing with children and young people."[8] There is much we can learn from this letter, so I'll quote it in length below.

Did I answer your letter about Brunner? I don't really remember. When you wrote you seemed pretty impressed by the book; I read up to about the last sixty pages, where I gave up because I didn't expect much more after finding the entire book extremely disappointing. . . . Today I encountered a . . . unique case in my pastoral counseling, which I'd like to recount to you briefly and which *despite its simplicity really made me think*. At 11:00 AM there was a knock at my door and a ten-year-old boy came into my room with something I had requested from his parents. I noticed that something was amiss with the boy, who is usually cheerfulness personified. And soon it came out: he broke down in tears, completely beside himself, and I could hear only the words: "Mister Wolf is dead," and then he cried and cried. "But who is Mister Wolf?" As it turns out, it is a young German shepherd dog that was sick for eight days and had just died a half-hour ago. So the boy, ill consolable, sat down on my knee and could hardly regain his composure; he told me how the dog died and how everything is lost now. He played only with the dog, each morning the dog came to the boy's bed and awakened him—and now the dog was dead. What could I say? So he talked to me about it for quite a while. Then suddenly his wrenching crying became very quiet and he said: "But I know he's not dead at all." "What do you mean?" "His spirit is now in heaven, where it is happy. Once in class a boy asked the religion teacher what heaven was like, and she said she had not been there yet; but tell me now, will I see 'Mister Wolf' again? He's certainly in heaven." So there I stood and was supposed to answer him yes or no. If I said "No, I don't know" that would have meant "no." So here was someone who wanted to find out, and that is always unfortunate. So I quickly made up my mind and said to him: Look, God created human beings and also animals, and I'm sure he also loves animals. And I believe that with God it is such that all who loved each other on earth—genuinely loved each other—will remain together with God, for to love is part of God. Just how that happens, though, we admittedly don't know. You should have seen the happy face on this boy; he had completely stopped crying. "So then I'll see Mister Wolf again when I am dead; then we can play together again"—in a word, he was ecstatic. I repeated to him a couple

8. Schlingensiepen, *Dietrich Bonhoeffer 1906–1945*, 43.

of times that we don't really know how this happens. He, however, knew, and knew it quite definitely in thought. After a few minutes, he said: "Today I really scolded Adam and Eve; if they had not eaten the apple, Mister Wolf would not have died." This whole affair was as important to the young boy as things are for one of us when something really bad happens. But I am almost surprised—moved—by the naiveté of the piety that awakens at such a moment in an otherwise completely wild young boy who is thinking of nothing. And there I stood—I who was supposed to "know the answer"—feeling quite small next to him; and I cannot forget the confident expression he had on his face when he left. One of those cases of "laughter amid tears," and doubtless a case of the sort that will not recur very frequently.[9]

This letter reveals so well the heart of Dietrich Bonhoeffer and why he is the forefather to the theological turn in youth ministry. It begins with a heavy-handed critique of the great twentieth-century Zurich theologian Emile Brunner, showing a young man doing youth ministry that is not shy to delve deeply into the ideas and theological perspectives of others. Bonhoeffer ultimately finds these pages of Brunner of little help, for they do not square with the *theological* demands of his ministry. And his ministry comes to him as an event of the concrete and lived experience in the person of a child.

Bonhoeffer has requested something from the boy's parents, and as the boy arrives, Bonhoeffer becomes attuned to him, sensing that there is something wrong, as the usually cheerful boy is not himself. The *theological* in youth ministry often has its impetus not in the formal but in the encounter of the experiential. Bonhoeffer has not organized a formal time of pastoral care, nor is he looking to teach the boy theology, but rather as minister he seeks to attune himself to the young person enough to seek the boy out, to ask the boy to speak of his experience.

This attunement shows the depth of Bonhoeffer's gifts for youth ministry and his desire to "carry" the boy. He does not see a one-dimensional child with flat and stupid concerns. Rather, as a forefather to the theological turn, Bonhoeffer contends that there is theological depth in the very concrete and lived experience of the boy—and his

9. Bonhoeffer, *Barcelona, Berlin, New York*, 138.

tears witness to it. Bonhoeffer is drawn into the boy's humanity, understanding that when this young person speaks of his experience, it will come to Bonhoeffer with theological depth. As Bonhoeffer invites the boy to speak, it eventually comes out, the tears flowing. Bonhoeffer hears through the gasps of sobs as the boy repeats, "Mr. Wolf is dead, Mr. Wolf is dead."

Bonhoeffer dwells deeply in the boy's suffering, sharing it by experiencing the loss the boy must feel, telling Walter Dress about the boy's deep emotional attachment to the dog. Bonhoeffer stands as the boy's *Stellvertreter*, as his place-sharer (a key theological concept in which Bonhoeffer, from beginning to end, will frame his theology). As his *Stellvertreter*, seeking to "carry" the boy, Bonhoeffer invites him to narrate his experience, to tell Bonhoeffer how it was that the boy loved the dog and how the dog awoke him in the morning, playing with him all day. It had now just been a half-hour since Mr. Wolf's death. Bonhoeffer hears the narration that is the revealing of the boy's humanity by embracing the boy and taking him to his knee, giving him his person in the midst of his suffering, being close enough to hear the boy, awaiting the deep theological questions the boy has, which are tied to his very concrete lived experience, to the deep questions of childhood, questions Bonhoeffer himself remembers from his own childhood.

Sitting with the boy, sharing in the boy as his place-sharer, the boy's sobbing is muted by the arrival of the theological; it wells up in him as his heavy experience is shared by another, as Bonhoeffer embraces the boy's suffering on his knee. Standing neck-deep together in the boy's experience, having this experience shared by Bonhoeffer, the boy says, "But I know he is not dead at all!"—the theological has arrived. The boy uses what he has heard other boys say about death in religion class, what his teacher has responded about heaven, and constructs his theory of hope that he will again see his beloved dog, Mr. Wolf. The boy then directly addresses Bonhoeffer, looking for an answer; seeking confirmation from his pastor on his theory, the boy says, "But tell me now, will I see 'Mr. Wolf' again? He's certainly in heaven."

Now, Bonhoeffer's *Stellvertretung*, his place-sharing, leads to the impulse of confession and proclamation. Bonhoeffer did not take the boy to his knee thinking, *the boy is weak, it is now time to convert him*. Rather, Bonhoeffer just shares in the boy's pain, embracing him, patient and present in every tear. But now that the boy's person has been joined, he seeks clarity. The boy seeks to offer his conception of what is real through his experience; he loved Mr. Wolf, so Mr. Wolf is in heaven, right? The theological bursts forth from within the experiential, growing from the fertile soil of shared humanity through the action of ministry.

What is Bonhoeffer to say? He is stuck between theology and the theological. He perceives that the boy wants a yes or no answer. He knows that it is ministerial malpractice to not give an answer, to somehow drown the boy's questions in Socratic methods of avoidance, offering the boy's direct question only the answer of another question that gets him off the hook. The boy has shared his experience and now seeks to make sense of it; he seeks the theological, and Bonhoeffer knows that the philosophical (answering a question with a question) or the heavy stone of theology that may give the right dogmatic answer but takes no concern for the stained cheeks of the boy, will not do.

Bonhoeffer essentially confesses to Walter Dress that children's/ youth ministry is a deep and challenging locale to do the *theological*. He explains to Dress how he struggled with what to say, forced through this experience to think deeply. And like so many of us in youth ministry, he explains at the end of the letter that he felt small next to the significance of the boy's deep theological question. It is more than ironic that the arrogant young man felt insecure next to the ten-year-old's question. Bonhoeffer never doubted himself in defense of his dissertation or while wrestling with Harnack in his seminars. But in the shadow of the ten-year-old and his cosmic question raised by the lived sorrow over his dead dog, the overly confident Bonhoeffer sits in fear and trembling. The letter begins with a twenty-two-year-old, fresh from his dissertation, unmercifully critiquing one of the greatest theologians of the twentieth century, but it ends with this same arrogant young man transformed into a minister who is made to feel small by the questions of a ten-year-old that pull him into a shared experience of the transcendent.

And this is so because it is next to the ten-year-old, not the old professor, that Bonhoeffer is pulled beyond theology and into the theological, beyond the academic and into the ministerial. It is here in youth ministry that he encounters the possibility of the encounter with Jesus Christ through the concrete humanity of being this ten-year-old boy's place-sharer.

So Bonhoeffer must give an answer, and a theological one at that; the boy will settle for nothing less. So Bonhoeffer connects the boy's love for Mr. Wolf and God's own being as love, explaining, in a way the boy can understand, how in the eschatological fulfillment all forms of love are redeemed and taken into the very love of God. "So I will play with Mr. Wolf again," is the boy's response, embracing the possibility in joy.

But, now that the boy has had his suffering shared in, leading him to ask his deepest theological questions—as he hears Bonhoeffer respond to him not with theology but with the theological—he cannot help but do the theological himself. He says to Bonhoeffer that he scolded Adam and Eve for bringing death into the world, for losing Mr. Wolf was an experience of a ruptured world that allows death to end love. The boy, too, takes a step toward the theological, and Bonhoeffer was forced by the boy's concrete experience into imaginative theological articulations. Witnessing Bonhoeffer standing in the theological, so too the boy is drawn into the theological; watching someone do the theological, the boy does the theological himself.

Dietrich Bonhoeffer is a forefather to the theological turn in youth ministry, and the story of Mr. Wolf stands as a shining example of what this means. The theological is first the ministerial; it is the taking of the boy to your knee and sharing in his suffering, allowing him to narrate his experience. It is never beating the boy over the head with theology, but seeking to give responses that attend to the experiential. It hopes not for assimilation of theology in the young person's brain but for the wrestling with God in the questions swirling within the young person.

Bonhoeffer even reflects at the end of the letter on how surprising it was to see a boy that he imagined as only wild and excitable come to such reflection. This is a boy who would resist theology, too wild to listen or care. But next to his experience, in sharing in his humanity, Bonhoeffer enters with him into the theological, igniting his imagination, seeing him transformed from a wild, uninterested boy to one who wrestles with God next to his deepest questions of lost love.

Mr. Wolf forced Bonhoeffer to be nimble, to be a true theological thinker. In our own day, so many in our own churches think they want a youth minister that can teach their kids theology, believing that if the youth worker knows theology their kids will be safe, good, and informed enough to never ask their parents or other adults the theological questions that inevitably make them feel, like Bonhoeffer, small and unsure in the thin air of inquisition. But it is in this very thin air of the theological that the transformational occurs; it is where weeping turns to laughter, as Bonhoeffer says at the end of the letter. It is here in the theological that we encounter the being and action of God in the concrete and lived. Bonhoeffer helps us see that a youth minister is not someone who heaves theology onto young people, getting them to know stuff, but is rather a minister of the gospel that stands near the concrete humanity of young people, sharing in their experience, helping them wrestle with God's action in and through their concrete lives.

---

(7)

The Child as Eschatological

Back to Berlin and On to New York

Just like Bonhoeffer's first youth ministry experience in Grunewald, things in Barcelona ended well.[1] There was talk—even pleading—that young pastor Bonhoeffer not leave Barcelona but move from intern to full-time pastor. But in the end, Bonhoeffer resisted, not yet ready to give his life completely over to the pulpit of pastoral ministry. The pull of the professor's lectern was still nagging at him, and nagging so fiercely that late in his time in Barcelona he offered his congregation, who had little concern or experience with the academic, a lecture series on ethics. Many people came, but more out of respect and love for Bonhoeffer than interest in the topic.

1. Fritz Olbricht says as much in his concluding internship report:
Let me humbly report that my vicar, Dr. Bonhoeffer, concluded his year on February 15 and then returned home. He demonstrated competency in every respect and helped me a great deal in my various activities. He was particularly good at engaging the children, who are enormously fond of him. In the end, an average of forty children attended his children's service. He also enjoyed immense popularity throughout the colony itself. I would be extremely grateful if the German Evangelical Church Committee could send me as soon as possible a new, competent vicar who could be active in the same way. Yours faithfully, F. Olbricht, Pastor. (Bonhoeffer, *Barcelona, Berlin, New York*, 171)

Toward the end of his time in Barcelona, not only had *Sanctorum Communio* been revised and published, but Bonhoeffer also began making plans for his *habilitation* (a second dissertation; in the German system, even today, the first dissertation qualifies you as doctor, the second is needed to qualify you as a lecturer in the university system). So instead of staying in Barcelona and continuing in his ministry, Bonhoeffer decided to return to Berlin and his parent's home to write his *habilitation*. Yet the biggest hurdle was the topic.

Working again with Seeberg, Bonhoeffer explained to him that he felt a deep urge to write on the consciousness of children, no doubt impacted by his ministry experience in Barcelona and maybe still wrestling with events like Mr. Wolf.[2] But Seeberg was against it, pushing Bonhoeffer to a more philosophical topic, which in the end he followed. His *habilitation* became his second book, *Act and Being*, a rich text that places Martin Heidegger and Karl Barth in conversation, critiquing and affirming both scholars' epic contributions, as he placed them into service of his own theological vision for the concrete social constitution of the church-community presented in *Sanctorum Communio*. But still at the very end of the text the reader can see remnants of Bonhoeffer's initial desire, as the book ends with a section called "The Definition of Being in Christ by Means of the Future: The Child."[3] Bonhoeffer's youth ministry experience was becoming

2. Bethge explains:
The choice of topic, "Act and Being, Transcendental Philosophy and Ontology in Systematic Theology," was not influenced by either Seeberg or Lutgert. At an early stage Bonhoeffer had written from Barcelona: "I . . . think about a postdoctoral thesis every now and then." The subject of his reflections during those hot summer weeks, the "problem of the child," became the formula for the conclusion and climax of the book: the description of the new being in Christ that unites act and being under the heading of "The Child." Here he forced the hostile brothers together—be they transcendentalists and ontologists, or theologians of act and theologians of being, or Barthians and Lutherans. His understanding of the church was still dominated by his idea of "Christ existing as church-community." (*Dietrich Bonhoeffer*, 132)

3. I have no proof to substantiate this, but my hunch is that Moltmann's little book *In the End—The Beginning: The Life of Hope* (Minneapolis: Fortress, 2004), which draws on children as eschatological beings, has its creative inception in Bonhoeffer's thought in *Act and Being*. After all, it is Moltmann's book *Two Studies in the Theology of Bonhoeffer* that put Moltmann on the English-speaking theological scene.

more and more inextricable from his academic projects. And one can imagine without too much trouble that if the academic environment had allowed for the study of the theological and young people (as it does today in North America, parts of Europe, and beyond), Bonhoeffer may have found his way into such conversations.[4]

Childhood as Eschatological Gift

Act and Being shows unequivocally that Bonhoeffer had the chops to be an academic theologian. While Karl Barth was a significant inspiration in *Sanctorum Communio*, in *Act and Being* Bonhoeffer reveals what he sees as the weakness of Barth's act theology,[5] asserting that in Barth's theology, act is heralded so loudly that all considerations of being are drowned out in its reverberations.[6] Bonhoeffer's own experience in youth ministry led him to seek a place for being. As I said above, he wished to do this by making children and consciousness the topic of his *habilitation*. But Seeberg balked, leading Bonhoeffer to smuggle the theme of children into the final pages of *Act and Being*.

4. An example of this global conversation is the International Association for the Study of Youth Ministry. It is a global, though mostly American and European, group that publishes the *Journal of Youth and Theology*.

5. Michael P. DeJonge has offered a wonderful book on Bonhoeffer's distinction from Barth at these points. I only have room to offer one quote. "From Bonhoeffer's point of view, person-theology is superior to Barth's act-theology because it can account for the fullness of Christian life. Put otherwise, person-theology can solve the problem of act and being" (*Bonhoeffer's Theological Formation: Berlin, Barth, and Protestant Theology* [Oxford: Oxford University Press, 2012], 77).

6. Andreas Pangritz presents not only how Bonhoeffer desired for his *habilitation* to focus on children but also how Barth plays a central role within it:

> Writing to W. Dress on 14 June 1928, Bonhoeffer ponders the idea of writing his habilitation dissertation on the topic of "the child and theology." But even where he feels that he has to oppose him, Barth remains the standard by which he measures his work. Bonhoeffer is searching for a way of making the doctrine of the "sinlessness" of Christ fruitful for pastoral care, "so that one no longer looks to one's sin but only to Christ and that conscience ceases to be seen as the voice of God but as that of the tempter who only wants to fasten attention to the past instead of the present and what is to come. I find these ideas quite redeeming and liberating, however unBarthian they are." (*Karl Barth in the Theology of Dietrich Bonhoeffer* [Grand Rapids: Eerdmans, 1989], 25)

It just may be that experiences like those of Mr. Wolf are simply too important to Bonhoeffer to leave behind, witnessing to a theological reality that he must at least lean toward. So while he could not make the whole project revolve around children, as he wished, he could nevertheless bring them in at the end of this dense academic piece.[7]

And so Bonhoeffer does bring children in, returning to discussions of infant baptism that he had raised in *Sanctorum Communio*, but now pushing infant baptism in the direction of being (*Dasein*) and in so doing toward the eschatological, toward the fullness of God's act. The child *is* through the act of the will, but this act must be grounded in the communion of being encountering being. The child has a home from action, but this act of parents to *be* together forges a home and becomes a substantive place within which the child's being rests.[8] Bonhoeffer says in *Act and Being*, "Home is the community [*Gemeinde*] of Christ, always 'future', present 'in faith' because we are children of the future—always act, because it is being; always being, because it is act."[9] Baptism itself is an act of God done by human beings, but

7. Sabine Dramm gives some historical context to Bonhoeffer's focus on the child: Bonhoeffer had, from time to time, been intensely preoccupied with the theme of the child as a metaphor for man standing before God, and it becomes more and more crystalized in these concluding statements, reminding us that his original idea had been to write about the "problem of the child in theology." This work, which he never wrote might have ended in much the same way as the one he did finish. In any case, it is indeed an unusual way for an Evangelical theology to conclude a professorial dissertation in the year 1930. After all, he had been educated through the sternly rational school of Evangelical theology, which was ever mindful of its chosen duty to be "scientific"! He writes, "Here a new creation emerges in faith and is completed in contemplation: the new man of the future who longer reflects on himself but looks only away from himself to the revelation of God—to Christ—and who is (re)born out of the confines of this world into the wideness of the heavens; who becomes, whatever he was or even never was before, a creature of God, a child." (*Dietrich Bonhoeffer: An Introduction to His Thoughts* [Peabody, MA: Hendrickson, 2007], 79)

8. My own project *The Children of Divorce* (Grand Rapids: Baker Academic, 2010) has great resonance with this perspective.

9. Dietrich Bonhoeffer, *Act and Being: Transcendental Philosophy and Ontology in Systematic Theology*, Dietrich Bonhoeffer Works (Minneapolis: Fortress, 1996), 2:161. Pangritz adds texture:

Consequently, Bonhoeffer could not possibly adopt for his purpose the programmatic statement of Barth's Tambach address: "We live most deeply in the No than in the Yes, more deeply in criticism and protest than in naivete, more deeply in longing for the future than in participation on the present."

because it is, it leads to being, being community, being together, being the ones that "carry" the child. The mother is mother through act, but this act cannot be separated from her being, and it is her act that creates a community of being.

So baptism, Bonhoeffer says at the end of *Act and Being*, makes us all children, making our eschatological form that of the child, for the child *is* through both act and being. He says, "Baptism is the call to the human being into childhood, a call that can be understood only eschatologically."[10] Here Bonhoeffer makes not only a significant theological argument for the essential importance of children but also asserts that it is the very form of the child that is normative. The child, then, must stand at the center of the church-community, for the child is the eschatological form of humanity; the child *is* through both divine and human act and being. It may be, following Bonhoeffer, that a sign of a congregation's faithfulness, its very act to *be* toward *eschatos*, is not big buildings or full membership roles but its willingness to embrace children.

This is as far as Bonhoeffer pushes in *Act and Being*, leaving us with more questions than answers, leaving us so wishing Seeberg had permitted Bonhoeffer to explore his original desire. But what cannot be missed is the central importance of the child in the thought of Bonhoeffer. And this centrality of the child seems clearly born from Bonhoeffer's ministry experience. For the thoughts that came together in *Act and Being* actually had their origins while he was still in Barcelona. The second lecture Bonhoeffer gave to his congregation in Barcelona on December 11, 1928 (a handful of months after the Mr. Wolf event was recorded in a letter marked September 1, 1928), asserted that Jesus himself is the creator of childhood, making childhood the form and shape of his discipleship. Bonhoeffer says,

> Once when Jesus is out with his disciples and they are arguing over the rewards they will receive for living in this discipleship, Jesus "called a

---

In relation to the church, Bonhoeffer would stress the exact opposite. In the community of faith, the naivete of the child is quite possible; "Home is the community of Christ, always 'future' because we are children of the future . . ." (AB, 116). Here what is yet to come is already present and—albeit in a preliminary way—at our disposal "in faith" (AB, 112). (*Karl Barth in the Theology of Dietrich Bonhoeffer*, 29)

10. Bonhoeffer, *Act and Being*, 159.

child, whom he put among them, and said, 'Truly I tell you, unless you change and become like children, you will never enter the kingdom of heaven'" (Matt. 18:2–3), or "if any of you put a stumbling block before one of these little ones who believe in me, it would be better for you if a great millstone were hung around your neck and you were thrown into the sea" (Mark 9:42). *For Jesus the child is not merely a transitional stage on the way to adulthood, something to be overcome; quite the contrary, he or she is something utterly unique before which the adult should have the utmost respect. For indeed, God is closer to children than to adults. In this sense, Jesus becomes the discoverer of the child.* He sees the children and wants to belong to them; who would block his path? God belongs to children, the good news belongs to children, and joy in the kingdom of heaven belongs to children. "Woe to anyone who puts a stumbling block before one of these little ones." This notion is so utterly alien to the sensibility of antiquity that only one other might seem even more alien, namely, that Jesus, this man of the ruthless either-or, goes not only to children but also to sinners. He traffics with the socially despised, the outcasts, the tax collectors, the deceivers, and the prostitutes.[11]

And revealing that these are *not* the flitting thoughts of a young man too overcome with early experiences in ministry, fourteen years later (in 1942) Bonhoeffer wrote a position paper on the question of baptism, and in it he said nearly the same as in Barcelona in 1928:

Nowhere in the NT are children slighted in regard to salvation, the in breaking reign of God; on the contrary, that kind of attempt by the disciples (!) runs up against the "indignation"—i.e., the outrage—of Jesus. *Jesus' acceptance of children like that of the blind, lame, poor, signifies an eschatological event of salvation. It occurs, therefore, precisely not on the basis of some sort of natural, psychologically understood innocence of children—a thoroughly modern idea—but rather as the miracle of God, who humbles the lofty and raises up the lowly.* The "innocence" of children is a gift of Christ but never a natural state by means of which the gifts of Christ—such as baptism, for instance—becomes superfluous. The eschatological character of Jesus' acceptance of children calls instead for their baptism by the church.[12]

11. Bonhoeffer, *Barcelona, Berlin, New York*, 352; my italics.
12. Bonhoeffer, *Conspiracy and Imprisonment*, 555; my italics.

These are profound words on the significance of the child, ones that those of us in youth ministry today should hear. Bonhoeffer stands squarely as forefather to the theological turn in youth ministry because he sees the child and childhood (and, one could add, adolescence) not (primarily) as a developmental category but as a theological gift given to the church to live eschatologically through both act and being. The child is not less-than for Bonhoeffer but the very form (the very being) of the followers of Jesus. The child is the one who experiences most fully the act of God in Christ; only the poor and outcast are as dear to Jesus as the child, Bonhoeffer says in the 1928 lecture. It is the child as being that brings the act of God near. And we all are welcomed into this act and being of God's very eschatological self, for all of us have been children and now are called to "carry" and care for them. But "carry" and care for them not as innocent—an untheological modern idea—but as eschatological, as those who witness to the act and being of God.

It may be, following the logic of Bonhoeffer, that the churches that honor children, giving them a place at the center of their life-community, carrying them in love, bear the sign of the true community. It is the child, the outcast, and the broken that reveal a church that is not a volunteer society (a *Gesellschaft*) but a community that is Jesus Christ existing as church-community.

This Time across the Atlantic

The *habilitation* was accepted in 1930, but still Bonhoeffer was only twenty-four and not yet at the qualifying age for ordination, nor could he find an open lecturer position. He had found an assistant lecturer post, but this consisted of little more than menial work, such as filing, correcting papers, and, if he were lucky, some precept work with students. It was a foot in the door, and Bonhoeffer was willing to do it, but he took little joy in it.

Max Diestel again took center stage in directing Bonhoeffer's future, encouraging him to embark on another international experience, this time leaving Europe and taking a year in America. At first Bonhoeffer resisted, excited to travel but worried that in America, because of

his young age, he would have to enter as a seminary student. He not
only already possessed a doctorate but was qualified to be a faculty
member in Germany. The elite prodigy didn't like the idea of being
only a student in the classroom of an American university, let alone
a seminary. The thought of taking tests and sitting in classes wasn't
completely compelling to the young man. Bonhoeffer's brother Karl-
Friedrich, the physicist, had been on a lecture tour in America already
and encouraged him to wait some time before going so that he might
enter the American scene as a professor and not a student.

Yet in the end Diestel's advice won out, and Bonhoeffer boarded
a ship for a year in New York as a Sloan Fellow. Bonhoeffer's great
gift with young people could not be contained even on the voyage
across the Atlantic. Schlingensiepen reports that Bonhoeffer met the
Ern family, spending time with them as they crossed; the Erns' "ten-
year-old son Richard . . . became attached to Bonhoeffer during the
Atlantic crossing on the Columbus, and [began] writing to him since
then."[13] Upon arrival Bonhoeffer said good-bye to the Erns and entered
a New York City existing in the reverberating aftermath of a stock
market collapse. As he made his way uptown to Union Theological
Seminary, he passed the Empire State Building as it was being erected
beam by beam.

At Union Theological Seminary

His year in New York radically changed Bonhoeffer's life. The cata-
lyst for the transformation was not the curriculum of Union but the
significant friendships forged in the rooms and halls of the Upper
West Side seminary and the many experiences within the city itself.

There were four friendships—with two Americans and two fellow
Europeans—that would deeply impact Bonhoeffer. Paul Lehmann was
an American doctoral student at Union who had come from a German immigrant family in which his parents spoke only the language
of the homeland. Paul and his wife, Marion, became Bonhoeffer's
unofficial hosts, taking him into their apartment for evenings to escape

13. Schlingensiepen, *Dietrich Bonhoeffer 1906–1945*, 71.

American dorm living. Bonhoeffer was used to living in the private atmosphere of his parents' home, an environment that only became more private as his sisters and brothers married and moved out. The talkative American students and their open-door policy in the dorms was often more than the elite Berliner could take. The Lehmanns offered Bonhoeffer a little taste of home and a dose of peace and quiet.

The two Europeans were Erwin Sutz and Jean Lasserre. Sutz was a Swiss national who was in the middle of working on his doctorate. He had studied under Karl Barth and knew him quite well. Sutz impacted Bonhoeffer's future by being the contact that eventually connected Bonhoeffer and Barth, a relationship that would be of significant personal impact on Bonhoeffer during the church struggle and the war.

Jean Lasserre was a Frenchman. Standing on American soil between the two world wars, it is not a superficial point to highlight the odd and transformational friendship of these German and French nationals. Bonhoeffer was only a child, about the age of the boy in the Mr. Wolf incident, when the First World War broke forth and eventually took his brother Walter. World War I, which started with dreams of excitement and possibility, ended in a nightmare that Germany would not awaken from for the rest of Bonhoeffer's days. Not only did Germany lose the war, and with it many boys like Walter, but the Treaty of Versailles kept the nation sedated and stuck in its nightmare.

Political coups, inflation, and the shame of national defeat were the night terrors that Germany could not be shaken from. Bonhoeffer had personal experience with all these realities, hearing the shooting of Walther Rathenau, the foreign minister of the Weimer Republic, from his gymnasium window. And if it wasn't for Karl Bonhoeffer's ability to take in foreign patients, accepting their foreign currency, Bonhoeffer's upper-middle-class family would have found it hard to make ends met, as the deutsch mark inflated to such an extent that it took nearly a wheelbarrow of currency to buy milk and cheese. And these realities were the bitter marinade soaking a national shame of defeat that would allow fringe political groups like the Nazis to find a hearing and voice. Even a decade and a half after the ceasefire in the European trenches, the feeling of German hatred toward the French had not been diluted.

So the friendship between Bonhoeffer and Jean Lasserre started out choppy but grew into deep mutual respect. It was Lasserre who would turn Bonhoeffer to the Sermon on the Mount and its call for obedience in discipleship. Without their friendship, starting in 1930, Bonhoeffer's classic *Discipleship* may never have been written (or may have been written in a very different form).

Lehmann and Sutz continued to stay in touch with Bonhoeffer after his time in New York. Bonhoeffer wrote a number of letters to Sutz, and even returned the hosting favors of the Lehmanns by taking Paul and his wife into his family home in Berlin during the Lehmanns' European study trip just before the Second World War.

Jean Lasserre did not stay as connected with Bonhoeffer as did Lehmann and Sutz after their time in America. But Bonhoeffer and Lasserre nevertheless did find the opportunity to reconnect, and they did so through youth ministry. As Bonhoeffer became secretary to youth in the ecumenical movement and planned a number of youth conferences across Europe, he partnered with Lasserre in engaging the youth of France.

Yet it was the fourth relationship (the second American) that took Bonhoeffer back into youth ministry. Frank Fisher was an African American who had come to Union Seminary after studying at Howard University in Washington, DC. Bonhoeffer and Fisher could not have been more unlike in background, but this did not stop them from forging a rich friendship. Fisher became Bonhoeffer's guide and traveling companion into worlds Bonhoeffer never knew existed before his arrival in New York. Fisher took Bonhoeffer not only to Washington and into the nascent civil rights conversations at Howard University but also, even more impactful, into the storefront churches in Harlem.

During his early weeks at Union, Bonhoeffer visited most of the prominent and powerful churches of New York, hearing all the great white preachers the New World's biggest city had to offer. Yet Bonhoeffer was unimpressed; writing back to Diestel, he reported that American preaching was theologically bankrupt and self-indulgent. He says boldly in a letter back to Germany, "In New York, they preach about virtually everything; only one thing is not addressed, or is addressed so rarely that I have as yet been able to hear it, namely, the gospel of Jesus Christ, the cross, sin and forgiveness, death and life."[14] In another letter to Diestel, he states, "Things are not much different in the church. The sermon has been reduced to parenthetical church remarks about newspaper events. As long as I've been here, I have heard only one sermon in which you could hear something like a genuine proclamation, and that was delivered by a Negro (indeed, in general I'm increasingly discovering greater religious power and originality in Negroes)."[15] Bonhoeffer would not find consistent "good" preaching and vibrant church life until Frank Fisher led him to Harlem's Abyssinian Baptist Church.

Once Bonhoeffer visited Abyssinian, he stayed, getting deeply involved. He was moved by the skill in preaching and the passion of life together.[16] As before, Bonhoeffer sank his stakes in a church community by following his greatest ministerial gift, ministering to young people. The tall, athletic German, who at this time spoke proficient English punctuated by broken phrases and tinged with a deep German accent, sat with African American children in Harlem, more than three decades before the civil rights movement, leading the Abyssinian Baptist Church's Sunday school. Bonhoeffer must have seemed out of place in 1930s Harlem. But he seemed to thrive in such an environment.

Schlingensiepen points out more specifically both the youth ministry Bonhoeffer did and the impact he had within the congregation. "Almost every Sunday, and also during the week, [Bonhoeffer] could be found at the Abyssinian Baptist Church on West 138th Street in Harlem, where he taught a Sunday school class. He took part in countless discussions and in excursions with the church youth. Ruth Zerner, an American who worked at the same church in the 1960s, found that a number of the church members still remembered the blond pastor from Germany who had been part of their congregation 30 years earlier."[17]

14. Bonhoeffer, *Barcelona, Berlin, New York*, 313.
15. Ibid., 266.
16. Staats says, "In this young church of the African American working class, [Bonhoeffer] encountered a form of Christianity that was exemplary in its focus on preaching and on church life" (afterword to ibid., 606).
17. Schlingensiepen, *Dietrich Bonhoeffer 1906–1945*, 65.

Bonhoeffer's experience in the black church pushed him deeper to see not only the social orientation of church but also the theological. With great admiration, similar to his experience in Rome as a late adolescent, Bonhoeffer was moved by how the lived and concrete became the locale for reflection, for the theological. Bonhoeffer saw this theological commitment not only in the preaching and children's/youth ministry of the black church but also, most powerfully, in the music.

Bonhoeffer had particular gifts as a musician; his father actually had hoped that it would be his skill on the piano and a career as a concert pianist that would release the theological hook from his youngest son's mouth. But Bonhoeffer's fingers were too short, which in the end was no matter, for the theological hook had already been swallowed. The Negro spiritual bound together Bonhoeffer's two passions of music and the theological. Bonhoeffer ended up buying a crate of records of Negro spirituals in New York, which became one of the greatest treasures and essential tools for ministry for the rest of his life. The spiritual appeared in his ministry with his confirmands in Wedding, his university students in Berlin, his youth group in London, and, powerfully, in Finkenwalde at the illegal seminary.[18] Bonhoeffer says in a letter to his brother Karl-Friedrich, "I still believe that the spiritual songs of the southern Negroes represent some of the greatest artistic achievements in America."[19]

18. Wind says, "Reinhold Niebuhr recommended his students to read black American literature. Dietrich was deeply impressed by it. Later he was to make his students and probationary ministers familiar with the music of black America" (*Dietrich Bonhoeffer*, 51).

19. Bonhoeffer, *Barcelona, Berlin, New York*, 269. In Bonhoeffer's own words, The strongest contribution of the Negroes for American Christendom lies in their spiritual songs ("Negro spirituals"), in which they sing with moving expression about the distress and liberation of the people of Israel ("Go down, Moses . . ."), the misery and distress of the human heart ("Nobody knows the trouble I have seen . . .") and love for the Redeemer and yearning for the kingdom of heaven ("Swing low, sweet chariot . . ."). Every white American knows, loves, and sings these songs. It is difficult to understand how famous Negro singers can sing these songs in the overcrowded concert halls of white people and receive resounding applause, while at the same time the same men and women find no acceptance in the communities of the whites because of social discrimination. We should furthermore point out that nowhere else is revivalist preaching still so alive and widespread as it is for Negroes; here the gospel of Jesus Christ, the Savior of sinners, is truly preached and received

Bonhoeffer had experienced in Harlem a social-relational community that encountered Jesus Christ deeply in the concrete and lived, and that wrestled constantly with the theological, seeking to do so by "carrying" its children. The spiritual was the musical artifact of this theological reality for this community (and so many more). Bonhoeffer then used the spiritual as a way of helping his own young people do the theological and hear the theological voice of others as they sought for God next to and within their concrete and lived experience. Using the spiritual, Bonhoeffer invited young people to enter the theological themselves, to speak with the pathos of the spiritual as the faithful way of doing the theological.[20]

Bonhoeffer's positive experience in Harlem youth ministry, coupled with his negative experience of white mainline preaching, led him to see what he called "phraseology" as the great enemy of the confession of Jesus Christ, for phraseology hides us from the real. Phraseology was the enemy because it was theology cut loose from real life; it was theology that could make no difference or had no concern for the concrete and lived experience of young people. Clifford Green explains what Bonhoeffer means.

> What is "phraseological?" And why is it lacking in reality? The "phraseological" is theology that exists in words, that is not integral with life, that is therefore abstract, at home in an academic career, not

---

with great welcome and visible emotion. The issue of the Negro is one of the most decisive future tasks for the white churches. (*Theological Education Underground: 1937–1940*, Dietrich Bonhoeffer Works [Minneapolis: Fortress, 2012], 15:458)

20. Wolf-Dieter Zimmermann writes, "On one of the open evenings he played records of Negro spirituals. It was for us an entirely unknown, strange and frightening world. He told us of his coloured friend with whom he had travelled through the States; how hotels and restaurants had refused admittance even to him as a white man when he was accompanied by his black friend. He told of the piety of the Negroes, their worship and their theology. There, he thought, was a Christianity in reformation" (*I Knew Dietrich Bonhoeffer* [New York: Harper & Row, 1966], 64). Zimmermann says further: "He spoke of themes for sermons, expositions of sermons. And he played the spirituals, translated them, explained them, interpreted them. A strange new world was beckoning to us. At the end of the evening he said: 'When I took leave of my black friend, he said to me: "Make our sufferings known in Germany, tell them what is happening to us, and show them what we are like," I wanted to fulfill this obligation tonight'" (ibid., 65).

embodied in personal faith; the "real" is faith and theology that are at one, that are embedded in and formative of life, just as *Discipleship* has it: "Only the one who believes is obedient and only the one who is obedient believes."[21]

It was the "real" and the movement away from the "phraseological" that so impacted Bonhoeffer in Harlem. Abyssinian Baptist Church was a place that drove deeply into the theological, seeking the real in and through Jesus Christ.

Youth Ministry and the Real

In youth ministry the theological turn is a turn into the real; it is the seeking divine action in and through the concrete and lived experience of young people. Bonhoeffer's experiences in New York provide a great lesson for those us of seeking the theological turn in youth ministry today. It shows us the negative so that we might move into the constructive. We hear that the theological cannot become the phraseological and that we must take every step with our young people to avoid all loose phrases that are not bound in their experience of wrestling with God. To fall into the phraseological blinds us, as youth workers, from seeing the concrete humanity of young people and helping them see the humanity of others. "Youth ministry can so often overlook the reality of the suffering other, avoiding the challenges of reality in favor of safe programmatic language, settling for a drive toward religious socialization."[22]

The theological turn in youth ministry does not simply use the language of theology or religion. Rather, the theological turn in youth ministry seeks the living revelatory encounter with Jesus Christ (the *real*, as Bonhoeffer says). And Bonhoeffer's New York experience not only gives us the negative, a warning to stay away from the phraseological, but also pushes us into the constructive and practical. Watching Bonhoeffer, we see how forms of art (like the spiritual for him)

21. Clifford Green, editor's introduction to Bonhoeffer, *Barcelona, Berlin, New York*, 39.
22. Dan Adams, personal correspondence, August 8, 2013.

capture the deep expressions of others' concrete and lived experience. Bonhoeffer's own youth ministry, which moved from the phraseological to the real, from the abstract to the concrete, from theology to the theological, involved inviting young people to reflect on art (deep expressions of pathos) as an introduction to young people themselves doing the theological, seeking God in the midst of their own deep questions and experiences.

Bonhoeffer was not trying to get young people to like art, to become fans of the spiritual, but was inviting them to step inside it as a concrete articulation of the human experience, to dwell in the experience for its corollaries to their own concrete and lived experience of Negroes, to seek the God who suffers the experience of exclusion. He wanted them to seek God's act and being in and through Jesus Christ within the experience, to speak of the presence and absence of God within the concrete and lived as the way of doing the theological.

During his time in Harlem, youth ministry remained and even deepened as Bonhoeffer's ministerial focus. But as such it also became more integrated. Bonhoeffer took his rich theological conceptions of sociality and *Stellvertretung* and pushed further into the concrete. The spiritual and Harlem helped move in this direction. Even his classes at Union, the classes he was reluctant to take when arriving, turned him to the practical. As a doctoral student in Berlin, Bonhoeffer had been drawn to practical theology courses, and at Union he found that such practical theological classes moved him into further reflection on youth work.[23]

23. Bethge writes about the classes Bonhoeffer took at Union, discussing how Webber's class focused on youth work and how intrigued Bonhoeffer was with it. Bethge says, "Webber's course covered labor problems, restriction of profits, civil rights, juvenile crime, and the activity of the churches in these fields. . . . The Boy Scouts, Big Brother, and Big Sister movements interested them because of their success in fighting delinquency; the students learned that, while there were 1,313 youth 'gangs' in Chicago alone, only 7 percent of the members cared for by groups like Big Brothers returned to the gangs" (*Dietrich Bonhoeffer*, 163).

8

Back to Berlin—Again

Bonhoeffer's American experience gravitated around New York, but despite being in the New World for only a year, he was able to see much more than just the Big Apple. As mentioned, Bonhoeffer accompanied Frank Fisher to Washington, DC; and before this trip he had spent time with relatives in Philadelphia. On Christmas Day he traveled by train through the South to sail the short distance to Cuba.[1] And as his time in America came to an end, he drove through the Midwest with his European friends and Paul Lehmann in a run-down Oldsmobile (procured for him by his Atlantic-crossing friends, the Erns), dropping Lehmann in Chicago. Soon after, before making it to St. Louis, Sutz turned back, leaving just Lasserre and Bonhoeffer to drive through Texas. At the border they ditched their car like outlaws for a train deep into Mexico. Bonhoeffer's time in America wasn't restricted to New York, and his time in North America wasn't restricted to the United States.

In the summer of 1931 it was time to return to the Continent and Berlin. Things had changed for Bonhoeffer. The pull of pastoral ministry was gaining momentum within him and his own piety

---

1. This was a pre-Castro time and many Americans vacationed in Cuba.

and spiritual life had been ignited in a way it never had before his time in the New World. Bonhoeffer was clear that he had not been overtaken by American emotionalism and the infatuation with the "personal" religious experience. He was way too German, the son of his father, and engaged in Barthian thought to ever be tempted in this direction. Nevertheless, upon returning, *something* had changed; as Bethge boldly says, "the theologian became the Christian."[2] The life of Christian devotion—of Bible reading, prayer, and regular worship participation—had now sunk into Bonhoeffer's life. Even Paul Lehmann noticed it when he visited Bonhoeffer in Berlin, making comments about the difference in the Bonhoeffer of the early weeks in the Union dorms, who was blasé about such spiritual practices, and the devotion of the Bonhoeffer he met in Berlin in 1933.[3]

As Bonhoeffer landed back in Germany in the summer of 1931, fresh from his American experience, not only was he personally in the midst of change but so too was Germany. Bonhoeffer had been receiving word from his brothers throughout his voyages in Spain and America that the country was flirting with fascism, a diabolic thought for the elite Bonhoeffer family. And as Bonhoeffer returned from America it seemed that the Nazis, no longer a fringe group, had made their way to the center stage of German politics and were gaining power daily. Their power came into its own in 1933 as Hitler became both chancellor and president, and therefore supreme leader, of Germany.

To Bonn and Barth

Bonhoeffer for the most part had little concern about the political situation pre-1933, but was soon drawn into it full force. But before then there was time for him to meet Karl Barth. So in July of 1931 Bonhoeffer, barely unpacked from America, jumped on a train to Bonn seeking a seat in Barth's classroom. Erwin Sutz had made arrangements for Bonhoeffer to participate in one of Barth's notorious seminars. Bonhoeffer's parents tried to plead with him to stay home

2. See the heading on p. 202 of Bethge, *Bonhoeffer*.
3. See Bethge, *Bonhoeffer*, 264.

or retreat to their summer cottage and relax after his voyage into Mexico and across the United States, but Bonhoeffer could not be stopped. Like a man on a mission, he couldn't waste any more time before hearing Karl Barth for himself. Bonhoeffer had been a great defender of Barth at Union; with Sutz, he was one of the first heralds on North American soil of the Barthian revolution. And this heralding of Barth came with great American ridicule, pushing Bonhoeffer all the deeper into Barth's thought. He could wait no longer to hear him for himself. So after a short stop to see his oldest brother and his brother's growing children, Bonhoeffer was in Bonn as a short-term visiting student.

Barth was known for being kind but suspicious of such visiting students, especially those from Berlin and the womb of the liberal theology he was moving against. But, unknown in the Bonn seminar, Bonhoeffer raised his hand and made a statement, quoting Luther, in response to Barth's question. If Barth was known for being suspicious of newcomers, he was just as notorious for being swayed from suspicion to friendship by one comment in class. Bonhoeffer had hit the nail on the head, and from this statement he was invited to dinner and evenings with the great theologian and his students.[4]

Before Bonhoeffer left Bonn, Barth invited him for a few one-on-one discussions. Both men found a common ground, and soon their encounters bloomed into a significant friendship. Bonhoeffer found Barth even deeper in person and personal conversation than in his writing, impressed that Barth never wavered from thinking things through theologically, and Bonhoeffer was amazed that Barth was always open (even non-defensive) about being pushed in his conceptions and perspectives. And Barth saw Bonhoeffer as a German's German, a confident and capable young man with extraordinary gifts. Bonhoeffer now had his second true mentor, and one that would become deeply important as the Nazis came to power and sought to envelop the church within their political pursuits.

4. A very similar occurrence happened to Eberhard Jüngel decades later; when the East German came to Basil, he was met first with suspicion and then after one good question and dialogue, Jungel awoke the next morning to a complimentary stack of volumes of *Church Dogmatics* sitting at his door with an invitation for Barth's "new East German friend," as the letter said, to come to Barth's home for dinner.

After America and his short trip to Bonn, it no longer seemed to be an either/or for Bonhoeffer between the academy and the church but a both/and.[5] This movement into the both/and no doubt had its impetus in Harlem and the deep theological reflection done with youth at Abyssinian Baptist, but this move to the both/and may also have been pushed over some kind of threshold by Bonhoeffer's personal engagement with Barth. For Barth himself was a pastor turned academic who finally found his own theological lens, after some stops and starts, in the church, not in following classical dogmatic formulations but in thinking about God's action in, through, and for the church in the world. Barth, too, was exploring not theology but the theological, arguing that theology was always finally an act of the church, and therefore theological.

Max Diestel, Bonhoeffer's first mentor, had been gently molding Bonhoeffer for such a both/and ministry, believing an experience or two abroad would help the young man into imagining how he could be both scholar and churchman. And it so happened that Diestel was exactly right. Now back home and having met Barth, Bonhoeffer was ready for ordination and a lectureship at the university.

The Second Half of 1931

Bonhoeffer had asked his ordination committee if he could take a few months upon his return to Berlin from New York to regain his bearings, see Barth, and begin preparing lectures. He was comfortable with a both/and vocation, but, nevertheless, now being appointed lecturer in theology at the University of Berlin, he would need time to prepare. Bonhoeffer had assisted other professors and lecturers,

5. Justification for saying that the "both/and" was entered into by Bonhoeffer in the time in New York can be seen here through Bethge's words: "Church events played a more incidental role in the New York correspondence. Still, Bonhoeffer wrote Diestel: 'I'm attracted more and more by the ministry'" (*Dietrich Bonhoeffer*, 167). Bethge speaks further about the conflict within Bonhoeffer: "The choice between the ministry and an academic career lay open to him. His family took it for granted that he would choose the latter, where few obstacles and only friendly advancement awaited him. But his problem was not how to enter the academic world, it was how to escape it. The pulpit appealed to him more than the professor's lectern" (ibid., 96).

but now he would be given a classroom of his own. The young man, not much older than his students, was now ready to give his own lectures. The committee was divided on whether it was appropriate for the candidate, on the eve of a November ordination, to be given leave. After all, he had already been gone as Sloane Fellow for large parts of 1930 and 1931.

Yet again Diestel came to Bonhoeffer's aid, working out the leave, but arranging it with one contingency: that Bonhoeffer accompany him to Cambridge, England, for the conference of the ecumenical movement. So Bonhoeffer went, and by the end of his time there was voted the new secretary to youth of the European division of the ecumenical movement.[6] It would now be Bonhoeffer's job to work with European young people within the movement, organizing youth conferences throughout the Continent. Bonhoeffer had already proven himself a gifted congregational youth worker, and now as secretary to youth his youth work would stretch across Europe. Youth ministry now became formally central to who Bonhoeffer was. Of course, it had never *not* been; Bonhoeffer had little to no interaction with the church that did not come through doing youth ministry. And the members of the conference could see his passion and giftedness for youth ministry, leading them to vote the newcomer into leadership.

A Catechism

Bonhoeffer had needed a few months off before starting back into ministry in Berlin to prepare lectures. But the pull of youth ministry was just too strong within Bonhoeffer for him to be able to focus all his attention on just academic theology.[7] So between the July trip to see Barth and the

6. "Through Diestel's efforts, Bonhoeffer attended the Cambridge conference and returned as one of three international youth secretaries for the work of the World Alliance in Europe. In this position, Bonhoeffer became a member of the Provisional Bureau for Ecumenical Youth Work, a coordinating body in Germany for the various Protestant groups committed to ecumenical work" (Michael B. Lukens, editor's introduction to Dietrich Bonhoeffer, *Ecumenical, Academic and Pastoral Work: 1931–1932*, Dietrich Bonhoeffer Works [Minneapolis: Fortress, 2012], 11:9).

7. "Between his visit to Bonn in July 1931 and the trip to Cambridge in September, Bonhoeffer worked on 'a Lutheran catechism,' entitled 'By Faith Alone.' It is a

September Cambridge conference, Bonhoeffer and Franz Hildebrandt embarked on writing an updated catechism. Bonhoeffer had known Hildebrandt since 1927. Hildebrandt had been a fellow student in some of Bonhoeffer's final seminars at the university. It is not exaggerated to call Hildebrandt Bonhoeffer's first true friend, even though they didn't meet until Bonhoeffer was twenty. Until then, nearly all Bonhoeffer's close relationships were with relatives, whether brothers and sisters, brothers-in-law, or cousins, like Christophe von Hase. Hildebrandt would be the first to break through Bonhoeffer's self-enclosure inside his family, giving him his first taste of friendship beyond it.

Hildebrandt and Bonhoeffer shared deep academic interests coupled with an unquenchable pull toward pastoral ministry. As the church conflict started after 1933, Hildebrandt and Bonhoeffer became deeply engaged, together pushing the older pastors to think more radically and to take bolder steps to differentiate the church from National Socialism and the German Christians.

But these ambitious endeavors were still far in the future in the summer of 1931, when all the two young pastor-theologians desired was an updated catechism for use in youth ministry. Schlingensiepen explains both how the two friends got started on the project and the form that the catechism itself took. The last sentence of the quote below shows how the *theological* lived itself out in the catechism project. Like with Mr. Wolf and the spirituals in Harlem (and even like the discussion groups in Grunewald and his adolescent interactions with his brothers-in-law), Bonhoeffer saw youth ministry as seeking God's action in Jesus Christ within the concrete and lived experience of young people themselves, within sharing in their being. The catechism was designed to help create relational sharing through discussion. Schlingensiepen says,

> Hildebrandt had become pastoral assistant in Dobrilugk, in the rural
> Mark Brandenburg, the province surrounding Berlin, and was grappling

---

short document, showing the great freedom with which Bonhoeffer devoted himself to a work that lay between systematic theology and praxis. He did not do it as part of any teaching duties; as yet Bonhoeffer knew nothing of the confirmation class in Wedding he would take several months later. Franz Hildebrandt, who was now a practicing clergyman, had suggested he do it, and worked on it together with him" (Bethge, *Dietrich Bonhoeffer*, 186).

with the problem of how to make the Christian faith relevant to youth preparing for confirmation. At that time, confirmation classes were taught using Luther's Shorter Catechism, a series of questions and answers to be learned by heart, explaining the Ten Commandments, the creed and the Lord's Prayer. Pupils also had to memorize many hymns from the church's hymnal. This way of teaching youngsters was being increasingly criticized; so Hildebrandt suddenly descended on his friend with a plan to develop a new catechism, containing the "Lutheran faith for today." Bonhoeffer, with his wealth of experience with youth, was immediately captivated by the idea. . . . *They used the traditional format of questions and answers, but these were not to be learned by heart, becoming instead a stimulus for discussion with the young people.*[8]

Failures and the Lecture Hall

By late fall of 1931 Bonhoeffer was balancing the appointments of the both/and. He started his ordained appointment as chaplain to a technical college in October. There is more than a little irony that the elite Berliner from a highly achieving university family would become the chaplain to students seeking the skills for blue-collar labor.

Overall, things did not go well, and disconnect in shared context was possibly part of it. Bonhoeffer had experienced nothing less than success in all his other ministerial endeavors, but ministry at the technical college was a nut he seemed unable to crack.

Bonhoeffer clearly was still in the orbit of youth ministry, still working with young people, but these young adults seemed reluctant to connect with him. He was called to provide pastoral care to the students at the college, but they had little interest in knowing Bonhoeffer, let alone seeking him out for pastoral care.[9] Bonhoeffer's failure had nothing to do with a lack of trying, but nevertheless failure came. As Schlingensiepen says, "The program events he offered were poorly

8. Schlingensiepen, *Dietrich Bonhoeffer 1906–1945*, 79–80; my italics.

9. In a letter from Emil A. O. Karow, Bonhoeffer is given his official call. It says, "Your official duties will consist of providing pastoral care for the students at the Technical College" (Bonhoeffer, *Ecumenical, Academic and Pastoral Work 1931–1932*, 31).

attended; often no one came at all."[10] This is quite a different picture we have of Bonhoeffer's ministry from the other snapshots we have been given, glimpses of him turning dead ministries into rooms filled with excited and engaged ten-year-olds, and living rooms filled with deep and engaged conversation with seventeen-year-olds. Here we see a young man in an empty room, checking his watch as no one comes to share in the refreshments he has carefully placed on the table behind him.

There is some comfort for those of us taking the theological turn in youth ministry to hear of Bonhoeffer's own failures, especially with young adults. We also often find it hard to create the spaces to connect with young adults. And if Bonhoeffer is our forefather, it is important to recognize his failures as much as his glowing successes.

Bonhoeffer's own challenge had something to do with the number of students at the technical college who had joined the Nazi student organization and were (like in our day) simply ambivalent, unsure that anything the church offered would connect. Schlingensiepen explains that this ministry for Bonhoeffer "turned out to be extremely difficult. First of all, Bonhoeffer had to inform the students, two-thirds of whom already belonged to the Nazi student organization, that he was available to them as pastor." To do this Bonhoeffer placed "a notice . . . on the bulletin board," but in an incident I find particularly funny, these notices were "removed several times by unknown hands. Finally Bonhoeffer replaced it with a note attached [saying]: 'Dear fellow student, Why always the same joke, why not come round to see me some time? We might not do so badly talking with one another.' "[11] But even this last-ditch plea was met with silence, and in the end the young adult ministry in the technical college had to be chalked up as Bonhoeffer's first real disappointment—even failure—doing youth ministry.

But while the chaplaincy was sinking, the lectures at the university were soaring. Bonhoeffer was starting to make a name for himself with students as the calendar turned to 1932. His lectures were thoughtful, unique, and seemed to always move out into practice. As a matter of fact, Bethge says of these lectures, "His listeners were

10. Schlingensiepen, *Dietrich Bonhoeffer 1906–1945*, 104.
11. Ibid.

captivated because with each chapter the systematic thinker came so surprisingly close to practical theology."[12] And he moved so close to practical theology because, like a dog with a bone, he would not drop the questions of the *theological*. From Rome to Mr. Wolf to Harlem, Bonhoeffer sought to speak of the revelation of God in the concrete and lived. And it was youth ministry, the lives of young people in Barcelona, New York, Grunewald, and now the ecumenical movement, that became the concrete and lived context to explore the revelation of Jesus Christ for us today. Wolf-Dieter Zimmermann, one of the students in these lectures who remained connected with Bonhoeffer deep into the Confessing Church days, says of these early lectures:

> There was a lot of systematic theology in the lectures, as well as dogmatics and symbolics; but they served as occasions for dealing with the main question. And this was: What has God done? Where is he? How does he meet us and what does he expect from us? To answer these questions, the doctrine of the church was necessary; it had no meaning in itself [as just theology], it was part of the explanation of how God became man, and saved man [the theological].[13]

The uniqueness of Bonhoeffer's courses were that they pushed out beyond the classroom—and not only in lecture material but also in shared life. Bonhoeffer had learned something else in his youth ministry experience; he had learned that times of reflection that are transformational (that truly push forth the theological) happen in and through time spent together in fellowship.

So the young professor formed a pedagogy for his university classroom that he had learned in youth ministry and invited his students to meet informally for evenings of discussion and times of recreation. So a group of students began meeting in Wolf-Dieter Zimmermann's room weekly, discussing everything from church politics to Christology. There was even a night when Bonhoeffer, for the first of many times, played his spirituals, telling the students stories of African Americans in America, pushing through this experience to invite his students to think theologically about their own context. Zimmermann

---

12. Bethge, *Dietrich Bonhoeffer*, 213.
13. Zimmermann, *I Knew Dietrich Bonhoeffer*, 61.

explains that those evenings "did not produce anything, but taught us to 'theologize.' "[14] Bonhoeffer was taking his university students from theology and turning them to the theological. After their discussion they'd all go together to a pub to finish the night with an ale. Renate Wind sums up the implications of this group:

> The [young] lecturer was experimenting with new, unfamiliar forms of "social learning." He went into the country with his students and invited them to "open evenings"—a "Bonhoeffer group" formed which not only did theology but talked about the racial conflict in the USA and [more]. Evidently for Dietrich the question of credible Christian praxis and community was more important than his academic career.[15]

14. Ibid.
15. Wind, *Dietrich Bonhoeffer*, 61. Wind continues with an interesting fact about the group: "About a third of his group were women students; that says something at a time when the proportion of female theological students was 3 percent" (ibid.).

9

They Killed
Their Last Teacher!

The Wedding Confirmation Class

Perhaps the church authorities were aware that things were not going so well at the technical college. Maybe General Superintendent Karow was encouraged to get Bonhoeffer back into the sweet spot of his ministry gifts, to get him back with both feet in youth ministry. But this, most likely, is giving the leadership more foresight than they had. Rather, it is more probable that Superintendent Karow was in desperate need of someone, anyone, to take over a particular ministry, and Bonhoeffer came to mind as having specific skill with ministering to young people. After all, the leadership was not suggesting that Bonhoeffer resign from the technical college but rather that he add another responsibility to his busy schedule.

And this responsibility was to take over an out-of-control confirmation class in the low-income Wedding district of Berlin. We are unsure why they chose Bonhoeffer, other than his sparkling record within the church for doing excellent youth ministry and the reality that this particular class was seriously out of control. The level of mayhem was so high that, in no exaggeration, these boys had killed their first teacher. Bonhoeffer was taking over because Johannes Maller simply could not handle the boys, leading him to great distress. A few weeks after handing the class over to Bonhoeffer, Pastor Maller had a heart attack and died. So it's not out of the question to suggest that Bonhoeffer was taking over a class that was so out of control that they had killed their last teacher.[1]

In no time at all Bonhoeffer witnessed the level of bedlam for himself. When old Pastor Maller took him to the class for the first time, the boys waited on the top floor as Bonhoeffer and Maller slowly climbed the stairs to reach them. As they approached, the boys chose to serenade them with screams, stomping, and a confetti welcome of paper and banana peels. Upon reaching the top, Maller screamed and shoved the boys into the classroom (not good for his ailing heart, I am sure). Maller then shouted that Pastor Dr. Bonhoeffer was now their teacher. And with the screamed announcement the boys began chanting "Bon, Bon, Bon," and Maller turned and walked briskly to the door, shutting it behind him, leaving Bonhoeffer alone in the lion's den.

As Pastor Maller continued down the stairs and the shouts of "Bon, Bon, Bon" echoed in the rhythm of his footsteps, he must have wondered if the boys would tear Bonhoeffer limb from limb; but then, again, he wasn't willing to stick around to find out. Bonhoeffer just stood in the front, unfazed by the chanting, allowing it to continue for a few more minutes. He then began to speak very quietly, telling a story from his experience in Harlem. Like a wave that moved from front of the room to the rear, one by one each boy quieted down and moved his head forward to hear what Bonhoeffer was saying. Soon the whole room fell quiet and Bonhoeffer continued with stories from New York. And with his stories a new spirit was injected into the

---

1. Bethge says, "The class was out of control; the minister responsible was at the end of his tether, and in fact died several weeks later. Bonhoeffer wrote Sutz that they had 'quite literally harassed [him] to death'" (*Dietrich Bonhoeffer*, 226). Schlingen- siepen adds: "The old pastor whom they had literally annoyed to death was carried to his grave not long after he had handed over the class to its new teacher. Bonhoeffer cancelled an important meeting in order to take all the boys to the funeral" (*Dietrich Bonhoeffer 1906–1945*, 105).

group. Bonhoeffer dismissed them that day with the promise of more stories to come.

Even in this first meeting, Bonhoeffer was living out place-sharing (*Stellvertretung*); he was using his own stories to create a space for these boys to enter, to come and share in him, as he promised to share in them. Bonhoeffer continued with two core commitments with this class. He remained calm and composed, and he shared his own experience, his stories. As Richard Rother, one of the boys in the confirmation class said of Bonhoeffer years later, "[Pastor Bonhoeffer] was so composed that it was easy for him to guide us; he made us familiar with the catechism in quite a new way, making it alive for us by telling us of *many personal experiences*."[2]

Composure and Stories

These commitments to composure and stories were not simply the momentum of a hypnotizing pendulum used to enthrall the out-of-control boys. Rather, composure and stories became fertile ground for the theological, for the very experience of encountering Jesus Christ. Through stories Bonhoeffer invited the boys to share life together, to know him, so that they might in time give him the gift of knowing them, and in their mutual sharing of one to another, encounter the living Christ. It is no surprise that a year or so after his Wedding experience, Bonhoeffer wrote in his christological lectures (published in English as *Christ the Center*[3]) that Jesus exists ontologically for me, that Jesus is found with and for our neighbor, and that when we share in our neighbor we share in Christ himself.[4] It seems logical to

2. Richard Rother in Zimmermann, *I Knew Dietrich Bonhoeffer*, 57; my italics.
3. *Christ the Center* (San Francisco: Harpercollins, 1960).
4. From the christological lectures:
    This in turn means that I can think of Christ only in existential relationship to him and, at the same time, only within the church-community. Christ is not in-himself and also in the church-community, but the Christ who is the only Christ is the one present in the church-community pro-me. This pro-me should not be forgotten; according to Luther, 'Because it is one thing if God is present, and another if he is present in you.' It is not only useless to meditate on a Christ-in-himself but godless, precisely because Christ is not there in-himself,

assume that, at least in some way, the boys in Wedding were on his mind as he wrote these important christological ideas.

But the place-sharing (*Stellvertretung*) that Bonhoeffer was entering with his boys through the sharing of his stories was only possible if he remained composed. Rother says, "He was so composed that it was easy for him to guide us." It actually may be that composure is an (or *the*) essential disposition to leadership, maybe even a significant mark of the good youth minister. But when I say composure, I don't mean it as simply a personality trait but as the spiritual practice of prayerfully avoiding anxiety.

Anxiety, as neuropsychologists today tell us, is toxic; our brains are wired to avoid anxiety. Anxiety corrupts the chemistry of the brain and leads us to depart (emotionally or physically) from others to protect ourselves. Jesus's words to his disciples "to fear not" (Luke 8:50 NRSV) become of utmost significance. Anxiety is so acidic that it is nearly impossible to have relationship, to be a place-sharer, where the air is poisoned with it.

Bonhoeffer's calm and composure, even on the first day, signaled to the boys that he had no anxiety, no worry about lessons being unfinished or others thinking he was a failure. His composure signaled to them that it might be that he is really just here for them, rather than to fulfill some goal that they could frustrate (like getting them through the material). Bonhoeffer's composure tacitly indicated to the boys that he was more loyal to their concrete persons than any end others sought for them. Bonhoeffer's composure relayed to the boys, again implicitly, that he was there for them, that they could trust him, for he served not his own anxiety but was free to be there with and for them. And with anxiety absent and the stories flowing, they felt ever drawn to him, willing to be led (these un-lead-able) and guided because each step they were assured he would take them to a place where their humanity would be affirmed and their person embraced in relationship. It was Bonhoeffer's composure and stories that became the buoyant waters that "carried" the boys, allowing him to lead them.

but rather is there for you. (Dietrich Bonhoeffer, *Berlin: 1933*, Dietrich Bonhoeffer Works [Minneapolis: Fortress, 2009], 12:314)

And lead them Bonhoeffer did; he did not shy away from teaching them the catechism, and taking them deeply into the tradition of the Christian faith. But this faith had to be concrete and lived; its confession needed to be born from the impulse of their own narrative. So much like the catechism he wrote with Hildebrandt, now face-to-face with these young people, Bonhoeffer taught the core of the Christian story and creedal commitments through shared experience, weaving stories and biblical texts into a narration of life lived before one another and Jesus Christ.

Bonhoeffer even admitted in a letter to Erwin Sutz that he didn't over-prepare (or prepare much at all) for the classes. Rather, as he says, he talked with the boys and, knowing the material well, he sought to weave together through spontaneous sermonettes their stories and the tradition that already lived deeply within him. Bonhoeffer says to Sutz, "Something I almost hate to admit but which is true: I never prepared for the classes in detail. Of course, I knew the material very well, but then I just went there, talked with the boys for a couple of minutes before the class, and then just started. I didn't hesitate, quite often, just to preach to the children; I believe everything else is, in the final analysis, pedagogically doctrinaire."[5]

"Pedagogically doctrinaire" is to make the material more important than the concrete lives of the young people before us. Bonhoeffer's confirmation pedagogy sprung from these two dispositions of composure and stories. From his own personal encounter with the boys in a non-anxious way, he took the initiative to share himself by sharing his stories. It was these dispositions that allowed him to take the pedagogical step to hear the boys' own stories and weave these stories together with the biblical text and, in Bonhoeffer's case, Luther's Small Catechism. Place-sharing led to a form of teaching that embraced persons, drawing these persons into the Christian tradition through the stories of their own experience and the discipleship of the teacher. Bonhoeffer simply, but profoundly, was inviting the boys to witness and share with him as he followed Jesus Christ, as he lived his faith before them.

5. Bonhoeffer, *Ecumenical, Academic and Pastoral Work*, 98.

In another letter to Erwin Sutz, Bonhoeffer gives more texture on what he did with the boys and how they responded:[6] "At the beginning the boys were acting wild, so for the first time I really had discipline problems." He continues, "But here too one thing helped, namely, just simply telling the boys Bible stories in massive quantity, and especially eschatological passages. By the way, in doing this I also made use of the Negro spirituals. Now it is absolutely quiet, and the boys see to that themselves, so that I no longer have to fear the same fate as my predecessor, whom they rather literally aggravated to death."[7]

In our own ministry these two dispositions of composure and stories could be formative. Bonhoeffer may be our forefather into the theological turn into youth ministry, not only because he reminds us that we must form our ministries around explorations of the living Christ in the concrete and lived, but also because he points us to the very practical dispositions of *doing* youth ministry. We are encouraged to do youth ministry in and through the stories of our own faith life, and to prayerfully seek composure, a spirit of calm with young people, pushing us to see that this calm disposition, coupled with narration, creates fertile ground for place-sharing (*Stellvertretung*). And within place-sharing we are given a rich locale to discuss, wrestle with, and explore together the core of the Christian story.

Ministry in Wedding Continued

After the first wild start to his youth ministry in Wedding, it was official: Bonhoeffer was adding the work of confirmation teacher to his busy schedule. Yet with all the other commitments filling Bonhoeffer's week (like university lectures, scholarly papers, guest sermons, and technical college pastoral care), the confirmation class—the youth ministry—would become his most passionate commitment. Bonhoeffer's university students report that he was always organized and

6. Maybe because Bonhoeffer did such little preparation, "there are virtually no documents from his confirmation classes and student retreats, and many of his lecture manuscripts have been lost or exist only in fragmentary form" (Michael B. Lukens, editor's introduction to ibid., 6).

7. Ibid., 76–77.

on time as a lecturer. The only occurrence otherwise was one time when he showed up a few minutes late, hurried into the classroom and began by saying, "I am sorry I am late, one of my boys is in hospital and dying. My lateness could not be avoided."[8] The class knew admittedly who "his boys" were, for Bonhoeffer, especially at their informal evening of discussion, was not shy to talk about his confirmation class and the theological work he was doing with them through their life together.

In a letter to young Richard Ern, Bonhoeffer speaks of his busy schedule, but when he comes to "his boys" there is compassion and a deep pastor's heart that cares not for their simple instruction but for the very humanity of these young people. Bonhoeffer explains the difficult economic situation these boys find themselves in, explaining his desire, this first Christmas with them, to do something concrete for them. Echoing his youth ministry in Barcelona, when Bonhoeffer sought money from his father to buy his young people gifts, in Wedding he felt the urge to do the same. Bonhoeffer refused to disconnect the boys' concrete lived experience in poverty from Christian instruction; he told Richard Ern that he doesn't believe you can do one with out the other—this was no doubt a powerful lesson that began in Barcelona and came into full view in Harlem. In Harlem, Bonhoeffer's experience had been broadened; he had been taken out of his elite, upper-middle-class life to see poverty and struggle he had never experienced before. Now home and with these boys, he was drawn deeply into their concrete and lived experience, an experience so different than his own. He explains to Richard Ern why Richard would not be getting a Christmas present from Bonhoeffer this year.

8. Richard Rother was one of the students in the confirmation class. He says this of that time:

> I remember one incident from our confirmation time very clearly. One of us boys was dangerously ill. In spite of many other engagements pastor Dietrich Bonhoeffer visited him in the university hospital two or three times a week. Before the operation, he stayed with the boy to pray with him and to ask God to help him through those heavy hours. As it turned out, the boy's leg had not to be amputated after all; it was saved by the operation, and he made a complete recovery. On his confirmation Pastor Bonhoeffer gave him the text: "God is love, and he who abides in love abides in God, and God abides in him." (in Zimmermann, *I Knew Dietrich Bonhoeffer*, 58)

In addition to my work teaching at the university and working as a pastor for students [the technical college], I am now doing something else, which takes up all my time and attention; that is teaching a confirmation class for fifty boys in the northern part of Berlin. Most are children of unemployed fathers. There you see so much suffering and can only help a little. The boys don't get anything from home for Christmas, naturally, so I have to try, with the help of some friends, to give them something little that will make them happy. Often they don't have the most necessary things, shoes, trousers, etc. So that I can help out here, this time all my other friends to whom I would have liked very much to give Christmas gifts will have to forgo their gifts in favor of these boys. And I think that you, too, will understand that this time one of these boys will receive the gift that I otherwise would have sent to you. Once you have seen these people, you don't want anything else for yourself. You see then how well we are still doing, that we still have food, and clothes to wear, and coal for heating. These boys often don't have all of that. And it is unfair to talk to them all the time about love of your neighbor and do nothing. So this year you will have to make do with sincere greetings from me and think about one of the poor boys being well and happy.[9]

A Flat in Wedding

As the months of his youth ministry in Wedding continued, Bonhoeffer felt the pull to be more available to his boys, to actually step further into sharing in their lives. So he rented a flat, moving into the Wedding district himself, opening his door to the boys. Bonhoeffer's small flat became a place where the boys could come when needed, escaping the chaos of their lives. Schlingensiepen says, "On his free evenings, Bonhoeffer invited the boys to his room one or two at a time, shared a meal and played games with them. A few became enthusiastic chess players."[10] Bonhoeffer even told his landlady to open the door for the boys whenever they asked, and soon the landlady and her husband, who were skeptical at first of having pastor Bonhoeffer occupying one of their rooms, were sharing in the ministry, cooking meals for the boys

9. Bonhoeffer, *Ecumenical, Academic and Pastoral Work 1931–1932*, 74.
10. Schlingensiepen, *Dietrich Bonhoeffer 1906–1945*, 107.

and laughing with them. Bonhoeffer then was not only relationally connecting these boys to himself, but through his relationship with them, to others. Place-sharing was leading to *communio*.

This time spent in fellowship at Bonhoeffer's flat was about shared life together, and as such it embodied the catechesis Bonhoeffer sought. Bonhoeffer saw it as a false dichotomy to see youth ministry as an either/or—as either focused on the relational or focused on instruction. Rather, significant and direct instruction (teaching) happened in and through relationship. Writing again to Sutz, Bonhoeffer says,

> I have given almost all of the second half of the semester for the confirmands. Since New Year's, I've been living here in the north, so that I can have them by, here every evening, naturally not all at the same time. We eat dinner together; afterward we play something—I have taught them chess and now they're playing it with great enthusiasm. In general, any of them can also come without an appointment. And they all like to come. . . . At the close of each evening, I read something from the Bible, and following that we have a little catechetics, which is often very serious. The class instruction itself was such that I can hardly bear to leave it. Naturally, the boys were still often dumb [i.e., speechless] and didn't concentrate, but I actually liked that sometimes. Because, on the other hand, it was really possible to talk to them about central and profound things, and they listened, often with their jaws fairly dropping. It is simply new to them to have anything other than learning the catechism. I structured the entire class around the concept of church-community.[11]

But these nights at his flat would not be the fullness of Bonhoeffer's steps to share in the lives of the boys. He had moved to Wedding to share more fully in the boys' lives, and this would include more than just chess and dinners. Bonhoeffer was interested not in being the boys' pied piper but in truly sharing their place. And this meant knowing their families. So as part of his ministry Bonhoeffer took the time to do home visits with each confirmand.[12] These home visits

---

11. Bonhoeffer, *Ecumenical, Academic and Pastoral Work 1931–1932*, 97.
12. Bonhoeffer writes to Erwin Sutz:
> Since I will be keeping the boys until confirmation, I'll have to visit all fifty parents, and for this purpose I will move to that area for two months. I'm looking forward to this time very much. It's really work. Most of the home conditions are indescribable, poverty, disorder, immorality. Yet the children are still open.

were no doubt born in formal pastoral practice; it was common at the time for a German pastor to do them as confirmation approached. But Bonhoeffer's schedule was so full, he could have easily fudged this common task. Yet the home and the child within it had been significant themes in both *Act and Being* and *Sanctorum Communio*. Bonhoeffer took the steps to do these home visits for deeply integrated theological and ministerial reasons.

Visiting the boys' homes was an eye-opening experience for Bonhoeffer. He saw firsthand the difficult situation in which these boys were living. And standing before these parents struggling with poverty, he felt a deep loss of what to say or how to say it. Writing to Sutz he expresses his angst, comically stating in frustration that his theological training was no help in understanding these visits and how to do pastoral care at the end of Christendom. (It is amazing to see how Bonhoeffer's concrete experience leads him into deep contemplation, turning from the concrete to significant questions about God, the church, and the world—he is the forefather to the theological turn because it is from doing youth ministry that he enters so smoothly and deeply into idea construction that never loses the concrete and lived.) Bonhoeffer says to Sutz,

> I had the worst experience during my home visits. *I sometimes or even usually stand there and think I really might as well have studied chemistry.* Sometimes it seemed to me as if pastoral care was where our work broke down. What hours or minutes of torture often pass by when the other person or I try to have a pastoral conversation, and how hesitatingly and drearily it goes on. . . . Some will tell you completely without embarrassment and naively about their very dubious lifestyle, and you have the feeling that if you said anything about it they would just not understand you. In short, that is a very sad chapter, and I often try to console myself with the fact that I think this whole kind of pastoral care is also something that didn't exist even earlier and is completely unchristian. But maybe it really is the end of our kind of Christianity. . . . We have learned to preach again [here he is referring

---

I am often speechless at how it is possible that a boy is not completely ruined under these conditions, and, of course, you ask yourself at the same time how you would react to an environment like that. These people must have a very strong capacity for resilience—probably morally as well. (ibid., 77)

to the arrival of dialectical theology and the place of preaching in the thought of Barth, Brunner, and Bultmann], at least a very little bit, but pastoral care?[13]

Bonhoeffer continued to struggle with the home visits, but he kept at them. They were essential experiences that helped him understand his boys and therefore gave essential narrative shape to their lives. Meeting the parents helped reveal the boys more fully and may have shaken any unrealistic nostalgia of family from his theological conceptions. Bonhoeffer knew that to be these boys' place-sharer he needed to see, to experience, the relationships (whether tense or resilient) that made the boys. To know their person he needed to know them through the family. In our own youth ministry of place-sharing, Bonhoeffer reminds us that in doing the hard work of visiting our young people's homes, we are blessed with seeing them more deeply, understanding the shape of their most important relationships. And seeing them through their relationships we are invited, almost compelled, to share in them by being in relationship with them.

While the home visits remained difficult, Bonhoeffer found great joy in taking the boys out of Wedding. Bonhoeffer paid out of his own pocket to take the boys to his parents' cottage, giving many of them their first experience outside Berlin. The forest had been a great blessing to Bonhoeffer in his own youth. Like for many other middle-class children of the time of the German youth movement, the forest for Bonhoeffer was a place of adventure, relaxation, and life together. Bonhoeffer thought it a blessing his boys should experience. He writes to Sutz, "Recently I took several of them out of the city for two days; tomorrow it's another group's turn. This time together was very enjoyable for us."[14]

The Reverberations of Wedding

These experiences of youth ministry allowed Bonhoeffer to tangibly live out his theological ideas; the boys in Wedding became the

13. Ibid., 98; my italics.
14. Ibid., 77.

communio, the very place where "Jesus Christ existed as church community."[15] Bonhoeffer had been living out this theological reality with all the youth ministry he had been doing since 1925, but here in Wedding in 1932 he could give his youth ministry more shape than he had been able to before. And it is therefore logical to assert that the youth ministry in Wedding became the essential beginnings to the forming of the community that Bonhoeffer was able to create in Finkenwalde as principal of the underground Confessing Church seminary.

Without youth ministry, without Wedding, it is hard to see how this most creative community, that still captures our imaginations eighty years later, could have ever come to be. It was in youth ministry that *Stellvertretung* took its practical shape for Bonhoeffer. And it was in Wedding, through classroom instruction, nights of chess, home visits, and excursions to the forest, that Bonhoeffer saw that place-sharing (*Stellvertretung*)—a position he pushed forth in his dissertation while doing his first youth ministry in Grunewald—must move out into the world, into areas like Wedding, taking responsibility for it. This commitment to "response-ability" not only found its way into Bonhoeffer's *Ethics* in the 1940s; responsibility for those in the world also framed Bonhoeffer's resistance to the Nazis. The beginning, both intellectually and concretely, of the centrality of responsibility is born for Bonhoeffer in youth ministry in Wedding.

This move toward responsibility in the world, ignited by the confirmation class in Wedding, pushed Bonhoeffer deeper (if that was possible) into youth ministry in late 1932 and into 1933.[16] After confirming the class in Wedding, Bonhoeffer joined forces again with Hildebrandt and his youngest sister, Susanne, to start a youth center in Charlottenburg (another district where young people were suffering under severe economic conditions).[17] "The youth club sought to

15. See *Sanctorum Communio*.
16. Actually, the youth club began in the late part of 1932 and moved into 1933.
17. Bethge gives some texture: "The Wedding experience was soon supplemented by another: the Charlottenburg youth club. His acquaintance with Harry Ward's work in New York was behind this idea, as well as his contact with Siegmund-Schultze and his social work in east Berlin. Bonhoeffer's contact with Siegmund-Schultze grew out of Hildebrandt's connection to it and Bonhoeffer's own new ecumenical duties" (*Dietrich Bonhoeffer*, 229).

bring in unemployed young people from the streets and give them a place in which to meet, talk, and learn. The project was in no way tied to the church. Christians, Jews, and Socialists worked, discussed, and celebrated together."[18] This was youth ministry pushed out into world, foreshadowing in lived practice the words that Bonhoeffer wrote in his *Ethics* nearly a decade later, inspired further by his full entrance into the conspiracy.

Unfortunately, the youth club was short lived; "six months after it was founded, the youth club had to be closed because the roving commandos of the SA were on the streets."[19] Hitler was coming to power, making such gatherings that welcomed Jewish, communist, and proletariat young people problematic. Bonhoeffer's practice of youth ministry, here at the youth center, was one of his first direct frictions with National Socialism.

Concluding Wedding

Months before the youth center opened, Bonhoeffer needed to see his boys through confirmation. On March 13, 1932, Bonhoeffer saw his boys confirm their faith, transformed from delinquents to disciples by the act of Jesus Christ in and through their life together; through chess, dinners, walks in the forest, and stories about New York and the New Testament, they had encountered the living Christ. Days before the ceremony Bonhoeffer, out of his own pocket, bought yards of material, measured the boys, and cut and sewed their gowns himself.[20] He preached Genesis 32 and Jacob's wrestling with the angel of the Lord. Bonhoeffer exhorted his boys to not let go, to plead with God to bless them.

Bonhoeffer must have known that Sunday that not only were the boys already living among dark clouds but that a fierce storm was

18. Wind, *Dietrich Bonhoeffer*, 60.

19. Ibid.

20. "The young people understood him too, his confirmation class was devoted to him. His room in the Oderberg Strasse was often full of them in the afternoons. Not everybody has had the fun of seeing him cutting up a bale of cloth, which he had probably purchased cheap, for confirmation suits for those boys. I remember from that time some conversations with him about infant baptism" (Fritz Figur, in Zimmermann, *I Knew Dietrich Bonhoeffer*, 56).

brewing. Ominously, the same day the boys were confirmed, Germany held its election for president, and Hitler won a high enough percentage of the vote to secure a powerful place in the government.[21] Hitler's foot was now solidly in the door; within a year he'd be supreme leader of Germany.

21. Wind says, "The confirmation Sunday was 13 March 1932, the day of the German Presidential election. The voting was 49% for Hindenburg, 30% for Hitler, and 13% for Thalmann, the Communist candidate. The middle-class parties and the Social Democrats had supported Hindenburg, because they thought that he was the most promising candidate to defeat the radical right. The radical left warned, 'Those who vote for Hindenburg vote for Hitler, those who vote for Hitler, vote for war.' The parents of Dietrich's confirmation candidates voted for Thalmann" (*Dietrich Bonhoeffer*, 59).

---

(10)

The Younger Generation
and the Führer

Into the Political

Bonhoeffer would spend from summer 1931 to mid-1933 engulfed in youth ministry. Not only was he doing pastoral care with young adults at the technical college, teaching a confirmation class, and running a youth club, but he was also knee deep in the ecumenical movement as secretary to youth. It was his responsibility to organize and then lead a number of conferences around Europe. Juggling these responsibilities, he was still lecturing at the university and writing some of his most interesting material, which included not only the christological lectures but also his theological exegesis of Genesis, which would be released as the book *Creation and Fall*.

Hitler continued to gain power as 1932 turned into 1933. And when the Reichstag burned in February, Hitler's cold fingers wrapped themselves tightly around the neck of Germany. Even before the ashes of the Reichstag cooled, Hitler was both president and chancellor, with complete and unequivocal power of the great country. Bonhoeffer was animatedly opposed to Hitler from the beginning. Retrospectively, this doesn't seem to be noteworthy, but this is to stand on the other side of history. It needs to be remembered that most of Germany and even some who would become part of the Confessing Church after 1933 were initially behind Hitler and hoped for his success. Larry Rasmussen explains why some pastors would have celebrated Hitler's arrival.

> In the very early months of National Socialism, the party even encouraged Germans to rejoin the church (they did), and Hitler seemed to offer a pseudo-religious and populist, even mystical, transformation of politics itself. Clergy and laity in turn reciprocated with enthusiasm for what they regarded as the opportunity to re-evangelize the nation and rejuvenate the church. Then, with the burning of the strongest symbol of the German state, the Reichstag, on February 27, 1933, Hitler had the terrorist act he needed to move swiftly from a faltering democracy toward party control and dictatorship (some historians believe that the Nazi party itself was behind the fire).[1]

Even some pastors who would become part of the Confessing Church simply thought Hitler had overreached in his desire to control the churches. Coming from the humiliation of World War I and the Treaty of Versailles, Hitler's passion and fight seemed to many to be just the kind of leadership the beleaguered nation needed.

But never the Bonhoeffers. From the beginning they stood in opposition to Hitler. Bonhoeffer's own disdain no doubt came from the direct experience his brothers and brothers-in-law had with the National Socialists through their political positions. But Bonhoeffer, too, had his own experience, watching brown-shirted Hitler Youth and SA loyalists intimidate and harass the young Jews and communists from the youth center, while also recruiting, playing on the vulnerabilities of the boys like those in Wedding.

As Hitler came to power, he moved to take control of the institutions of Germany, seeking to put his own loyalists in charge of the church. Hitler's influence on the church was too much for some, so resistance began. Bonhoeffer and Hildebrandt, two of the youngest pastors, dug their feet in particularly deep, fervently calling the church to push back against the Nazis, to not allow them to place their own

---

1. Larry Rasmussen, editor's introduction to Bonhoeffer, *Berlin*, 11.

man Ludwig Muller, a patsy of Hitler's, in charge of the state church. Bonhoeffer rallied his young people to help campaign against Muller as the church elections came near. But it was to no avail, and soon the church had been Nazified. Thus began the pastor emergency league that turned into the Confessing Church. For these pastors could no longer continue in a state church that equated loyalty to the government with obedience to God.

In 1937, after four long years of resistance and fighting for the Confessing Church, Bonhoeffer would write one of the only books of his that would receive a reading during his lifetime, *Discipleship*. As we'll see in part 2, the book is focused on the theme of obedience, the importance of the disciple following the living Christ; "Only the believer obeys," Bonhoeffer says, "but only the obedient believe."[2] The classic book cannot be read apart from the church struggle and its pressure to stand up under the force of a government that demanded loyalty to itself over obedience to the Word of God.

Bonhoeffer and Hildebrandt were the most radical of the pastors in the Confessing Church. Martin Niemoller was the leader and face of the movement, but behind the scenes it was Bonhoeffer and Hildebrandt who pushed for the most direct action. Most of the other pastors were uncomfortable with the zeal of the young men, feeling that the Nazis had to be asked to step down from their control of the church, but not outright opposed. In other words, even pastors in the Confessing Church thought Hitler may be bad for the church but overall good for Germany. So they would support him broadly, just not his church involvement.

Bonhoeffer and Hildebrandt saw things very differently, believing that Hitler's government needed to be opposed completely and fully. There was no compromise in them, and this lack of bend had everything to do with their experience of the Aryan clause. Soon after Hitler took control in 1933 he ruled non-Aryans ineligible for university and pastoral positions—any position that would be receiving government funds. This meant even baptized Christians who had any Jewish blood, even pastors like Hildebrandt himself, lost their jobs. And Bonhoeffer had direct experience with this not only through Hildebrandt but also

2. Bonhoeffer, *Discipleship*, 63.

through his twin sister, Sabine. Sabine's husband, Gerhard Leibholz, was removed from his teaching position as professor of law at Göttingen. Eventually, the Leibholz family escaped to London. Bonhoeffer's twin sister felt the sting of the Nazis directly and experienced the first steps of their plan to exterminate the Jews.

Bonhoeffer spent most of 1933 pushing those who would become the Confessing Church to radical action. Even before the church elections and the departure from the state church, Bonhoeffer, with Hildebrandt, asked the sympathetic pastors to take on nonviolent action, similar to that learned from Gandhi, and to refuse to do any baptisms or funerals, essentially refusing to do the functions the state needed, until they were heard.[3] But even the sympathetic pastors found this too radical.[4]

Yet Bonhoeffer continued to push, and did so as a youth minister who was a theologian, a theologian who ministered to youth. Just after Hitler had taken full power in 1933, Bonhoeffer gave a radio lecture (the only one of his life) titled "The Younger Generation's Altered View of the Concept of Führer," no doubt a controversial title since "Führer" was the nomenclature Hitler had given himself.

The lecture never directly addressed the new government, yet its themes did push against its ideologies. Bonhoeffer's main concern was

3. Schlingensiepen gives more texture to this:

Bonhoeffer and Franz Hildebrandt then proposed an interdict, a sort of "strike" by pastors. There would be no more church funerals in Germany until the state restored the Church's rights under law. A better moment could not have been chosen to take such a decision. Hitler wanted to show the world that he had brought his German revolution to a successful conclusion; so alongside the solemn signing on 20 July of the Concordat between the Reich government and the Vatican, an uproar in the Protestant church was really not what he wanted. If such pressure had been applied right at that moment, Hitler would have had to yield. But everyone to whom Bonhoeffer and Hildebrandt turned with the idea was shocked and wouldn't even consider it. So then the two friends wondered together whether the time had not come for them to leave the church which had ordained them as pastors. (*Dietrich Bonhoeffer 1906–1945*, 132)

4. "With Hildebrandt, Bonhoeffer had tried in 1933 to protest against the appalling general assent to what went under the heading of the 'Aryan paragraph' and the promptly beginning exclusion of Jewish Christians from a church that failed so miserably in this question. Through his ties with Hildebrandt, Bonhoeffer became highly sensitive early on to what was played down as 'the Jewish question'" (Sabine Dramm, *Dietrich Bonhoeffer and the Resistance* [Minneapolis: Fortress, 2009], 9).

how the German youth movement of the 1920s and earlier had made young people susceptible to the disposition of a messianic leader. And this government, Bonhoeffer felt, was profoundly but diabolically using this weakness in the youth of Germany. The Nazis had particular skill at using adolescent passion and clamorings for a leader for their own gain (Hitler's very use of the title "Führer" was drawn from the spirit of the German youth movement). Bethge explains that in the lecture, "Bonhoeffer analyzed the development of the Führer concept and the changes it had undergone in the postwar [World War I] Youth movement. He made no secret of his contempt for the 'unnatural narcissism of . . . the youth made vain by old fools.' "[5] Without naming this directly, Bonhoeffer spoke against the youth of his day being used as pawns for the Nazis. So this was a lecture no doubt crafted in light of Hitler's seizing of power, but it also drew deeply from Bonhoeffer's youth ministry experience in Wedding, Charlottenburg, and the ecumenical movement.

As Bonhoeffer made these points over the broadcast, with just minutes remaining and as the presentation moved to its sharpest point, it went to dead air. There is no proof that it was Goebbels who cut the feed or that there was any censor. It may in the end have been technical difficulties, but, regardless, the incident points to Bonhoeffer's boldness in confronting the government, and doing so as a theologian with young people on his mind, as a youth pastor delving into resistance.

But this was not the only way in 1933 that Bonhoeffer's youth ministry led him to resistance. Through contacts in the ecumenical movement and the conferences with youth, Bonhoeffer alerted others to the issues and struggles inside Germany, helping them to see that the German Christians (the state church) were not to be trusted and that this breakoff group, the Confessing Church, needed the ecumenical movement's support. As secretary to youth, Bonhoeffer placed the big questions facing Europe before young people at conferences in Gland, Fano, and beyond. He called young people into reflection and action, and to do so theologically, as those called by Jesus Christ to follow Jesus Christ, and follow him deeply into the world.

5. Bethge, *Dietrich Bonhoeffer*, 259.

These months of early conflict, with Bonhoeffer on the leading edge of resistance and so young, led to exhaustion. His schedule had been incredibly full since his return to Berlin in 1931, and the first half of 1933 only led to more stress as the young youth pastor and theologian pushed and pushed for his older colleagues to take definitive action against the government and the state church. Feeling he had done all he could inside Germany, and frustrated, Bonhoeffer decided to step away and take a pastorate of a German-speaking congregation in London.

This was part retreat and part recalibrated strategy. Now in London, Bonhoeffer not only could return to youth ministry, and do so as pastor to the whole congregation, but using his ecumenical contacts he could also meet with many in England, advocating for the Confessing Church. He informed and persuaded them to see the apostasy of the German Christians and recognize what the Third Reich meant for Europe and the world.

---

(11)

"Eight Theses on Youth Work"

In London Exile

Bonhoeffer's move to London was not understood by many within the Confessing Church; Karl Barth—who had become Bonhoeffer's mentor, even more so in the months of the church struggle—criticized him for departing Germany when the church there needed him most. But while this move strained Bonhoeffer's relationship with Barth, it allowed for the occasion of a new mentor to enter Bonhoeffer's life—the bishop of Chichester, George Bell.[1] Bell would play an essential part in Bonhoeffer's resistance from 1933 until the end of his life. As a matter of fact, it was Bell, even before Bonhoeffer's parents, who received word that Bonhoeffer had been killed in April 1945. Bell had direct contacts in the English government, and when Bonhoeffer became a double-agent spy, it was through Bell that he would relay information of plans of an impending coup d'état. But in these early days of late 1933 and 1934, Bonhoeffer sought only to inform Bell of the spirit of the church struggle in Germany, asking the

---

1. "Karl Barth and George Bell were the only men whose authority he ever truly accepted—although even then he struggled alone to reach the decisions he believed to be right" (Bethge, *Dietrich Bonhoeffer*, 72).

bishop to advocate for the Confessing Church within the ecumenical movement.

As Bonhoeffer dove into his pastoral responsibilities in London, he felt free. The busy schedule of 1931 to 1933 and his many tasks were greatly lessened. And the balancing he now faced between congregational responsibilities, informal ambassador of the Confessing Church, and youth secretary were shared by Hildebrandt, as his young friend had decided to follow him to London. Bonhoeffer was able to spend time traveling throughout Britain and preparing his youth conference sermons because Hildebrandt was willing to cover the congregational responsibilities.

Bell would call these two young pastors living in the run-down, mice-infested parsonage of the congregation his boys. And it was as boys that they lived—sleeping until late in the afternoon, as they'd rise to breakfast and the *London Times*, catching up on the news of the church struggle in Germany, before working independently throughout the afternoon and evening, and then reconvening for late nights of talks, song, and debate. Finally, around 3:00 a.m. they would end their day.

Like every other phase of Bonhoeffer's ministry, here too in London youth ministry was central. His responsibilities clearly stretched beyond youth ministry, but he continued with organizing youth discussion groups, having youth from the congregation over to the parsonage for Bible reading, music, and conversation. And now his responsibilities as secretary to youth in the ecumenical movement deepened his thought about the shape of youth ministry broadly.

It may be during this time that Bonhoeffer wrote his piece called "Eight Theses on Youth Work." I say *may be* because we are not sure when it was written, but it seems that the two most logical possibilities are that the piece was either crafted in the height of his 1932–33 youth ministry or in this period of London exile. It could be that, now in London with time and space to think, these theses are a way of reflecting back on his youth-ministry experience in Berlin;[2] but as the theses show, they look forward as a way of honing future engagement

---

2. For a discussion of when and where Bonhoeffer wrote this piece, see Bonhoeffer, *Berlin*, 515n1.

in youth ministry. Regardless, these eight theses may be informative for us as we in our own day take a theological turn in youth ministry. In these eight theses we see Bonhoeffer's own *theological* commitment to youth ministry, further substantiating my argument that he is the forefather of the theological turn in youth ministry.

Thesis 1

Thesis 1 reads:

> 1. Since the days of the youth movement, church youth work has often lacked that element of Christian sobriety that alone might enable it to recognize that the spirit of youth is not the Holy Spirit and that the future of the church is not youth itself but rather the Lord Jesus Christ alone. It is the task of youth not to reshape the church, but rather to listen to the Word of God; it is the task of the church not to capture the youth, but to teach and proclaim the Word of God.[3]

Bonhoeffer starts his theses with an explosion; he seeks to shake youth ministry free from the cultural accommodation to the youth movement. As we have seen, the German youth movement made the spirit of young people important, but this importance, Bonhoeffer believed, had been over-elevated (as he prophetically said in his radio address, "The Younger Generation's Altered View of the Concept of Führer"). This led many to believe that the future of the church was dependent on getting spirited young people engaged in it. Bonhoeffer asserts that it appears that the spirit of youth has overtaken the Holy Spirit, that the church's future is not dependent on being indwelled by the Spirit of Christ (the Holy Spirit) but by attracting the spirit of the young.

Bonhoeffer starts his theses on youth work by calling this idolatry. The future of the church is not dependent on youth, but only on Jesus Christ himself. The church must avoid the culture of youth—especially in our day, when we feel the decline of religious institutions. Bonhoeffer believes we can only minister to youth if we see our ministries as *not*

---

3. All quotes below come from ibid., 515.

for getting the spirit of young people into the church but for encountering the Holy Spirit with young people in the church-community. Bonhoeffer says twice in the last sentence of the first thesis that it is the Word of God, not young people themselves, that is the primary focus of youth ministry.[4]

Bonhoeffer is saying that it is the *theological*, it is encountering the living Christ through the Spirit in our concrete lives, not youth or youthfulness, that sets the terms for youth ministry. *Youth ministry is first and foremost a theological task*, Bonhoeffer asserts. It is not a sociological, cultural, or church-growth strategy; it is, rather, a ministry that seeks the encounter of the divine with the human.

In our time, just as in Bonhoeffer's day, we find ourselves struggling in the aftermath of a youth movement (even now nearly fifty years after its inception—which ironically is about the same amount of time between when Bonhoeffer wrote these theses and when the German youth movement began in the 1880s). Youth ministry in North America became full-blown after the 1950s evolution of a youth consumer culture, and it took significant congregational shape in response to a mid-1960s youth countercultural movement. The binding of the counterculture youth movement with a consumer society (see Thomas Frank's book *The Conquest of Cool*[5]) has embedded the power of a "youthful spirit" deep within our North American cultural consciousness.

Depending on the denomination and its political views, this spirited youth counterculture movement was interpreted either romantically or immorally; we needed young people in the church because their spirit was either so great or so corrupt. Either way, North American youth ministry was created to capture the spirit of youth for the church and often still exists for the same today. The spirit of youthfulness, not the theological, set the terms for youth ministry. Even today we claim that we need young people in the church, for their spirit will revitalize

4. This last line persuades me that the theses were written later, for these two statements about the Word of God seem to have correlation to the rhetoric of the language of the Confessing Church. This would point to a later drafting of these theses.

5. Thomas Frank, *The Conquest of Cool: Business Culture, Counterculture, and the Rise of Hip Consumerism* (Chicago: University of Chicago Press, 1998).

a dying institution, and if we don't have them in church then their spirit will be corrupted by the culture.

Bonhoeffer starts his theses by exhorting that such a starting point is not only misguided but also theologically problematic. Youth ministry does not have its beginnings in the spirit of youth, but in the unveiling of Godself in Jesus Christ through the Holy Spirit. Youth cannot save the church, for the church is not simply an institution in need of new members (even enthusiastic ones); the church is the very body of Jesus Christ in the world. Youth ministry, Bonhoeffer argues, does not start with the love of the spirit of young people.

In North America, youth-ministry gurus often passionately say that this is exactly where it starts. "Youth ministry is about loving kids," they shout at conferences. But this loving kids often means loving the youthful spirit of kids. And this love is rarely connected to the *theological*; it becomes only a passion for the youthful spirit, not a love bound in the being of God. It is not God's Word, which encounters us as the Holy Spirit, that is loved. Loving kids means loving their spirit, not loving them through the mystery of the Holy Spirit that encounters us as we take the responsibility to "carry" their concrete and lived humanity.

And this is a major shift that the theological turn in youth ministry wishes to push forth. The theological turn is not a strategy to engage young people—either for them to come to church or for the church to engage them. The theological turn in youth ministry is driven not by youth at all but by the very desire to articulate the revelation of Jesus Christ in the concrete and lived experience of young people.

The priority is on the act and being of God, which, we confess, encounters young people. It is not that we underplay loving young people or think it unimportant; the opposite is true. Bonhoeffer is not saying that love for young people is wrong. It is actually of utmost importance. What is problematic is, not loving young people, but the loving of the youthful spirit of young people. For in loving the youthful spirit we actually love *not* the young person, in his or her particularity, but what having the young person's youthful spirit in our churches can get us. (Too often this is why youth ministry exists in congregations; it exists because it gets more members on church rolls. Or it's why youth workers want big youth groups, so that in capturing the youthful spirit we might be perceived as successful or cool.)

Bonhoeffer was particularly sensitive to this because he saw how the National Socialists loved the spirit of the youth movement, using it for their own political gain, but had little concern for the concrete humanity of young people themselves. They wanted their passion without their humanity. But Bonhoeffer's point, a point the theological turn in youth ministry follows, is that the living Christ is found with and for the concrete humanity of young people revealing Godself to them (something even those who have become overly attentive to the youthful spirit desire deep down). Youth ministry, then (in the view of the theological turn), is never about harnessing the spirit of youth so that they might do good things, revitalize the church, or even evangelize the world. If these things happen, we rejoice, but youth ministry, as Bonhoeffer articulates in this first thesis, is for encountering the living Word of God with young people. If acts of justice, ecclesial revitalization, and evangelism are to happen, they will *not* be born from the spirit of young people; they will not run on the petrol of youthfulness. If they are to occur, they will come from the act of God through the Holy Spirit, as the Holy Spirit calls young people through their concrete humanity to love the world as they are loved by Jesus Christ. Bonhoeffer's first thesis reminds youth ministers that we are called not to attend to the spirit of youth but to seek the revelation of Jesus Christ in the concrete lived humanity of our young people.

Theses 2 and 3

Theses 2 and 3 read:

> 2. Our question is not: What is youth and what rights does it have, but rather: What is the church-community and what is the place of youth within it?
> 3. The church-community includes those on earth whom God's dominion has torn away from the dominion of death and evil, those who hear the Word concerning the establishment of God's dominion among human beings in Jesus Christ and who obediently assemble around this Word in faith. The church-community is Christ's presence

as the true Lord and Brother. Being in the church-community means being in Christ; being in Christ means being in the church-community. Sacrifice, intercession, and confession are the acts of fellowship in the church-community. *It is only within the church-community that one can pass judgment on the church-community. By nature the church-community cannot be judged from the outside.* (italics added)

In 1927, while Bonhoeffer was both writing his dissertation, *Sanctorum Communio*, and doing his first youth ministry at the church in Grunewald, he argued in print and lived out in ministry with children and youth that "Jesus Christ exists as church-community." He asserted in his dissertation and embodied in his ministry that it is *not* in the institution of the church that Jesus Christ is found, but in the communion of persons that we encounter the living Christ among us. Jesus is not found in the bricks and mortar of the church, or even in its ideologies and positions. Jesus Christ is found in the meeting and sharing in persons; we encounter the living Christ concretely in the life-community of the church.

Bonhoeffer continues this theme in theses 2 and 3, now somewhere between 1932 and 1934. He asserts here that it is in persons sharing in each other through sacrifice, intercession, and confession—in other words, through sacraments, prayer, and preaching, given to us by our brothers and sisters—that we encounter the living Christ among us; this is the church community.

Following this, youth ministry begins, Bonhoeffer asserts, by asking not "What is youth?" but "What is the church-community?" Bonhoeffer does not mean this as some kind of clerical or doctrinal cul-de-sac. Rather, he means it as a way of fleshing out his first thesis; youth ministry is for participating in the revelation of Jesus Christ in the concrete lives of young people. And this revelation happens for Bonhoeffer not in the institutional church (*Kirchen*) but in the church-community (*Gemeinde*), in the place where persons share in each other's lives; for the Spirit of Christ comes to our person from the personhood of others who are our *Stellvertreter* (our place-sharer).

The youth minister, then, as this second thesis states, is to be captivated not by the spirit of youth and his or her culture but by the church-community. For the church-community is the place where the divine and human meet in personhood—there can be little that is more captivating. For as the third thesis says, the church-community is not simply a religious organization that he or she works for but a cosmic and yet concrete community in the world that claims and experiences God's Word as the living presence of Jesus Christ. And this Word has the power to bring life out of death. It is the Word that is the primary attention for the youth worker, but, according to Bonhoeffer, the youth worker can only encounter this Word, giving him or herself to it, in the church-community.

So the theological turn claims that youth ministry is *not* seeking to affiliate the spirit of youth with the institutional church. Nor is youth ministry simply a hanging appendage of the church. Rather, youth ministry stands at the center of the church-community, for youth ministry seeks to participate with youth in the Word of God in the church-community (we saw this ramification hidden in the text of both *Sanctorum Communio* and *Act and Being*). The job of the youth worker, according to Bonhoeffer, is not to re-create an institutional church for youth but to help and advocate for the young to be found at the center of the church-community's life—for it is here that young people encounter the presence of Christ.

This is why the second thesis ends with saying, "What is the church-community and what is the place of youth within it?" Bonhoeffer means that the job of the youth worker is never to oppose the church with the spirit of youth. This sometimes happens in contemporary youth ministry; the youth ministry in frustration reviles the church, and the youth worker says things like, "I love my youth; I just hate the church." Bonhoeffer would find such statements deeply problematic, because for him the youth minister's job can never be to use the youthful spirit of the young to undercut the church-community, and there is no way of doing youth *ministry* outside the church-community. For to oppose the church-community is to lose the concrete locale of Christ's presence in the world; it is to make youth ministry for something other than encountering the Word of the living God. Rather, the youth worker's calling as minister is to make space for the humanity of young people to be embraced at the center of the church-community, so that together we might participate in the life and work of Christ.

And this is what the theological turn in youth ministry asserts as well. It does not believe that you have to follow Bonhoeffer in his own articulation of the concrete presence of Christ in the church-community ("Jesus Christ existing as church-community"), but it does mean that the youth minister seeks to understand the shape of God's revelation in the world, to articulate that shape *theologically* next to the concrete lives of young people. This is why Bonhoeffer wants the youth worker to first ask, "What is the church-community?" for it is in the church-community, in the concrete and lived locale of shared life, that young people encounter the living Word of God.

Youth ministry, in the theological turn, seeks to take the concrete shape of our lived experience with the revelation of God. We seek to take on practices (even programs) *not* for the sake of drawing (capturing for the church) the youthful spirit. Rather, we seek practices and programs that move us into the presence of the living Christ. What we do in ministry is framed not by the question "Will the kids (the spirit of youth) like this?" but rather "Does this practice, activity, or program take the shape of our confession of God's unveiling in the world?" The theological turn, again, is about moving away from overattention on the spirit of youth and reflecting instead on the places where young people concretely experience the Spirit of Christ.

And, following Bonhoeffer, the theological turn asserts that the church-community plays a significant role in God's unveiling in the world. This has the deep ramification of shifting the job of the youth worker from hunter and gatherer of the spirit of youth to pastor of the church-community that calls all its members to hear, see, and respond to the humanity of children (by carrying them), inviting children and youth deep into the church-community's life as a way of sharing in Jesus Christ (Matt. 19:14).

Theses 4 and 5

Theses 4 and 5 read:

> 4. The church-community suspends the generational problem. Youth enjoys no special privilege in the church-community. It is to serve the

church-community by hearing, learning, and practicing the Word. God's Spirit in the church has nothing to do with youthful criticism of the church, the radical nature of God's claim on human beings has nothing to do with youthful radicalism, and the commandment for sanctification nothing to do with youthful impulse to better the world. "Christian" and "youth" is a rather harsh and not very credible word combination. The issue is not "modern" or "old fashioned," but rather solely our thinking concerning and from the perspective of the church.

5. The Bible judges youth quite soberly: Genesis 8:21; Isaiah 3:5; Jeremiah 1:6; Ecclesiastes 11:10; 1 Peter 5:5; 2 Timothy 2:2 et passim.

Thesis 4 starts with a bold statement that, if lived out, throws contemporary youth ministry into question, but it is only by following this bold statement in thesis 4 that we can get any traction to move in the direction Bonhoeffer pushes in theses 2 and 3. Here in thesis 4, Bonhoeffer says that "the church-community suspends the generational problem." Youth movements (whether the German youth movement of the late nineteenth and early twentieth century or the American youth movement of the late 1960s and after) are created because of, and then often exacerbate, the generational gap. Youth ministry is called upon (really created in the first place) to stand within the gap; youth ministry often exists only because there is a gap (this seems true in both Germany and America). The gap forces parents and church members to believe they need a special program or specialist to connect to the (odd and strange) youthful spirit of their children. *Youth ministry is to stand in the gap, but youth ministry is only created (and perpetuated) because there is a gap.*

Standing in this gap, it is no wonder that youth ministers often feel peripheral or unsupported. Our calling is not bound to any theological commitments at the center of the church-community, but is seen as a device (a technology) used to solve the problem of the generation gap. Youth workers are like plumbers called in to fix a leak, to fill the gap, but rarely do we invite the plumber fixing the gap in our bathroom waterline to dinner, into the heart of our communion. We appreciate the technical work of solving the problem of the gap but are not sure outside this technical know-how what purpose they have in our family. So we appreciate the technical ends the plumber wins for us but keep him from the center of our family life.

Because the youth minister is called into service due to the problem of the generation gap, she will always have a hard time being seen as a *minister*, as one who brings (young) people before the Word of God. The church will always feel the temptation of treating her as less (or as different), for her place in the church is technical; it is to fix the problem of the gap, to be the church's generational-gap plumber. Her identity as youth worker is captured by technical ends, undercutting her theological identity, keeping her from being seen as a minister who wrestles with the revelation of Jesus Christ in the concrete experience of young people, their parents, and all those in the church-community.

So Bonhoeffer asserts that we should "suspend with the generational problem," that the church should refuse to anxiously see our young people as divided from us, because once we do our children become a problem (a leaking pipe) and the youth worker, like a plumber, becomes only a specialist with a task to fix *the problem* (*fix our children*) and then leave. When the church-community obsesses about the generation gap, seeing it always as a problem, the youth worker is obscured from being seen as an essential minister to the whole congregation with particular responsibilities for the young.

And the youth ministry itself quite literally becomes a stopgap. Stopgaps are never essential but are only called into service because of an emergency, because the existing structure has sprung a leak. The youth ministry born out of the anxiety of the generation gap can never stand at the center of the church's identity but can only be a specialty used to mind the gap. And when children are moved from the center of the church, it reveals significant theological issues, as Bonhoeffer has shown in his two earlier works.

For Bonhoeffer, outside the center of church-community the Word of God is lost, for it is in the church-community that young people (really, all people) concretely encounter the living Christ through the Holy Spirit (theses 2 and 3). To focus on the generation problem is to push both the youth and the youth worker from the center of the church-community, spinning the youth worker away into technical functions. The theological turn in youth ministry invites youth workers to turn back and return to the center of the church-community. But the theological turn in youth ministry recognizes that this turning back can only be done by embracing the *theological*, for the theological, according to Bonhoeffer, is the center of the church-community—it is where we encounter the living Christ.

When the church becomes anxiously overattentive to the generation gap, believing it needs a specialist (a plumber), the youth worker is slighted, giving him reason* to become more loyal to the youthful spirit than to the church, pushing him to actually add to the gap rather than close it. Bonhoeffer's suggestion is for the church-community, because it is a community of persons bound in *Stellvertretung* (place-sharing), to refuse to acknowledge the gap. This is not simply a strategy of the church burying its head in the cultural sand. The church acknowledges that there is a gap, and even hires a youth worker because the gap exists. But at the same time, the church-community refuses to define its young through the gap and the youth worker as a technician. The church embraces both the child as eschatological and its own essential practical life of carrying all children as mother. It chooses to see young people not through the lens of youth culture, not as *teenagers*, but as *disciples*, as followers of Christ, as human beings wrestling with the presence and absence of God. And because young people are seen this way, and not as a problem, what they need is not a technician but a theologian, who can invite young people into the presence of the Spirit who covers all gaps (Gal. 3:28) through the *Stellvertretung* of Christ. This leads the youth worker back to the center of the church-community because young people are now found at the center. They are no longer problems but persons wrestling with God's presence and absence; they are at the center because it is Jesus Christ, not the generation gap, who creates childhood.

So taking the theological turn, it may be that a huge part of the youth minister's job is to work with the whole church-community, reminding the adults that they need not—that they theologically should not—define their children through the generation gap, but instead should see them as human beings needing a *Stellvertreter* (a place-sharer). The youth minister may need to point again and again to the biblical and theological truth that Jesus Christ, not the cultural generation gap, is the creator of childhood.

This may actually be the central calling of the youth worker. Instead of being a functional plumber, her job as *theological minister* is to encourage the whole church-community to desist with the generational problem and embrace the humanity of the young as bound at the center of the church-community. Her job as youth worker is to actually bring youth and adults together through the theological; she seeks to create spaces for the young and old to wrestle together with the absence and presence of God in their shared and distinct, concrete and lived experience. She may even start by simply getting the young and old to pray for and with each other, for it is in prayer that we invite others into our concrete and lived experience, together bringing it before God through the Holy Spirit.

Bonhoeffer says further in thesis 4 that "youth enjoy no special privilege in the church-community." There is no special privilege of youth given to them by the cultural youth movements; they are not special in the sense of distinct, but embraced fully in their form as children. This may actually be the starting point of leading young people back to the center of the church-community. Ironically, where the youth minister may misstep is in claiming "the special privilege of youth." We often think a major part of our job description as youth ministers is to claim the special privilege of the young. But the irony is that when we claim such a position we do more harm than good. For in claiming a privileged space in the church for the young we fortify the generation gap, pushing young people off into youth ministry programs and away from the center of the congregation, making the very form of childhood no longer eschatological but fully cultural. "Special privilege" may be used to segregate young people away from others in their own special youth rooms and youth ministries. Youth are "so special" to the church that they become a major line item in the annual budget, but in the end this specialness only pushes them farther from the center of church-community. And to make them "so special" is to divide them from their parents and other adults, for *only* those with special knowledge can teach them the faith and even relate to them at all.

The youth worker then becomes caught in a vicious cycle. We feel ostracized and frustrated because our pleas for "special privilege" have actually been heard. But they have sounded an alarm of a distinct generation gap that needs specialties and specialists to solve it, so they lead to a special privileged space that disqualifies youth and the youth worker from the center of the life of the church-community.

It may then be that, following Bonhoeffer, the best way to advocate for youth and therefore do youth ministry is to continually reiterate to the church-community that their young ones have no privileged space and therefore must be taken deep into the life of the community to find *Stellvertretung* with all the adults of the community. They have no special privilege, so they should be invited into friendship at the center of the community, as together we bend our lives toward the unveiling of Jesus Christ in our midst.

It is a paradigm shift but, following Bonhoeffer, it may be that the paid youth worker's job (her ministry to and for the young of the church) is to remind the church that "there is no privileged space for its children, that its children must be taken into its life." Her calling as youth worker is to advocate for youth not by idealizing their youthful spirit but by calling the church to look past it and embrace their humanity. And if we should miss that youth have no privileged space in church, in thesis 5 Bonhoeffer lists texts of the sober view of youth in the Bible, to remind us that, indeed, youth have no privileged space outside the center of the church-community itself.

Yet Bonhoeffer is not finished pushing this point; he wishes to push so far that he finds it theologically misguided to even put together "Christian" and "youth" as a privileged label, for Jesus is not the inventor of *Christian* children but of childhood universal (as an eschatological reality). To put such words as "Christian" and "youth" together *undercuts*, in Bonhoeffer's mind, the importance of young people themselves. It is a problem because when we put together "Christian" and "youth," young people are no longer "Christians," disciples and full participants in the church-community through baptism. Rather, they are a distinct species called "Christian youth." And when the "youthful" label no longer fits, as it dissipates with age, then so too might the "Christian." To label the young "Christian youth," Bonhoeffer believes, is to make faith bound not in their humanity and eschatological work of Christ, not in the wrestling of their being, but in this episodic time of "special privilege" created by culture. It makes faith a fashion, a particular, distinct time that you are loyal to something before moving on to something else. Your "Christian-ness" is bound in your "youthfulness." Once the youthfulness is made problematic by age or new lifestyle commitments, so too is "Christian."

It is interesting that in contemporary youth ministry, issues of drifting faith have become of central attention. Youth ministry has been digging deeply for new perspectives to keep young people connected and affiliated to the faith they had as "Christian youth." Young adulthood seems to shake the "Christian" out of the young person, like a wet dog shakes the water away after a bath. But it may be that the reason it is so relatively easy to shake "Christian" loose from the young adult is because we've allowed "Christian" to be fused to "youth," allowing a privileged space for "Christian youth" in our congregations. The problem is that once "youth" is thrown into question, so too is "Christian." "Christian" was an adjective used as a description of one's high school days, and now, materially, as one has outgrown the privileged space (especially outgrown the youth group), now that one is no longer a "youth," the "Christian" is also thrown into question.

Following Bonhoeffer, the theological turn in youth ministry seeks, through theological reflection, to do youth ministry, but to do so by undercutting youth ministry as a privileged space. It desires instead to move the young into the center of the church-community; for the young, like their parents, experience of presence and absence of God. The theological turn in youth ministry seeks not to help make "Christian youth" but to participate in the humanity of the young as they encounter the living Christ. Its attention is not on strategies to produce "Christian youth" that hold onto the fashion and stay loyal to the brand. Instead it seeks to invite young people, not into a privileged or special space, but into the cruciform space of *Stellvertretung* (of place-sharing) that is concretely lived out by the community of persons (by the church-community). In the privileged space young people are given the fashion of being Christian youth for a time, but in the cruciform space, in *Stellvertretung*, they are given a shared space, a space of persons sharing in persons, of being not a Christian youth but a person bound to others in faith, hope, and love, which they do not outgrow. So in the theological turn, young people are given a shared space to encounter the living Christ who meets them not with a call into a fashion but with an invitation to follow, to be disciples of the crucified and now-living Christ.

Theses 6 and 7

Theses 6 and 7 read:

> 6. Church youth work is possible only on the basis of addressing young people concerning their baptism and with the exclusive goal of having them hear God's Word. It remains the act of the church-community toward its members. Every transgression of this boundary constitutes a betrayal of Christ's church-community.
>
> 7. It may well be that the youth do have the right to protest against their elders. If that be the case, however, the authenticity of such protest will be demonstrated by youth's willingness to maintain solidarity with the guilt of the church-community and to bear that burden in love, abiding in penitence before God's Word.

Bonhoeffer gives further justification for his position in theses 4 and 5 here in thesis 6. In thesis 6, Bonhoeffer explains that there is no privileged space and therefore no such thing as "Christian youth." Since 1927 Bonhoeffer had offered a rich theological perspective through the lens of baptism. Baptism, Bonhoeffer asserts, takes us into the life, death, and resurrection of Jesus Christ. And having been taken through his life, death, and resurrection, we are placed in the body of Christ forever. For as our body has died in baptism and been made alive by the Spirit of Christ, we are given Christ's very life, his very Spirit, by being given his body. And his body, as Bonhoeffer goes to great pains to articulate in the whole of his theology, is the church-community. There is no generation gap, there is no "Christian youth," because all—young and old—are taken into the church-community through baptism (thesis 6 points to similar themes Bonhoeffer articulated in *Sanctorum Communio* and the end of *Act and Being*). In baptism, we are dead in Christ and now made alive (Eph. 2:5) to live one to another in and through the Holy Spirit. To add restrictions and labels beyond baptism is to betray Christ's church-community, says Bonhoeffer.

So the youth worker taking the theological turn is the one who calls the church-community as a whole to move past the generation gap and include its children at the center of its life. She does this not for reasons of posterity but for theological ones; for the act of God in baptism becomes a deeper reality than the generation gap. And the identity of being once dead and now alive in Christ is deeper than the fashion of "Christian youth." But it must be said that, in Bonhoeffer's mind, the youth worker makes this push through baptism not as guardian of pure liturgy, saying, "Listen congregation, you made baptismal promises (religious promises of obligation) to this child—so now care for her!" This is not what Bonhoeffer means by "carrying." Rather, the youth worker turns the congregation to the baptismal reality as a theologian, reminding the congregation of what the Spirit of Christ has done and continues to do in the life of this young one before them. This young one, like all of them, has been taken into Christ; this young one has died with Christ and now is made alive with Christ. This young one is wrestling with the living Christ within her concrete and lived experience, and baptism makes this so, for baptism is a concrete and lived experience that pulls her humanity into the concrete and lived experience of Christ himself. The same Spirit that works in the adults works in and through this young one. There is no generation gap because in her baptism all boundaries are crossed, making this young person one with all persons in the church-community through the one Spirit. And therefore through her baptism she should be seen not as a "Christian youth" but only as a disciple, as one in Christ. Bonhoeffer asserts that to hold to the generation gap, "Christian youth," or a privileged space, is to undercut the *theological* reality of being baptized into Christ.

In these first six theses, Bonhoeffer has given us some strong words that are meant to push us toward unity, moving our youth ministries to resist division. Yet in thesis 7 Bonhoeffer does acknowledge that the young may need to take a prophetic stance against their elders, even within the church-community. After all, he and Hildebrandt were willing to stand and push their elder-pastors to take on more radical action against the Nazis. And at the youth conferences Bonhoeffer led, he pressed young people to speak for peace and refuse violence, to be a prophetic voice in their church-communities.

But this prophetic stance, Bonhoeffer explains in thesis 7, must not surrender to the inflated youthful spirit. Bonhoeffer believes that if the young need to stand against their elders, the youth should not do so with an attitude that they can do more and better, for all *doing* (whether of justice, evangelism, or meaningful worship) is, first and finally, the work of the Spirit of Christ. Nevertheless, a time may come to protest against their elders, but its "authenticity," Bonhoeffer says, will be bound *not* in the young's willingness to protest and speak but in their solidarity, in their willingness to share in guilt. And this sharing of guilt is necessary, even in protest, for the heart of the church-community is *Stellvertretung*, place-sharing. And the place-sharer enters so deeply into the other's life, as Bonhoeffer articulates in his *Ethics*, that he shares the guilt of this other (here, a central point of *Ethics*, written after 1939, is being first worked out in reflection on youth ministry). Because the church-community is bound in personhood, we no doubt confront the persons we love, but we do so *for love*, standing against their attitudes and actions, but always for the purpose of standing with them. Sharing with their person we share in their guilt, for we embrace them, and this embrace is in itself a strong protest that nevertheless leads to the reconciling work of the Spirit.

If Bonhoeffer's first six theses have been helpful, it may be that theses 7 and 8 need critique. Some may see in these two final theses Bonhoeffer's conservative disposition and his desire for conventionality. This, no doubt, is part of his personality and his upper-middle-class perspective and is a legitimate critique. And while this ethos clearly gets attached to these last two theses, still within them we can see that Bonhoeffer is seeking to make his case theologically.

Thesis 8

Thesis 8 reads:

> 8. There is no real "church association"; there is only the church. The church youth association is not the youth of the church-community; that youth includes, rather, all baptized young people. Every church

association as such already discredits the cause of the church. Such associations can only be perceived as makeshift entities, which as such have only relative significance.

It is possible that Bonhoeffer wrote these theses for a presentation to the London YMCA. If he did, it would not be unreasonable to imagine that he was booed from the podium. Bonhoeffer has not minced words in any of the above theses; this lack of nuance could be a problem, and if so, none are more problematic than this final thesis.

Bonhoeffer is in deep either/or mode; as Hitler is taking power and the church is giving in at every turn, Bonhoeffer's rhetoric is strong (maybe too strong!). In most of the sentences of this final thesis, Bonhoeffer rails against the "church association"—that is, the YMCA and other parachurch youth ministries (as we would call them). He rails against them for undercutting the church and therefore, in his mind, only being *relatively* significant. Many of us in present-day North America would push back against Bonhoeffer's harsh words.

But where Bonhoeffer's hyperbolic words are helpful is in reminding us that these "church associations" do face the temptation of seeing themselves as simply free organizations allowed to engage the spirit of youth. Bonhoeffer's hyperbolic final thesis reminds us that instead these "youth associations" must recognize that they, too, if they come in the name of Jesus Christ, are involved in a deeply theological task; for these associations wrestle with the revelation of Jesus Christ in the concrete lives of young people.

And if they do recognize this, they must wrestle with their relation to church-community too, for the church-community is the body of Christ. Bonhoeffer's words remind those running important youth ministry organizations to also take the theological turn and think about how it is that they are related not simply to religious institutions (i.e., how do we help the young people we evangelize become members of a church?) but also to the multigenerational church-community that lives in prophetic denial of the generation gap. It may be that in such thinking these organizations can read Bonhoeffer's first line of thesis 8 ("There is no real 'church association'; there is only the church") as a positive theological anchoring of their work. This is exactly how Ray Anderson has read this statement in his important (and rarely read) book *Minding God's Business*. Anderson recasts the "church association" within a rich theological perspective that grounds its ministry within the church-community itself.[6]

6. Ray Anderson, *Minding God's Business* (Pasadena, CA: Fuller Seminary Press, 1986). Anderson offers a reenvisioning of parachurch ministers through a deeply theological ecclesiology.

12

Finkenwalde

*From Youth Ministry into
Intentional Community*

In London, Bonhoeffer lived out many of the above theses on youth work. He blended his pastoral responsibilities so deeply with his youth work that they were nearly indistinguishable. There was no generation gap or privileged space for his London youth; they were taken, with the help of Hildebrandt, to the center of the church-community. And these commitments could be seen on a more global (or at least more Continental) level through Bonhoeffer's presentations at the Fano youth conference in August 1934.

Now a year into Hitler's rule, with war seeming to build on the horizon of Europe, Bonhoeffer preached his "Peace Sermon," calling European young people to serve the church-community by standing for a gospel of peace. In the sermon Bonhoeffer makes the bold statement that safety and peace cannot always coexist, and that an obsession with safety will only lead to further violence. The statement not only foreshadows Bonhoeffer's own future but also is amazingly relevant in our post–9/11 America. Reading the sermon today, you could almost be convinced that it was written in 2004, not 1934.

Throughout the sermon, Bonhoeffer does not shy away from drawing young people into the heart of the issues facing the church, calling
them to faithful action. And Bonhoeffer did this from the pulpit, and
also in conversation in the Fano sand dunes as he talked peace, war,
and pacifism with the conference's young people. It was one of these
young people who asked Pastor Bonhoeffer what he'd do if he were
called to fight in the war. He responded that he would "pray that
he would have the strength to resist." This stance became a turning
point in Bonhoeffer's own history after 1937, for the Nazis had only
a bullet for conscientious objectors.

As Bonhoeffer continued with his congregational work in London
and prepared for the Fano youth conference, the Confessing Church
galvanized and officially departed from the state church, writing the
Barmen Declaration in May of 1934, just months before the Fano
conference. The *Declaration* now stands as one of the most important
pieces produced by the church in the twentieth century. And while
Bonhoeffer had been centrally involved in the church struggle, he was
absent from the crafting of the declaration at Barmen, away in London
exile. It was his mentor Karl Barth who was the creative force behind
it. The document asserts with great boldness that the church has one
Lord, Jesus Christ. And anything or anyone that seeks to rival this
one Lord, even a state or ideology, must be denied. The publication
of *Barmen* made the split between the Confessing Church and the
German Christians (the state church and its Reich bishop) official,
making the Confessing Church illegal.

Sitting in London, Bonhoeffer celebrated the *Barmen Declaration*.
And as he did, he again began to feel the pull to visit India and Gandhi. He had tried after his return from New York, but logistically it
was impossible at that time. Now, the itch returned; Bonhoeffer saw
even more clearly how Gandhi's nonviolent resistance could be of
use in Germany.

But as Bonhoeffer was exploring travel options, the Confessing
Church was reorganizing its educational system. Now that the univer-
sities' theology faculties had been Nazified and the other seminaries of
the state church could not be trusted, the Confessing Church needed
its own schools. So it was decided to form five independent and illegal
seminaries for the training of the Confessing Church pastors.

In 1935 Bonhoeffer's plans to go to India were thwarted again, this time by the invitation to be the principal of one of these illegal seminaries. It was a call Bonhoeffer could not pass up; he would be free to create his own curriculum, preparing these young men (nearly his age) for the great challenge of pastoring illegal churches throughout Germany, in direct conflict with the government.

So Bonhoeffer left Hildebrandt in London with the German-speaking congregation and returned to Germany. But before he did, he spent his last months in Britain visiting monasteries and intentional communities of faith, seeking ideas, perspectives, and forms that might be used in his new educational endeavor.[1]

In 1932 in Wedding, Bonhoeffer had sought to give his youth ministry a feel of intentional community. He'd moved into a flat and nightly invited his confirmands over for games, conversation, and shared meals. He then pushed this intentional community deeper by taking them for excursions away from Berlin and into the forest. This youth ministry may have been the most fulfilling pastoral work of Bonhoeffer's short life. But it still did not connect the pulpit with the lectern.

It was the call to run one of the illegal seminaries for the Confessing Church that finally fused the church and academy, pulpit and lectern, pastor and professor within Bonhoeffer. It was as principal of an illegal seminary that Bonhoeffer found what he was looking for since his time in Barcelona. To give his new endeavor shape, he returned to his youth ministry experience in Wedding, seeking to push further into intentional community, now using the practices he had learned in the monasteries of Britain.

The seminary began in April of 1935 in Zingsthof, near the Baltic Sea. Yet within a few months it moved to its permanent location at Finkenwalde, taking up residence in an old primary school. Bonhoeffer had his library, records, and piano sent to the school, making his own personal treasures freely available to the community. And it

---

1. Keith Clements says Bonhoeffer "had already visited Methodist and Baptist colleges in the London area, and George Bell made introductions for him to visit several Anglican religious houses and theological colleges. Before leaving for Germany in April 1935, therefore, he and his friend Julius Rieger made a tour and visited the Cowley Fathers in Oxford, the Society of the Sacred Mission at Kilham and the Community of the Resurrection in Mirefield, Yorkshire. Mirefield's daily routine of prayer especially impressed him" (*The SPCK Introduction to Bonhoeffer* [London: SPCK, 2010], 16).

was into a community that Bonhoeffer sought to form this group of divergent young men, who sought leadership as illegals in the Confessing Church. Fusing the spiritual practices of the monastery and the relational life of his youth ministry experience, Finkenwalde took dynamic shape.

All participants, including Bonhoeffer as principal, were asked to call each other "brothers," and these brothers were asked to spend significant time each day in meditation on Scripture, periods of quiet, and confessing their sin to one another. These German Lutheran young men thought their teacher had gone far too Catholic and initially resisted these monastic practices, until Bonhoeffer informed them that they were not optional. The rhythms of the community's life were essential, but these rhythms needed to rest on a deep relational commitment to one another. In the coming pastoral environment in Nazi Germany, where mistrust, misinformation, and possible persecution would be commonplace, Bonhoeffer demanded honesty and brotherly love as the core of the community at Finkenwalde.

This spirit was encompassed in what Bethge calls "the one rule," which was to "never speak about another [brother] in that person's absence or to tell that person about it afterward when such a thing did happen." Bethge continues, "The participants learned almost as much from the failure to observe this simple rule, and from the renewed resolution to keep it, as they did from the sermons and exegeses. Bonhoeffer was able to impose this discipline on the seminary because he also left sufficient room for pleasure and outspoken discussions."[2]

Bonhoeffer was aware that the situation in which these young pastors would find themselves in the future would be one of great challenge, a test that could be met *not* by sheer intellectual book knowledge but only through a deep theological commitment that formed in them a rich spirituality. Bonhoeffer pushed them academically, bringing to bear the full weight of his academic credentials. But he did not do so outside of prayer, meditation, and confession. The students needed to encounter the living Christ as much as learn about him.[3] Bonhoeffer would not settle for theology in his school but demanded

2. Bethge, *Dietrich Bonhoeffer*, 428.
3. Bethge, a student in Finkenwalde, the place he met Bonhoeffer, explains the rhythm of the day:

a move into the *theological*, into concrete spiritual experiences of the living Christ.

Bonhoeffer sought a curriculum that would prepare students to follow Jesus, and follow (*Nachfolge*) him all the way to the cross, even into persecution and death.[4] The students prepared for this through prayer and confession, and studied it in the classroom as Bonhoeffer crafted the lectures that became his book *Discipleship*. The book was published just a month after Finkenwalde was closed and the students were exposed to the full weight of the Nazi takeover of the church.

But Bonhoeffer coupled these monastic practices and demanding lectures with the actions he had learned in youth ministry. While the rule of life was a demanding one, and lectures on *Discipleship* heavy, Bonhoeffer followed the pattern he had used in Wedding to infuse the Finkenwalde community with a true brotherhood. Times of music, chess, and deep conversation were as central as the monastic rule of life. It was demanded that the young men meditate, but coupled with this were open spaces to discuss political topics, sing, and laugh.[5] Reminiscent of Bonhoeffer's flat in Wedding, the Finkenwalders shared deeply in each other's lives. And it was not uncommon on warm days for Bonhoeffer to cancel courses to spend the day in recreation, playing soccer or tennis. Actually, as Bethge says, "On Sundays [Bonhoeffer]

The day began and ended with two long services. In the morning the service was followed by a half-hour meditation, an exercise that was maintained even during the seminary's move, when their only furniture consisted of packing cases and youth hostel bunks. The services did not take place in church but around the ordinary dinner table. They invariably began with a choral psalm and a hymn selected for that day. This was followed by a lesson from the Old Testament, a set verse from a hymn (sung daily for several weeks), a New Testament lesson, a period of extempore prayer, and the recital of the Lord's Prayer. . . . Bonhoeffer believed this sequence of readings and prayers was the most natural and suitable form of worship for theologians. Only on Saturdays did he include a sermon, which was usually very direct. (ibid.)

4. Bethge explains, "Only one theme distinguished Bonhoeffer's seminary from the rest for the first two and a half years: the series of lectures on discipleship. After only a few hours newcomers realized that this was the heart of everything, and they realized they were witnessing a theological event that would stimulate every area of their professional life" (ibid., 441).

5. "One evening a week was devoted to the discussion of current issues; the politics of the day supplied more than enough subject matter. Despite its seclusion, the seminary community could not withdraw from the political situation" (ibid., 431).

didn't permit any class work to be done, but organized all kinds of games."[6] Following his youth ministry experience, Bonhoeffer had no second thoughts about playing sports with his students; he knew it was through such experiences that relational connection grew—and it didn't hurt that he was better than most of them at the sports they played!

It was through games, discussion, and confession that Bonhoeffer formed the deepest friendship of his life. Besides the men he met in New York (Lehmann, Sutz, and the others), up to that point his only other true friend outside his family was Franz Hildebrandt. But Hildebrandt was still in London, and his Jewish heritage would keep him there throughout the war. Just months after the opening of Finkenwalde, one of its students, Eberhard Bethge, arrived and soon became Bonhoeffer's closest friend. Bethge was the son of a rural pastor. He arrived at Finkenwalde never having heard of Dietrich Bonhoeffer. And as a matter of fact, Bethge was shocked at how young—not yet thirty—his principal and primary professor was. But as the months at Finkenwalde unfolded, Bethge and Bonhoeffer became dear friends. And as the seminary was closed and war arrived, Bethge remained at Bonhoeffer's side, supporting him as he entered the conspiracy. Bethge even joined the Bonhoeffer family when he married Dietrich's niece Renate (the daughter of Dietrich's oldest sister, Ursula, and Rudiger Schleicher), and Bethge was recipient of most of Bonhoeffer's letters in prison. In Finkenwalde Bethge became Bonhoeffer's confessor, and through a friendship forged in monastic practice and the kind of relational engagement that Bonhoeffer had learned in youth ministry, Bethge remained so the rest of Bonhoeffer's life.

Finkenwalde, then, was part monastery and part youth ministry, but it was no cut-off "church association."[7] The community was actually deeply connected to the Confessing Churches around the region of the school. Members of these churches provided food and furniture, and at times came for a visit. One of the school's most passionate supporters was an older woman, a grandmother named Ruth von Kleist-Retzow. "Ruth von Kleist-Retzow . . . was a remarkable woman. Throughout her life she was sympathetic toward movements that brought fresh life

6. Ibid., 429.
7. This connects to thesis 8 of Bonhoeffer's theses on youth work. See above.

to the church, and even in her old age she read every new book written by Karl Barth. She had a good sense for quality and substance, and never hesitated to say exactly what she thought." Bethge continues, explaining that when "Bonhoeffer arrived [he] . . . introduced a new spiritual stimulus into her life, and she promoted his interests with every means at her disposal. With feminine candor she would remind patrons of their duties and would persist until they had really done something to help."[8] It was Frau Kleist-Retzow more than anyone else who made sure that the Finkenwalde students had what they needed and were supported by the congregations of the Confessing Church. From 1935 onward this grandmother was one of Dietrich Bonhoeffer's greatest supporters, giving him space in her estate to holiday and write, always wanting to think *theologically* with him.[9]

Frau Kleist-Retzow saw such vitality in the Finkenwalde community that she found the time and energy to get not only herself to its worship services but soon was dragging along her grandchildren as well. Bethge explains, "Between 1935 and 1937 the Kleist-Retzow grandchildren frequently attended services in Finkenwalde, afterward enjoying games of table tennis in the garden with the [students]."[10] So even here in Finkenwalde young people made an appearance. Not only was Bonhoeffer using practices he had learned in youth ministry to shape this community, he was still inviting young people into its life.

When the illegal seminaries began in 1935, the Gestapo and SS looked the other way for the most part. They were illegal, but the thought inside the government was that the Confessing Church was more of an ecclesial conflict than a political rival. But as 1935 moved into 1936, and 1936 into 1937, any assembly not sponsored

8. Bethge, *Bonhoeffer*, 439.
9. Dramm provides more flesh to this relationship:

Of her loyalty he could be certain. Bonhoeffer had met the elderly lady five years before. In fact, it was the other way around; it was she who decided to meet him, the new pastor of the Confessing Church, in the new preachers' seminary in Finkenwalde. At that time she was living in Stettin, looking after five of her grandchildren who were attending the high school there. On the last Sunday in September 1935 she came to Finkenwalde by train, her grandchildren in tow, to attend public worship in the preachers' seminary. Ruth von Kleist-Retzow was a highly interested and committed woman, both theologically and in the church. (*Dietrich Bonhoeffer and the Resistance*, 58)

10. Bethge, *Dietrich Bonhoeffer*, 439.

by government needed to be shut down. And it was the Gestapo's job to do so.

Even then, for the most part Finkenwalde remained in the shadows. Yet, even in the shadows, things were anything but comfortable. Students lived with the pressure of being illegal and getting no financial help or support, and there was always the pull that any of these seminarians could leave the Confessing Church and become legal with just a little paperwork, which would bring a pension, salary, and the relief that prison would not be in their future. Some of Bonhoeffer's students indeed went "legal," but most, through prayer and fellowship, remained strong.

In early 1936, however, the school was exposed to the heat of the Gestapo. With Bonhoeffer's thirtieth birthday coming and having heard so many of Bonhoeffer's tales of travel, the students suggested a trip. Through Bonhoeffer's ecumenical contacts they set up a trip to Sweden, ignoring government restrictions. The trip received news coverage in the Scandinavian nation that high-ranking Swedish church officials were hosting the illegal seminarians. The trip brought significant attention to the seminary, and within a year and a half the Gestapo nailed shut its doors.

13

Back to Youth Ministry

When the Gestapo closed Finkenwalde in November 1937, Bonhoeffer was often forced to move between his parents' home in Berlin and Ruth Kleist-Retzow's estate. In January of 1938 Bonhoeffer would actually be kicked out of Berlin and told he could not live there, receiving permission only to visit and stay with his parents. Yet Bonhoeffer continued to work for the Confessing Church, trying his best to continue to educate Confessing Church pastors. But this was extremely difficult now that they could not assemble together; therefore, he sent circular letters seeking to continue the Finkenwalde experience, and each letter ended with biblical texts for meditation.

Most of the students remained in the Pomeranian area, and Bonhoeffer was keen to be in the same locale as much as possible, which made Ruth Kleist-Retzow's estate logistically appealing and its comfortable surroundings and her emotional support intoxicating. Bonhoeffer was invited to use her estate not only as home base for clandestine Confessing Church activities in Pomerania but also as a retreat to write. At Kleist-Retzow's estate Bonhoeffer wrote his circular letters and prepared his lectures on discipleship for publication.

In 1938 Bonhoeffer crafted his short but immensely popular little book *Life Together*. The book served as a kind of theological reflection on the shape of the Finkenwalde experience. Bonhoeffer wanted to publish it both to communicate what this community was about and to remind his dispersed students, now in the growing heat of persecution, to continue with the lessons learned. *Life Together*, like *Discipleship*, also received a reading in Bonhoeffer's own day, though due to a writing sanction thrust on him by the Nazis, it did not have the direct impact in the years of Bonhoeffer's life that *Discipleship* did, having been published two years earlier. Yet since Bonhoeffer's death it has remained one of his most treasured writings, and particularly embraced by youth ministers. Therefore, in part 2 I will offer, coupled with *Discipleship*, a kind of youth worker's guide to *Life Together*.

Before *Life Together* was published, in early 1938, Frau Kleist-Retzow convinced Bonhoeffer to catechize three of her grandchildren. Bethge explains humorously that she may have convinced Bonhoeffer not only for the gain of her grandchildren but also for her own. Bethge says, "In 1938 their grandmother—perhaps with the ulterior motive of attending some of the classes herself—was able to persuade Bonhoeffer to prepare three of the children for confirmation."[1] The next sixteen to eighteen months were incredibly significant ones for the fate of Dietrich Bonhoeffer. And like most of the rest of his adult life, these important months started with youth ministry.[2]

In April of 1938 Bonhoeffer finished the confirmation classes and prepared the young people for the confirmation service. On April 9 he preached their confirmation sermon, on Mark 9:24: "Immediately the boy's father exclaimed, 'I do believe; help my unbelief.'" The sermon, preached against the backdrop of the pending war and the failure of the Confessing Church to hold back the wave of Nazification, is powerful.

> This confirmation day is an important day for you and for us all. It is not an insignificant thing that you profess your Christian faith today

1. Bethge, *Dietrich Bonhoeffer*, 439.
2. "Worship service held on the occasion of the confirmation of Maximilian von Wedemeyer, Spes von Bismarck, and Hans-Friedrich von Kleist-Retzow in Kieckow, at the estate of the Kleist-Retzow family, on April 9, 1938. After Hans-Friedrich von Kleist-Retzow died in July 1941 in Russia, Bonhoeffer held the memorial service for him in Kieckow with a homily based on his confirmation verse, Prov. 23:26" (Dietrich Bonhoeffer, *Theological Education Underground: 1937–1940*, Dietrich Bonhoeffer Works [Minneapolis: Fortress, 2012], 15:476n1).

before the all-knowing God and before the ears of the Christian church-community. For the rest of your life, you shall think back on this day with joy. But for that very reason I admonish you today to full Christian soberness. You shall not and may not say or do anything on this day that you will remember later with bitterness and remorse, having said and promised more in an hour of inner emotion than a human being can and may ever say. Your faith is still weak and untried and very much in the beginning. Therefore, when later on you speak the confession of your faith, do not rely on yourselves and on your good intentions and on the strength of your faith, but rely only on the one whom you confess, on God the Father, on Jesus Christ, and on the Holy Spirit. And pray in your hearts: I believe, dear Lord, help my unbelief. Who among us adults would not and should not pray the same with you? . . .

. . . Let us be thankful that God grants us this hour of common confessing in the church. But all of this will only become utterly serious, utterly real after confirmation, when daily life returns, our daily life with all its decisions. Then it will become evident whether even this day was serious. You do not have your faith once and for all. The faith that you will confess today with all your hearts needs to be regained tomorrow and the day after tomorrow, indeed, every day anew. We receive from God only as much faith as we need for the present day. Faith is the *daily* bread that God gives us. You know the story about manna. This is what the children of Israel received daily in the desert. But when they wanted to store it for the next day, it was rotten. This is how it is with all the gifts of God. This is how it is with faith as well. Either we receive it daily anew or it rots. One day is just long enough to preserve the faith. Every morning it is a new struggle to fight through all unbelief, faintheartedness, lack of clarity and confusion, anxiety and uncertainty, in order to arrive at faith and to wrest it from God. Every morning in your life the same prayer will be necessary. I believe, dear Lord, help my unbelief.[3] (italics added)

Ramifications for Our Day

In contemporary youth ministry we talk much of faith formation or desiring that young people receive a faith that will last and is therefore

---

3. This is only an excerpt of the sermon. The full sermon is available in Bonhoeffer, *Theological Education Underground*, 476–82. All subsequent quotations are from this edition.

vital or meaningful.[4] Yet we do all this talking and rarely stop to ask "What is faith?" and "What is its theological DNA?" In this sermon, Bonhoeffer frames faith as a lived reality that is deeply theological; through this sermon Bonhoeffer gives us a handle on what faith actually is and how it relates to youth ministry.

This sermon, like *Discipleship*, cannot be read outside the backdrop of the church struggle; there is a soberness to the sermon, which seeks to call youth themselves into such sobriety. These young people before Bonhoeffer are being confirmed and made part of a church that is under great temptation. Therefore, their faith will inevitably face doubt; they may even face prisons and firing squads. And it must face doubt because they are being confirmed into faith in Christ Jesus, held not by a stable institution but by a persecuted and threatened community. Like the father in the text, so too these young people face the possibility of suffering, and their faith will only be faith when such times come and they trust in spite of doubt surrounding them—when they believe, though they doubt. Faith itself, Bonhoeffer asserts, is only found in pleas of doubt.

Bonhoeffer starts the sermon in a kind of anti-pep-talk way, calling his youth not to think too highly of the commitment they are making, to not confuse the ceremony of this confirmation with the need to profess Jesus Christ in the world. He is inviting them to base their faith not on theology but on the theological, to confess Christ not as an idea but as a living reality that will be found in their daily life.[5] Bonhoeffer is disconnecting faith from institutionalized Christianity and binding it to the lived and concrete existence of Christ in the world.

If so many North American confirmation services feel like adolescent church graduation ceremonies, like young people having

---

4. Lisa Dahill gives us insight on Bonhoeffer's own conceptions of spiritual formation: "As a Lutheran, Bonhoeffer asserts that the primary emphasis in the discourse of spiritual formation needs to fall on the formational power of Jesus Christ in us, rather than on the ways we attempt to form ourselves or the world in his image 'Christ remains the only one who forms, . . . [forming] human beings to a form the same as [his] own'" (*Reading from the Underside of Selfhood: Bonhoeffer and Spiritual Formation* [Eugene, OR: Pickwick, 2009], 15).

5. The contrast between Jesus Christ as idea and as living reality had been central to Bonhoeffer's thought since his christological lectures (*Christ the Center*); this contrast shines its brightest in *Discipleship*.

completed something, then Bonhoeffer's sermon to these youth stands in direct opposition. He says boldly that this ceremony means little. It is done before God; it is worship and therefore significant, but it will not be in this service that these young people will confirm their faith. They will confirm their faith only in the world, only in places of doubt and conflict, only where suffering is near. This service is no triumphal finish, for these young people are at just the beginning. This confirmation service is only the processional into the world; it is in the world that they will find Jesus Christ.

This confirmation sermon connects back to Bonhoeffer's theses on youth work; in this sermon he does not glorify the spirit of youth, giving them a pep talk on *their* possibility, on what *they* can do (even) with Jesus. Bonhoeffer believes that this is not faith in the crucified Christ, and if it is anything other than institutional grandstanding, then it is faith in the youthful spirit. But Bonhoeffer knows that the youthful spirit, even made religious, is no match for a world where demons crush little boys, throwing them in the fire to destroy them. Faith must *be*, not against the backdrop of youthful possibility, but against the backdrop of the impossibility of a broken world. It is only in shouting, "I believe, help my unbelief" that faith can be, for it is only in this statement that faith is bound to Christ and not to the potential and possibility of the spirit of youth.

Faith for Bonhoeffer can never be vital, vibrant, or any other adjective; faith can only be "weak"—not weak in the sense of pathetic, but weak because it takes the form of its Lord, found on a cross. Faith is weak because faith can never be solidified in sight or certainty, for the faith of the young person is only bound to the young person through their need, through their wrestling with God and the human condition. It is not their possibility that is the fertile ground of faith, but their weakness and need. It is their unbelief that is the soil, like the father in Mark 9, where faith bursts forth in bloom. If any adjective at all can be connected to faith it must be "weak," for the God that calls for faith comes into the world as the weak one, as crucified king. And this weak one calls us into faith in and through our own weakness, in and through our own unbelief.

So much of youth ministry in North America lacks the soberness that Bonhoeffer gives these young people, this confirming into the weakness of faith. Youth ministry often serves as pep rallies for institutional church commitment rather than a place of honest articulation of the struggles of faith itself. In contemporary youth ministry we like to remind kids of what *their faith* can do, of what difference they can make with commitment. But here Bonhoeffer throws water on the ambitious fire of youthful faith bound in the spirit of youth itself, calling his young people instead to a weak and sober faith that follows the lead of the father in Mark 9.

The Weakness of Faith

Bonhoeffer flat-out tells his confirmands that their "faith is weak," that getting to this day is beautiful, but it is not proof that their faith is strong. For it is only in the world, up against suffering like the father's in Mark 9, that they will experience faith, and only through their weakness (not around it or beyond it) that they will find the strength of faith.

Bonhoeffer does not call their faith weak to take the young people down a peg, to belittle youthful faith next to its adult version. Rather, he says, "Who among us adults would not and should not pray the same with you?" And this prayer Bonhoeffer wishes them to pray is the sober prayer of belief next to doubt; it is faith born, not just for the young but for all, through weakness, through the unbelief of our wrestling with God in the world. These young people are not being confirmed into strong faith, turning their commitment from foam to steel. Bonhoeffer believes there is no such thing; there is only the trust that up against the weakness of human impossibility the act of Christ comes, transforming what is dead into life. These young people are being confirmed into the theological vision of seeking God in weak places, having faith that in their own weakness Jesus comes to them with a word of new life.

And Bonhoeffer explains that this faith must be *prayed faith*, that their prayer must be the same as all the adults: "I believe, help my unbelief." Adult faith is prayer; it is not chest-beating commitment but the weak act of praying constantly. And it is prayer because in prayer we are reminded that faith is not our doing, that we cannot in our power, potency, or potential create faith. It is only the act of God, next to our impossibility (like Sarah's womb, Heb. 11:11), that brings faith. Youth ministry cannot call young people to create faith for themselves. Youth ministry, Bonhoeffer believes, can only invite young people to prayerfully confess their unbelief, so that the church-community might share in their unbelief and that through the confession of this unbelief God might give faith to young people.

Bonhoeffer says in the sermon, "Therefore, when later on you speak the confession of your faith, do not rely on yourselves and on your good intentions and on the strength of your faith, but rely only on the one whom you confess, on God the Father, on Jesus Christ, and on the Holy Spirit. And pray in your hearts: I believe, dear Lord, help my unbelief."[6]

Faith is the gift of God, given by the Holy Spirit to those who seek God through the crucified Christ, through weakness and impossibility. Bonhoeffer tells us that when young people confess their faith, we should encourage them to confess it in soberness, not as a place of arrival but as deeper invitation into the mystery (the unbelievable mystery) of the love of the Triune God. Faith is not something young people produce; it is not something youth workers can forge. It is the gift of God given to those who will seek God in doubt and fear.

From Faith Banking to Manna

And because this faith is the gift of God, it comes like manna, Bonhoeffer says. So often we see contemporary youth ministry as faith banking. Believing that vital, vibrant, or essential youth ministries will increase the dividends of the faith bond that young people commit themselves to, we act as though the very point of youth ministry is to enrich young people with enough faith in their bank account that when they enter adulthood they can live off its interest. But this is to see faith as locked within human possibilities; it is a perspective that believes that faith is something that human beings create through investment.

6. To see what this might look like in youth ministry, see chapter 14 in Root and Dean, *Theological Turn in Youth Ministry*, called "Doubt and Confirmation."

But when faith is the gift of God, it cannot be banked, only received as a daily gift. For faith can never be arrived at but is always becoming. We are always moving into faith, praying for the gift of enough faith to make it through the day. Because faith is a gift of God, given like manna, it cannot be saved up. When gifts are banked and interest accrued, we are often deceived into believing that it was we, through our own wisdom or talent, that made our own fortune, forgetting the one who gave the gift.

Faith that is the gift of the Triune God comes only daily, like manna, moving us through our weakness to the very side of Christ. Contemporary youth ministry often is framed more by the mistake of seeking to bank faith, trying to produce in young people faith reserves, than by the goal of teaching them to trust daily for the bread of faith that comes from the hand of God. Youth ministry that takes the daily gift of faith is a youth ministry of prayer and confession, praying to God to give this day the bread of faith next to and with their many doubts; it's a youth ministry that looks a little bit like Finkenwalde.

Too often we want strong youth ministries as investments for the future, so our kids will have faith in the future (and therefore the congregation itself will stay afloat into the next generation). But if faith is only for the future, there will be no faith, for like manna, faith saved spoils. It is only by learning to prayerfully confess their weakness in sobriety each day that young people learn to take the gift of faith that comes from the hand of the Triune God. American youth ministry often looks beautiful on the surface, with big youth rooms and conferences full of excited kids, but underneath the shine is rot, for the youth ministry has been more about mammon than manna, more about investment in banked faith than about inviting young people to partake with parents and other adults in the daily gift of faith that comes to us all as we pray and confess, "I believe. Help [our] unbelief."

$$\overline{}\;\;\left(14\right)\;\;\overline{}$$

Toward a Destiny

From Youth Pastor to Spy

Through the rest of 1938 Bonhoeffer continued to support and educate his students through circular letters and personal visits (when possible). But the ethos of Germany was becoming so toxic as Hitler moved toward all-out war that Bonhoeffer could barely breathe. And now not only were the church and Bonhoeffer's many students suffocating under National Socialism but so too was his family. As 1938 unfolded it became clear that Bonhoeffer's twin, Sabine, who was married to Gerhard Leibholz, a baptized Christian who was part-Jewish, would need to emigrate, and quickly.

With Bonhoeffer's help the Leibholz family awoke early one morning to travel into Switzerland, before making it to the safety of London. It was too risky to tell the children of their plans even on the morning of their departure. Later, after the war, the Leibholz children explained that they were told nothing of the plan and permanent move but knew something was up because their mother dressed them in layer after layer, forcing them to even wear two jackets.

Bonhoeffer was of great use as his sister and her family landed in London. His contacts were so strong there that he had many people, including Bishop Bell, watching after his beloved twin and her family.

Gerhard Leibholz would even become a kind of advisor to Bell, as Bell sought to relay the political situation in Germany through his own political contacts in the British government. Leibholz had been a professor of law before being removed because of his Jewish blood and therefore provided great assistance to the English (particularly Bell) in understanding the German political realm.

Bonhoeffer had known since 1933 that Hitler meant war for all of Europe.[1] And now as 1938 moved into 1939 it was clear to everyone. With war looming it would not be long until the mantle of compulsory military service would land on Bonhoeffer. So in March of 1939 Bonhoeffer traveled to England under the auspices of ecumenical work. While there he not only looked in on his sister but also met with Bishop Bell and Reinhold Niebuhr, who was in Britain giving his Gifford Lectures.

Bonhoeffer discussed with them his situation and was encouraged to find a way out of Germany. Niebuhr suggested that Bonhoeffer go back to New York where summer school lectures could be set for him to give. The idea was that once in New York, lectures and presentations could be set up across the United States, keeping Bonhoeffer busy for a year or more, providing him the contacts that could lead to a professorship in America and complete shelter from the war. Through correspondence with Niebuhr, Paul Lehmann, now located in the Midwest, got to work, writing to professors and presidents of seminaries and colleges to introduce Bonhoeffer and to encourage them to invite the unknown German Confessing Church pastor to their school.

On June 2 of 1939 Bonhoeffer boarded a ship for New York. It was over! He was now safe and would survive the war, returning to Germany only after Europe was in rubble. The relief should have been palpable; his letters and travel journal should have spoken of release and happiness as each minute moved him farther and farther into safety. But it was quite the opposite. Almost immediately, regret swarmed in on him like hornets, and second-guessing stung him raw. As the ship pointed toward the New York harbor, Bonhoeffer's mind could not be steered away from Germany.

1. Bethge states this in his biography.

Within weeks of his time in New York the regret was too much; he was not meant to be there. After spending the first handful of days at the home of the Union Seminary president, Bonhoeffer moved into the guest lodging of the seminary, taking a bed in what was called the "Prophets Chamber." In that small room Bonhoeffer wrestled with the pull to return, scribbling notes and smoking mass quantities of cigarettes. But there was no getting around it; he needed to return—and quickly, before the war started and travel was made impossible.

In his own travel journal Bonhoeffer writes, "With all this, there is only Germany lacking, the brethren. The first lonely hours are difficult. I do not know why I am here. . . . The short prayer in which we remembered the German brethren almost overwhelmed me. . . . This inactivity, or activity, as the case may be, has really become simply unbearable to [me] when [I] think of the brethren and the precious time. The whole weight of self-reproach because of a wrong decision comes back and almost chokes me."[2]

Bonhoeffer was convinced that he needed to immediately return to Germany. He wrote Niebuhr and Lehmann to inform them of his decision. Both men were confused, and Lehmann, particularly, was left with a schedule filled with lectures and presentations that he would now need to cancel. But the ticket was booked, and in early July, just over a month after his arrival, Bonhoeffer returned to Germany. Both Niebuhr and Lehmann pleaded with him to reconsider, reminding Bonhoeffer of the great danger. But it was the danger that propelled Bonhoeffer back; as he told Niebuhr, no one who refused to suffer with Germany could be of help in rebuilding Germany. Bonhoeffer could not sit out this suffering, for his students, family, and fellow brothers and sisters in the faith had to bear an awful either/or. They had to hope either for the victory of their nation and therefore the end of Christianity in Germany, or the defeat of their nation and the continuation of Christianity. Bonhoeffer could not sit out this conflict. Lehmann rushed as quickly as he could to New York, trying one last time, face-to-face, to dissuade Bonhoeffer from departing. But it was to no avail. And with the embrace of Christian brotherhood Bonhoeffer said good-bye, and Lehmann worried it would be the last time

2. Quoted in Wind, *Dietrich Bonhoeffer*, 133.

he'd see his German friend. Lehmann was right; with the waves of bon voyage, Lehmann would never see his friend again.

From Pastor to Spy

Bonhoeffer returned to Germany with a new and different resolve. Even before leaving for New York he had been in conversation with his brother-in-law Hans von Dohnanyi, and on his return he knew his next moves would be more directly political.[3] Regardless, Bonhoeffer continued to have the problem of military service. So within weeks of being back, using his prestigious maternal family name, he sought to land a military chaplaincy. In the end, this fell through. But, as it did, Dohnanyi, a high-ranking official in the office of the Abwehr—the intelligence agency, somewhat like the CIA—made it possible for Bonhoeffer to become an agent. Due to his ecumenical connections, Bonhoeffer could avoid military service by becoming a spy, traveling to Switzerland and Scandinavia on missions couched as ecumenical church work. What the government failed to recognize—and what Bonhoeffer had known for quite some time—was that the Abwehr had flipped, as the whole office sought to remove Hitler through a coup d'état.

Bonhoeffer was now a man with cover on top of cover. He continued with his Confessing Church duties, seeking to encourage pastors, writing his students, and making ecumenical contact throughout Europe. While at the core this remained Bonhoeffer's greatest commitment, it also served as a cover for espionage; but this entrance into espionage also served as cover for direct action to overthrow Hitler. As double-agent spy, Bonhoeffer's most direct action was to get word to Bishop Bell of the Abwehr's plans, asking Bell to get word from Churchill assuring the resisters that if a new German government would come to be, the war would end with the allies stepping down.

The cover on top of cover inevitably led to tension, as almost all of Bonhoeffer's church brethren and friends could not be let into the layers and pursuits of his new work. Many now even wondered if

---

3. For more on resistance and particularly Dohnanyi's place in it, see Dramm's *Dietrich Bonhoeffer and the Resistance*.

the bold pastor Bonhoeffer had been swayed over to the side of the Nazis. Even devoted friend and mentor Karl Barth had his suspicions as Bonhoeffer moved in and out of Switzerland with ease. It wouldn't be until Bonhoeffer sat with the Swiss theologian and told him everything that Barth's skepticism gave way to understanding and support.

But inevitably Bonhoeffer's most significant community shifted at this time, as the Confessing Church was battered and dispersed, and Bonhoeffer entered headlong into the conspiracy as an Abwehr agent. Coming full circle, Bonhoeffer's most significant community again would become his family. Karl and Paula's home had always remained a gathering spot for the Bonhoeffer children, even after they had grown. The Dohnanyis—Christine's family—and the Dresses—Susanne's family—actually lived just houses away from the elder Bonhoeffers, and the Schleichers—Ursula's family—lived right next door, making Karl and Paula's house always the hub of children and grandchildren reuniting.

Yet now that the conspiracy was full-blown, and Dietrich was pulled in, joining not only Hans but also brother Klaus and brother-in-law Rudiger, the elder Bonhoeffer home became ground zero for plots, conversations, and support. Dietrich, like in his time in Finkenwalde, found deep community as his brothers and sisters gathered around their parents' dining room table and sought to take action for their neighbor, to seek, even to the risk of death, to be a *Stellvertreter* (a place-sharer) to the other. Like a kind of return to his own youth, brothers-in-law Hans and Rudiger, who had embraced Bonhoeffer and inspired his own practice of youth ministry, now took him fully into the conspiracy, seeking his counsel and insight. Bonhoeffer had spent his whole theological life writing about the concrete and lived reality of the church-community, exploring its relational action for the other as its way of encountering the living presence of Jesus Christ. While separated from church-community, Bonhoeffer was experiencing a witness to this community of place-sharing in his family.

Ethics

Now sitting with his brothers and sisters, outspoken agnostics who made no direct Christian confession, Bonhoeffer explored responsible action in the world, moving further in seeing Jesus Christ not bound in the church but always in the world. This renewed community with his family moved Bonhoeffer further into thinking past the cultural Lutheran doctrine of the two realms—a political and a church sphere—pushing Bonhoeffer to explore Jesus Christ as a single reality in the world. The world itself is not divided between church and state or sacred and secular, but all was united and intermingled, like the actions of pastor and that of agnostic brothers, in the single reality of Jesus Christ.

It was such concrete and lived experience with his family that energized him to put pen to paper, as during this time Bonhoeffer crafted essays and chapters that were gathered into the book *Ethics* after his death. Bonhoeffer never intended necessarily for the contents in *Ethics* we have today to be a book. But he did have a deep sense that now, in the 1940s, a piece on ethics was his intellectual task. Unfortunately, it would only be posthumously that it would come to light (thus having all the vitality and problems of fragmentary essays bound into one volume).

From the very beginning of Bonhoeffer's theological career he had been interested in ethics,[4] but it is particularly fitting that during this period, now that the pastor had become a spy, and the spy a double agent, he was forced to wrestle with questions of ethics. Yet as he sought to construct his ethics, even in its fragmentary form, he sought to do so as a theologian, as one who seeks the *theological*. Therefore, *Ethics* revolves around the statement that "ethics is not what is right or what is wrong, but what is the will of God."[5] It is by seeking the living Jesus in the world that we discover the ethical action that we must take. Place-sharing (*Stellvertretung*), as a theological reality, sets terms for ethics.

These were haunting thoughts for Bonhoeffer, for standing with his family it soon became clear that the only way to remove Hitler would be to kill Hitler. No successful coup would end the war and allow a new government to take place, they all believed, without the permanent removal of Hitler. What would be the will of God next to this radical step?

Sitting in his parents' dining room, Bonhoeffer was faced with the challenge of whether he, a pastor, would be willing to dirty his own

---

4. See the lectures he gave to his congregation in Barcelona.
5. *Ethics*, 209.

hands by pulling the trigger himself. When first confronted with the question, Bonhoeffer balked. But then his strong and agnostic sister Christine (Hans' wife and great confidant) said to her little brother, "Oh, you Christians! You'd celebrate if someone else's hands were dirtied by killing Hitler, but you are not willing to get your own hands dirty." Bonhoeffer was forced to think more deeply about what he indeed was willing to do, what he was *called* to do; what was the will of God? Guilt, responsibility, and preservation would bleed on to each page of the *Ethics*, for such questions hemorrhaged from the very life of Bonhoeffer.

As Bonhoeffer pondered whether he'd be willing to pull the trigger himself, he came to the conclusion that indeed he would, believing that in so doing he would become (never innocent but) a murderer. He decided in the end that he would rather take on this guilt, standing before God a murderer, than know unequivocally (from the documents of the Nazis themselves shown to him by Dohnanyi) that millions of Jews were being exterminated and he had done nothing.

In the end, the decision would never come to fruition. But if it had, Bonhoeffer explained that he would do it only leaving behind his pastoral office and taking this action on his own. No doubt, bound in his Christian commitments, he would act, but knowing it would be *always and forever* a guilty act, Bonhoeffer wished to do it outside the office of pastor.

The Coming End of Youth Ministry

From 1940 on, Bonhoeffer's time was spent either in intense acts of resistance or mundane periods of solitude grinding away on the *Ethics*. But as war fell over all of Europe and so many of the Confessing Church pastors found themselves swallowed into the German war machine and sent to the front, Bonhoeffer's direct pastoral duties came more and more to a close. And as they did, so too did his youth ministry. It is nearly impossible to see Bonhoeffer's pastoral work from 1925 to 1939 apart from youth ministry, but as his role moved from pastor to conspirator, his direct youth work was drowned out by resistance and espionage.

There are no clear occurrences of youth/children's ministry in this period after 1940, but I believe this is only because there are few direct occurrences of any pastoral ministry.[6] Bonhoeffer continued to serve the Confessing Church but now as itinerant educator, and he continued to reach out to ecumenical friends, but as resister. Yet even in this post-1940 period of Bonhoeffer's life there are signs of his continued care and enjoyment of young people. During this period, back deeply in the community of his family, Bonhoeffer spent significant time with his nephew Christopher von Dohnanyi, taking him under his wing as he had done for so many other young people in Grunewald, Wedding, and London. Christopher, fourteen at the time, actually wrote Bonhoeffer two letters while he was in prison. Bonhoeffer was so moved by them that he told his parents how much they meant to him and to thank the boy heartily.

Even as Bonhoeffer grappled with his own action to pull a trigger and kill, wrestling with these thoughts as he sat in his family bedroom while he wrote pages on ethics, we are told that Bonhoeffer often opened his window to throw chocolates to Susanne's children as they played in the yard below his window, making his espionage not only German secrets to the British but also chocolate to children without their mother seeing.[7] This would be a period of little youth work, but Bonhoeffer's care and enjoyment of young people remained.

6. Dan Adams has pointed out that the exception to this may be the ministry that Bonhoeffer did to and with the young prisoners he encountered in Tegel. Adams's own thesis is focused on this area, and he makes a convincing case. Two particular quotes from Bonhoeffer's *Ethics* point to this. "A few of the young prisoners seem to suffer to such a degree under the extended isolation and the long, dark evening hours that they break down completely under it. It is in fact insane to lock these people up for months without anything to keep them busy; truly in every possibly conceivable way this is nothing but demoralizing" (223). Bonhoeffer says further, "I also believe that in the face of *this* misery that reigns in this building, a remembrance of Christmas that is merely more or less only playfully sentimental is inappropriate. A good, personal word, a sermon, should accompany it. Without that, music on its own can in fact become dangerous. Don't imagine, by the way, that I am worrying about this on my own account in any way; that is truly not the case, but I feel sorry for the many helpless young soldiers in their cells" (ibid., 232).

7. William Kuhns says, "His sister Susanne lived only next door, and he used to toss chocolates to her children from the window of his room" (*In Pursuit of Dietrich Bonhoeffer* [Dayton, OH: Pflaum Press, 1967], 268).

To the Cell

Besides relaying messages of the possibility of the coming coup to his ecumenical contacts, Bonhoeffer's direct work in the Abwehr also included a mission called "Operation Seven," with the objective to smuggle seven Jews out of Germany and into Switzerland. The mission was successful.[8]

Much had changed both in Europe and in Bonhoeffer's life. It actually may have been due to the renewed time spent with his family, but during this period Bonhoeffer, the consummate bachelor, felt the pull toward marriage. Visiting Ruth Kleist-Retzow, Bonhoeffer saw again, but now really for the first time, another one of her granddaughters, Maria von Wedemeyer.[9] She was but nineteen, making her an unusual match for the thirty-six-year-old Bonhoeffer. But her wit, intelligence, and strength made her ever Bonhoeffer's equal. To the great delight of Frau Kleist-Retzow the two quickly fell in love. Yet while the grandmother was ecstatic, Maria's mother was not. Fearing the age gap, she asked Bonhoeffer to refrain from seeing her daughter, and if that request could not be met, at the very least to give the girl some space, because just months before Maria's romance with Bonhoeffer, her father had been killed in action. Bonhoeffer respected Maria's mother's request. But within weeks the rushing waters of their love spilled over the banks of her mother's restrictions as letters and finally an engagement followed.

8. Dramm explains more:
Bonhoeffer's involvement in Operation 7 must be seen with the appropriate objectivity, solely in its real extent, and must not be unrealistically exaggerated. It is a fact that the pseudo-agents of Operation 7 were able to remain in Switzerland and were thus able to survive. Fourteen people were saved from the ethnic murder of European Jews, and for this Hans von Dohnanyi's efforts were decisive. Bonhoeffer contributed as far as he could and used his contacts as far as was possible. Moltke wrote in March 1943 to England that the opposition saved the lives of individuals. "We cannot prevent wild commands from being given, but we can save individual people." (*Dietrich Bonhoeffer and the Resistance*, 236)

9. "In autumn 1935 the eleven-year-old Maria had passed the time during a church service by counting the times Pastor Bonhoeffer used the word God. At the beginning of June 1942 she had just passed her Abitur, the school leaving examination, and was spending a few days holiday with her grandmother, with whom she had an especially affectionate relationship" (ibid., 193).

In January of 1943 Bonhoeffer and Maria were secretly engaged, but tragically, before the secret of their engagement could be revealed, Bonhoeffer and his brother-in-law Hans von Dohnanyi were imprisoned. Bonhoeffer and Dohnanyi were arrested for suspicions around Operation Seven; yet the case against them was thin. As Bonhoeffer was placed in the Tegel prison, he was confident that he would be back with his family and fiancée soon. During the long and grueling hours of interrogation, the only concern now was not to contradict Dohnanyi's testimony and/or give up information about the deeper plots coming out of the Abwehr.

But even though the case was not strong against Bonhoeffer and Dohnanyi, the interrogators nevertheless thought both men were hiding something, as indeed they were. Therefore, both men were held. Bonhoeffer would, as much as possible, ease into prison life. After receiving very harsh treatment his first few days, the many months that followed soon gave way to opportunities, as Bonhoeffer befriended guards and was therefore allowed to minister to fellow prisoners. Finding his groove, Bonhoeffer was also able to write and read. He wrote a play and many essays. But it was his letters and papers that are remembered. In these letters and papers, he explored, mostly with Bethge, a "religionless Christianity," a world come of age, the need to move past a God of the gaps (the *deus ex machina*), and how only a suffering God can help. These were some of Bonhoeffer's most radical thoughts, written from the gray view of his prison cell and the coming bombs of the allies. They made their way to Bethge by being secretly snuck out of the Tegel prison.

"What Does It Mean to Tell the Truth?"

One of the first essays Bonhoeffer wrote in prison was a deeply contextual piece.[10] After being interrogated and therefore lying and hiding information, Bonhoeffer returned to his cell to theologically explore

---

10. This essay is so early in Bonhoeffer's time in prison that it actually is not in *Letters and Papers from Prison* but in *Conspiracy and Imprisonment*. It is the first, or at least one of the first, of what Bonhoeffer wrote in Tegel.

what it means to tell the truth.[11] Even nearly eighty years later the essay is filled with significant insights, as Bonhoeffer pushes for the concept of "truth" not to be seen as an abstract "ought," some external metaphysical form, but rather as a lived and concrete reality that therefore can only be determined in context.[12] Truth can only be discovered in the concrete place of lived life in the world. And this is so because truth is not an idea but a person—truth is Jesus Christ, and Jesus Christ is in the world. So truth itself can only be discovered in the concrete context of our lived worlds.

To make this point, Bonhoeffer returns, here at the end of his life, to the very place he began—to children. Bonhoeffer explains that we must be taught to tell the truth, and this begins in childhood. We must be taught to tell the truth, but we must be taught because truth is a fundamentally relational and lived reality; it is never natural or obvious, for truth is found in context. The child must learn to tell the truth because she must learn to discern context, discovering what is truthful in a situation.[13] Bonhoeffer says, "From this we can see immediately that 'telling the truth' means different things, depending on where one finds oneself."[14] So one must learn, starting in childhood, to discern "where one finds" him- or herself.

11. In footnote 1 we are given some historical context for this essay. It reads: "Presumably the essay reached the manuscript form in which it appears here by the time of his final report about it. Bonhoeffer doubtless began it under the impact of the interrogations and the urgent accompanying constraint to conceal the truth" (Bonhoeffer, *Conspiracy and Imprisonment 1940–1945*, 601).

12. Bonhoeffer grounded this contextual reality deeply within his Christology, as he does everything. He says, "Those who say 'God' are not allowed simply to cross out the given world in which they live; otherwise they would be speaking not of the God who in Jesus Christ came into the world but rather of some sort of metaphysical idol" (ibid., 602).

13. Footnote 2 gives a picture of some of Bonhoeffer's interesting deletions in this essay on children: "In the archival copy, on the second page of the rough draft of his Morning Prayer for Prisoners, written in Tegel prison fill Christmas 1943, the following words are crossed out: 'I [= Bonhoeffer's enumeration on this page] From that point in our life in which we are capable of creating coherent words and sentences, we are taught that our words must be true. This is the same period in which we are told about Santa Claus and the Easter bunny and in which Grimm's fairy tales are the air we breathe. What does it mean that our words must be true? What does 'telling the truth' mean? It means to say how something is in reality" (ibid., 601).

14. Ibid., 602.

Much like *Sanctorum Communio* and *Act and Being*, so too at the end of Bonhoeffer's life—at the very beginning of the prison experience—he draws from the child as the frame for deep theological perspectives. Delving into the situation of the child, Bonhoeffer asserts that from the child's perspective truth is ever monotone; the child reveals that telling the truth is situated and relational. Bonhoeffer states, "The truthfulness of the child toward parents is by its very nature something different from that of parents toward their child. While the life of the small child lies open to the parents and the child's word is to reveal all that is hidden and secret, the same cannot be true of the reverse relationship." He continues, "In regard to truthfulness, therefore, the parents' claim on the child is something different from that of the child on the parents."[15]

Bonhoeffer is saying that there are supposed "truths" that parents hide from the child not because the parents wish to deceive the child but because they love the concrete child. And what is truth must be born from the acknowledgment and embrace of their concrete lives one to another. Truth is not simply the disclosure of data but the relational sharing of persons. And this sharing means that sometimes the truth is the hiding of data. When parents hide information, or even lie to a child about where babies come from, for instance, it is a deception *that seeks truth*—the truth that the parent is first and foremost called to embrace the concrete humanity of the child, protecting him in the truth of their relationship. Therefore, sometimes it is necessary to lie to uphold the truth of relation—like how the answer to "Does this make me look fat?" should nearly always be "No." The words from my mouth do not necessarily correlate with my true feeling, and therefore it could be called a lie. But to simply blurt out the information would be to serve my own desires rather than to recognize the relationship that binds us to each other. Truth must first honor this relationship, just as the truth—that which is truthful—for parents is to uphold the relationship between them and their child.

Of course Bonhoeffer has a much more significant contextual situation on his mind than telling someone if they look okay in an outfit.

15. Ibid.

He is wrestling with what it means to tell the truth under the threat of death. He knows that if he does not lie to his interrogators, he will not be able to uphold the truth of his commitment to his family and Hans will meet his doom, and, if he discloses (because it is true) the plans of the coup, then he will betray the truthfulness of his *Stellvertretung* for the Jews.[16]

Bonhoeffer says, powerfully, " 'Revealing the truth' is therefore not a matter only of one's intention but also of accurate perception and of serious consideration of the real circumstances. The more diverse the life circumstances of people are, the more responsibility they have and the more difficult it is 'to tell the truth.' " Bonhoeffer returns to the child, saying, "The child, who stands in only one life relationship, namely, that with his or her parents, does not yet have anything to ponder and weigh. But already the next circle of life in which the child is placed, namely school, brings the first difficulties. Pedagogically it is therefore of the greatest importance that in some way . . . the parents clarify the differences of these circles of life to their child and make his or her responsibilities understandable."[17] It is into these expanding life circumstances that Bonhoeffer next pushes his essay, turning again to young people, this time an adolescent. Bonhoeffer provides the following parable.

> For example, a teacher asks a child in front of the class whether it is true that the child's father often comes home drunk. This is true, but the child denies it. The teacher's question brings the child into a situation that he or she does not yet have the maturity to handle. To be sure, the child perceives that this question is an unjustified invasion into the order of the family and must be warded off. What takes place in the family is not something that should be made known to the class. The family has its own secret that it must keep. The teacher disregards the reality of this order. In responding, the child would have to find a way to observe equally the orders of the family and those of the school. The child cannot do this yet; he or she lacks

16. Bonhoeffer says it this way: "A truthful word is not an entity constant in itself but is as lively as life itself. Where this word detaches itself from the relationship to the concrete other person, where 'the truth is told' without regard for the person to whom it is told, there it has only the appearance of truth" (ibid., 604).

17. Ibid., 603.

the experience, the discernment, and the capacity for appropriate expression. In flatly saying no to the teacher's question, the response becomes untrue, to be sure; at the same time, however, it expresses the truth that the family is an *order sui generis* where the teacher was not justified to intrude. Of course, one could call the child's answer a lie; all the same, this lie contains more truth—i.e., it corresponds more closely to the truth—than if the child had revealed the father's weakness before the class. The child acted rightly according to the measure of the child's perception. Yet it is the teacher alone who is guilty of the lie.[18]

Bonhoeffer's parable not only brings home his significant theological points, showing the deep layers of his questions about truth bound in the real world, but, again, Bonhoeffer uses young people and their lived experience as a stage for rich theological construction. Even here in the prison letters Bonhoeffer shows himself to be the father of the theological turn in youth ministry as he continues to delve into theological construction through the experience of children and youth. He teaches us that when we think of helping our own young people think ethically, it begins by helping them discern their contextual location, seeing their life circumstance in context. Bonhoeffer pushes us to see that ethical formation in youth ministry is a teaching exercise that helps young people, not to know foundational truths, but to discern contexts, situations, and episodes,[19] looking for how their own action joins the active presence of Christ found in the world.

18. Ibid., 606. Georg Huntemann offers more on this passage, linking to what has been said above:

> Kant, in his ethical rigorism, thought quite differently. He would have branded the child's statement a downright lie and called upon the child to be unconditionally truthful, that is, to betray its family and its father. Kant would not have hidden an innocent victim of persecution if that would have made it necessary for him to lie. In Bonhoeffer's judgment, this ethical rigorism is totally unchristian and inhumane. For Bonhoeffer it was very clear that one can, may, and should lie if one has to in order to save an innocent friend from murderers. The persecution of the Jews in the Third Reich provided illustrative examples of this in abundance. But Bonhoeffer also knew that all decisions involve the taking on of guilt. (*The Other Bonhoeffer: An Evangelical Reassessment of Dietrich Bonhoeffer* [Grand Rapids: Baker, 1989], 241)

19. I'm taking this from Richard Osmer's important book *Practical Theology: An Introduction* (Grand Rapids: Eerdmans, 2008).

Life in Prison

The essay "What Does It Mean to Tell the Truth?" was only the first of many letters and papers smuggled out of Tegel. Reading these letters even today you can feel the building anticipation as the date moves toward July 1944. It would be around this time that the Abwehr would take their grand step to remove Hitler and start the wave of the coup d'état. Bonhoeffer is confident, anticipating that once the mission is successful he will be freed, and more importantly, the war will be over. Yet, "On 20 July 1944 the news flash even reached the prison cells in Tegel: an attempt had been made on the life of the Führer. However, by nightfall all hopes had been dashed. Hitler had survived the attack; Colonel Stauffenberg, who had placed the bomb, had been shot along with his closest collaborators, and the first wave of arrests was already under way."[20]

From this day onward the tone of Bonhoeffer's letters changed; all the optimism of the future was swept from them. Bonhoeffer knew it would now only be a matter of time before proof of his involvement would be uncovered. In sober acceptance Bonhoeffer began to face the fact that he more than likely would never be free again.

In October 1944, the Zossen documents were found, connecting Hans, Dietrich, Klaus, and Rudiger to the conspiracy. What Bonhoeffer knew would happen in July now was upon him. Bonhoeffer's only hope of survival was escape. Dohnanyi, an astute lawyer, had been poisoning himself in another prison for weeks, allowing himself to be too ill to be interrogated. But now even his sickness would not keep him from the wrath of the Gestapo. With the help of a prison guard named Knobloch, Bonhoeffer and his family made arrangements for escape. But just before the plan was to be executed, Klaus and Rudiger were arrested; if Bonhoeffer were to escape now they would be severely beaten and tortured. Bonhoeffer's only hope became the arrival of the allies.

The End

By early October 1944 Bonhoeffer was taken from his Tegel prison, and the road to his death began. He was taken from his cell to the

20. Wind, *Dietrich Bonhoeffer*, 171.

Gestapo prison at Prinz-Albrecht-Strasse. The interrogation and tor-
ture continued into 1945. As 1944 turned into 1945, Bonhoeffer's
family, including Maria, had a harder and harder time keeping track
of his whereabouts. This became even more difficult in February as
Bonhoeffer was moved around concentration camps. Finally, on April
5, 1945, Hitler gave the decree that all involved in the Canaris resistance of the Abwehr—including Bonhoeffer, Klaus, Hans, and Rudiger—must be eliminated. So just weeks before the American military
took over Germany, Dietrich Bonhoeffer was taken to the Flossenbürg
concentration camp in the Bavarian forest, stripped naked, and hung.
Hans, Klaus, and Rudiger were also executed, bringing suffering upon
suffering to the Bonhoeffer family.

Bonhoeffer's dead body was burned and the ashes dumped, sharing the place with all the other ashes of Jews killed in the furnaces,
in a pit at the back of the camp. Though brutally cut short, Dietrich
Bonhoeffer's life and legacy continue to live on, for he died as martyr,
pastor, theologian—and youth worker.

Part
2

A Youth Worker's
Guide to *Discipleship*
and *Life Together*

15

Youth Ministry and
Discipleship

In part 1, we took a trip back to the first decades of the twentieth century, sketching out Bonhoeffer's history and exploring the consistent thread of youth ministry within it. I sought to show how, especially from 1925 to 1939, Bonhoeffer was a youth worker doing significant theological work, or a theologian with young people on his mind. I sought to highlight through both his life history and writings the many places where young people, and ministry to them, appear. My objective was to make a case for Dietrich Bonhoeffer being the forefather to the theological turn in youth ministry.

In these final two chapters my objective and approach will shift. Instead of seeking to lift out the threads of youth work in Bonhoeffer's writings—like, for example, the place of baptism in *Sanctorum Communio*, or to wrestle directly with his confirmation sermons and theses on youth work, pieces rarely examined in the Bonhoeffer corpus—I'll instead shift my focus to Bonhoeffer's two most popular books, *Discipleship* and *Life Together*. In this part, I will explore the central themes of these two works for their relevance to contemporary youth ministry. I'll leave behind the scent of youth work I've been chasing, like a beagle, in Bonhoeffer's work and life, and with these final two chapters do something different.

I have already tried in part 1 to show how both of these two classics have connection to Bonhoeffer's youth work. So my goal here in part 2 is to pull us from our voyage through the early decades of the twentieth century and return us back to our own time. Part 2, then, provides a kind of youth worker's guide to *Discipleship* and *Life Together*. It will be my job not to show how youth ministry is embedded in these books but to show how the themes of these books might frame our contemporary practice of youth ministry. But by calling this part a "guide" I do not mean "commentary"; in other words, these next two chapters will not be a chapter-by-chapter commentary on *Discipleship* and *Life Together*. Rather, in them I will raise several major themes of these books and connect them with our contemporary practice of youth ministry.

Both of these books rise to the top on lists of theological texts read by people in youth ministry. And they are often not simply read but used within ministries. *Discipleship* and *Life Together* have often been known as books youth ministry people read with young people or adult leaders. It is not uncommon for *Life Together* to be read with seniors before or during a summer backpacking trip, or a book study on *Discipleship* to fill the training and equipping time of months of leaders' meetings. It is my hope with these last two chapters, then, to provide dialogue between the themes of these books and contemporary youth ministry.

Often when it comes to these two books, youth workers will invite young people to read *Life Together* and encourage adults, such as volunteer leaders, to read *Discipleship*. This decision is usually made because of the difficulty of each text. *Discipleship* is a much denser theological text, while *Life Together* is more accessible—Bonhoeffer himself thought of it as a practical guide. While there is merit in choosing which book to study with whom this way, I actually see the themes in *Discipleship* to be more directly relevant to young people themselves, as Bonhoeffer explores faith, grace, and obedience. I find that *Life Together* more directly relates to the youth worker (volunteer) as a way of reflecting on his or her own person in ministry. Because of this, below I'll seek to connect the themes of *Discipleship* with the

direct practice of youth ministry and *Life Together* with the vocational
life of the youth worker as pastor.

Follow!

Discipleship is a rare book in its reach. Almost every church with a
library has at least one copy of it. I personally have made it a kind of
game for myself to enter the libraries of the churches I visit to see if
I can spot a dusty binding that reads *The Cost of Discipleship*. After
just a short look, I usually spot it staring back at me. It makes little
difference if the congregation is liberal or conservative, mainline or
evangelical, Lutheran or Pentecostal. It seems to matter little if the
other books that nestle next to it wear on their binding the names
of Marcus Borg or John Piper. Regardless, there seems to always be
at least one copy of *Discipleship*. In our time, where we've divided
ourselves so easily into categories and are so quickly offended by that
which doesn't support our narrow commitments, it is surprising that
seemingly everyone likes *Discipleship*.

The German title—the title Bonhoeffer himself picked for the
book—is *Nachfolge*, which means "follow." Only after the book was
translated into English after Bonhoeffer's death did it receive the more
descriptive title *The Cost of Discipleship*. The short and direct title
Nachfolge, Follow, signals the book's directness. The book nearly
shouts in capital letters to the reader of the need for the Christian to
"FOLLOW!" and follow solely and completely the call of Jesus Christ.

As part 1 above tried to show, *Discipleship* was written in the heat
of the church struggle, and Bonhoeffer's intensity can be read on
nearly every page. The book was published in 1937, as the Gestapo
was closing the doors of Bonhoeffer's beloved Finkenwalde. The book
is, essentially, Bonhoeffer's lecture notes. *Nachfolge* is in every way a
passionate pleading for his students to stay faithful to the gospel and
its call amid deep attack. It is a book that in almost no way is after
nuance, but only the provoking of direct, immediate, and faithful
following of Jesus Christ. Even Bonhoeffer, in his prison cell, admitted that the book's direct tone may be a danger to the reader. But
though dangerous, due to its lack of nuance and propensity to yell its

directive to FOLLOW, Bonhoeffer, even in his gray prison cell, stood behind every word. It is quite a surprise that over eighty years later its intensity draws readers (and readers across distinct groups) instead of fatiguing them to the point of abandoning the book to the table of garage sales with so many other early-twentieth-century theological projects that now seem so dated.

Cheap Grace

The book starts with its most provocative theme on its first pages. Bonhoeffer opens the book by contrasting cheap and costly grace. It was from these first pages that English publishers chose to title *Nachfloge* as *The Cost of Discipleship*. And this is understandable, for the contrasting of cheap and costly grace is not only engaging but radical in its prophetic call.

Bonhoeffer is concerned that the gospel has been drowned in a dirty puddle of cheap grace. Cheap grace, he says, is "grace as bargain-basement goods, cut-rate forgiveness, cut-rate comfort, and cut-rate sacraments."[1] Cheap grace is a knockoff handbag bought on the streets of New York City or Beijing. It is a fake gold chain purchased in Chicago or Singapore. It looks real; it appears at first glance to be the genuine article. But after wearing it for a day, it turns your neck green; after carrying it on your shoulder for just hours, its seams sag and gap.

Bonhoeffer believes that the church has become addicted to the knockoff. And this has happened for the same reasons that people choose to buy the knockoff Gucci handbag. They buy it because they

---

1. Bonhoeffer goes on:
   Cheap grace means grace as bargain-basement goods, cut-rate forgiveness, cut-rate comfort, cut-rate sacraments; grace as the church's inexhaustible pantry, from which it is doled out by careless hands without hesitation or limit. It is grace without a price, without costs. It is said that the essence of grace is that the bill for it is paid in advance for all time. Everything can be had for free, courtesy of that paid bill. The price paid is infinitely great and, therefore, the possibilities of taking advantage of and wasting grace are also infinitely great. What would grace be, if it were not cheap grace? (*Discipleship*, Dietrich Bonhoeffer Works [Minneapolis: Fortress, 2001], 4:43)

like the "idea" of Gucci; they like the idea that they are someone
who is loyal to this brand. It doesn't matter that the bag is not really
Gucci. Even the fact that they know it isn't real doesn't change that
it provides them a cheaper way to possess and broadcast the idea of
being connected to Gucci. The knockoff gives the "idea" they are
after, that they are the kind of person that has Gucci and therefore is
classy, wealthy, and important.

For Bonhoeffer cheap grace is grace as an idea. And when grace
becomes an "idea," it is only a lame knockoff of the real thing. Just
like with the knockoff Gucci, cheap grace is grace without the price,
without the cost. The church, Bonhoeffer believes, has chosen the
knockoff to the real thing, because the real thing costs too much.
It costs us our very lives, for to possess it is not to buy it, but to be
possessed by it. It is to *Nachfloge*, to follow,[2] leaving all behind, like
Peter and Levi, to follow Jesus.[3]

So cheap grace is grace that has amputated the act of following. It
is stagnant and has no motion; it is a dirty puddle. Cheap grace, like
the fake Gucci, has become bound in the idea of the brand; cheap
grace has made Christianity an idea. For Bonhoeffer faith is dead
when it is turned into an idea. Cheap grace, for instance, is the idea
of justification; it is the idea that sin is forgiven as a general truth, as
a nice notion, but which worries little about the justification of the
sinner. Or we could say it this way: justification, as cheap grace, seeks
not the forgiveness and liberation of sinners, but to win their loyalty
to *the idea of forgiveness*, to give them the idea of being forgiven
so that they need not follow but can enjoy their apathy. We like the

2. And this following for Bonhoeffer is immediate. When we hear the call we are to
drop our nets and follow, period. Bonhoeffer says boldly that any stopping to reflect
is disobedience. When Jesus calls, we must respond. Bonhoeffer continued even after
1937 and 1938 to stand behind these statements. But it is statements like these that
led him in prison to see the potential danger of *Discipleship*. As Bonhoeffer writes
these pages of *Discipleship* he is concerned that the church has used reflection to
justify inaction, and he wants to raise this as a strategy of disobedience. Just as it is
also true that, in another context, at another time, action without the beat or two of
reflection could be just as problematic.
3. "As long as Levi sits in the tax collector's booth and Peter at his nets, they would
do their work honestly and loyally, they would have old or new knowledge about
God. But if they want to learn to believe in God, they have to follow the Son of God
incarnate and walk with him" (ibid., 62).

idea of forgiveness, the idea that God loves us, but the idea is only a warm blanket that satiates inaction. Cheap grace is the candy-coating concept that makes our apathy sweet, deceiving us with a sugary rush that our apathy is actually noble or faithful. Faith itself becomes only an idea, a brand like Gucci.[4]

Grace as Principles, Programs, and Doctrines

When faith is turned into an idea, it can substantiate itself only in principles and programs.[5] Principles and programs become consumable outlets that prove that we are loyal to the idea.[6] For example, we may be loyal to the idea of Apple because we take on the principle that design and function should be one, that the aesthetic is essential to the experience of a product. And the deeper we take in the idea, being shaped by its principles, the more we're compelled to participate in its programs. We're convinced not only that we need a new iPad with every new version but that we should stay up all night, standing outside the store in line to get it. We could wait just thirty-six hours and get one online, but now that we have become loyal to the idea, embracing the principles, we're drawn to the program.

4. Feil states boldly, "Discipleship is contingent upon Christ's call, but Christ's call is without any mediation. When Christ calls, only he and his call are present without any mediation. Doctrine, principle, system, and reflection do not mediate" (*Theology of Dietrich Bonhoeffer*, 79).

5. Geffrey Kelly and John Godsey say it powerfully: "Costly grace demands not a new confession of faith, not a religious decision to be more regular in church attendance, but obedience to the call of Jesus Christ! Christian discipleship offers no program, no set of principles, no elitist ideal, no new set of laws. Discipleship means, quite simply, Jesus Christ and Jesus Christ alone; the sole content of discipleship is to 'follow Christ'" (editors' introduction to Bonhoeffer, *Discipleship*, 4).

6. Haddon Wittmer explains,

> Cheap grace arises when grace is universalised as a principle, for if God does anything universally, it can be taken as given, existing reality and as automatically available to human beings. They do not need to seek it, or to get themselves into any place where they will receive what is in God's gift. When grace is not automatically available, when it has to be asked for, the person apprehends himself as one who is exposed to God's freedom to give or not to give. This is a true encounter with God, the essential element of a right relation with God. ("Costly Discipleship," in John De Gruchy, *The Cambridge Companion to Dietrich Bonhoeffer* [Cambridge: Cambridge University Press, 1999], 177)

When faith is an idea, it is only another brand, forcing the church to worry about its loss of the market share, concerned with why it is that we are losing our young people. This pushes us to believe we need to up our idea, to make the idea of Christian faith more attractive and appealing to the young. We think we need youth ministry to market the idea of Christianity, believing that only when the idea is appealing will the loyalty come. And we are certain there is no loyalty because our children are not conforming to our principles; they do not assimilate to our doctrines and morals as we want them to. And, worse yet, they simply are not coming to our programs; our pews are lacking their presence.

But this is cheap grace! Bonhoeffer asserts that cheap grace is grace as principle, doctrine, and program. It is possible that much of North American youth ministry is actually the perpetuation of cheap grace; it is the arm of the church that offers the "idea" of Christianity to the young. Bonhoeffer may tell us if he were with us today that the problem with youth ministry is that it is addicted to cheap grace. It has been so captivated by the "idea" of Christianity, by the idea of getting young people committed and excited about the institutional church, that it has given itself over almost completely to principles and programs. Just take stock of the most popular blogs and speakers at youth ministry conventions. Often these are not theologians or ministers but those in the business of ideation; they tell youth workers that they can create the next big idea, that Christianity is an idea and that if we can just break through, following the right principles, we can create programs of loyalty that stretch as deep as Apple and Gucci.

Even if we in youth ministry recognize the superficiality of the move from idea to principle to program, we often fall into the trap of cheap grace as doctrine. Bonhoeffer says directly, "Cheap grace [is] grace as doctrine." He describes it this way: "Cheap grace means grace as doctrine, as principle, as system. It means forgiveness of sins as a general truth; it means God's love as merely a Christian idea of God."[7]

Doctrine is the danger of faith turned into the hard stone of an idea. We need not follow the living Jesus, for we have our doctrine. Unlike

---

7. Bonhoeffer, *Discipleship*, 43.

Peter in Acts (chap. 10), when doctrine is an idea, we refuse to ever budge from our principles, even when the living Christ calls us to eat. Bonhoeffer says it this way: "Because Jesus is the Christ, it has to be made clear from the beginning that his word is not a doctrine. Instead, it creates existence anew. The point [is] to really walk with Jesus."[8]

If youth ministry avoids the temptation to make itself into principles and programs, it too often falls into the rigidity of doctrine, believing that youth ministry is not about fun and entertainment but about getting kids to believe the right thing. But this "right thing" is often the narrow doctrine that pushes faith further into "idea."

This is why Bonhoeffer is no forefather to theology in youth ministry; theology can be the perpetuation of cheap grace. This happens when theology is equated with doctrine, and doctrine is seen as the ideas that make Christianity. Christianity is not its doctrines; Christianity is only Jesus Christ, and Jesus Christ is not a dead man locked in ideas now called doctrines. Jesus Christ, for Bonhoeffer, is the living, acting Lord in the world, calling us to follow. Bonhoeffer reminds us that we can have our theology right; we can know our doctrine, and never *Nachfolgen*, never follow the living Christ. We can teach young people all the answers to the *how* questions of their faith. But for Bonhoeffer, without the *who* of the living Christ there can be no faith.[9] To contend that if young people just knew the Bible and theology is not to give them the bread that is the living Jesus but a cold stone of ideas to break their teeth on (Matt. 7:9).

Grace at a Cost

If grace is cheap when it is an idea that can be perpetuated in principles, programs, and doctrines, then what is costly grace? And what makes it costly? Bonhoeffer seeks to show that grace is not produced only in and through the human being's work. Bonhoeffer makes no mistake in asserting that the church in Nazi Germany had become sedentary. It has grabbed with both hands the "idea" of the doctrine

8. Ibid., 62.
9. This contrasting of *how* and *who* is a rich argument Bonhoeffer began with his christological lectures. These lectures have been published as *Christ the Center*.

of justification, weighing itself down with the idea that we are saved by faith alone and not by our works. And holding to this idea, the church, the Christian, could sit quietly with little opposition, allowing the atrocities before them to occur, allowing concrete persons to be exterminated. The *idea* of justification, Bonhoeffer believes, tranquilizes the church. No one acted for fear that they would step outside grace. The idea that action corrupts grace cheapened it to its core. Bonhoeffer even says, in a deeply prophetic comment toward his German Lutheran heritage, "Cheap grace has ruined more Christians than any commandment about works."[10]

But even with this comment Bonhoeffer is *not* saying that costly grace is costly because it calls for our works to save us. Costly grace is not costly because it calls for human beings to work themselves to a sweat, so that they might save themselves. Bonhoeffer is not replacing the gospel with law.[11] What he is doing is shifting the frame. Returning to a deeply biblical perspective, he is making a case for us to see grace not from the frame of an idea but from the location of a person.[12] Peter is called not to follow an idea but to come and follow Jesus's person, not to take on ideas and principles but to join Jesus's very person in ministry in the world. "Come and follow me!" Jesus says. "Come and be my disciple by joining in my person."[13]

10. Bonhoeffer, *Discipleship*, 55.
11. Bonhoeffer's reference to Luther shows how his position stays faithful to Luther's own: "When Luther said that our deeds are in vain, even in the best of lives, and that, therefore, nothing is valid before God 'except grace and favor to forgive sins,' he said it as someone who knew himself called to follow Jesus, called to leave everything he had up until this moment, and in the same moment called anew to do it again" (ibid., 50).
12. For a helpful articulation of Bonhoeffer's person theology, see DeJonge, *Bonhoeffer's Theological Formation*.
13. Geffrey Kelly explains: "With Kierkegaard Bonhoeffer can affirm that Christianity is not a doctrine but a person to whom we entrust ourselves irrevocably" (*Reading Bonhoeffer: A Guide to His Spiritual Classics and Selected Writings on Peace* [Eugene, OR: Cascade, 2008], 80). Green and the evangelical Huntemann adds to this. Green says, "God comes to a person not as an idea, a philosophy, a religion, but as a human being in the Christian community of the new humanity" (*Bonhoeffer*, 158). Huntemann says, "Discipleship is not an idea or a plan of action. Discipleship is Christ's call. . . . Discipleship is possible only because a now living and here present Jesus Christ exists. Because Christ exists, there must be discipleship" (*The Other Bonhoeffer*, 190).

Bonhoeffer says it this way:

> Discipleship is commitment to Christ. Because Christ exists, he must be
> followed. An idea about Christ, a doctrinal system, a general religious
> recognition of grace or forgiveness of sins does not require disciple-
> ship. In truth, it even excludes discipleship; it is inimical to it. One
> enters into a relationship with an idea by way of knowledge, enthusi-
> asm, perhaps even by carrying it out, but never by personal obedient
> discipleship. Christianity without the living Jesus Christ remains neces-
> sarily a Christianity without discipleship; and a Christianity without
> discipleship is always a Christianity without Jesus Christ.[14]

Following, actually, can only become a work when it is based in an
idea, when it is assimilation to an ideology.[15] Hitler is not just person
but the personification of an ideology. He loves, not concrete persons
whom he encounters, but only those that assimilate his ideology. To
follow Hitler is not to follow his person in love, but to follow his ideology. He is a tyrant because he *uses* his personhood to win loyalty
to his idea, and those who refuse his idea are no longer persons in his
eyes, and therefore can be exterminated by the power of his ideology
that is perfected in his program (concentration camps) made possible
by his doctrine (the Aryan clause).

To get less dramatic, it is only through human effort and not by
grace that we can follow an idea—whether that idea be political or
religious. It may be that faith formation is difficult in youth ministry
because we have not seen how we have been more embedded in the
idea than focused on drawing young people through their person into
encounters with the person of Jesus Christ.

Youth ministry may be simply, but profoundly, the space that invites
young people to hear the personal call of Jesus Christ to come and
follow. Because youth ministry is bound in personhood, then, it is
always open and never finalized. Only ideas embedded in principles

14. Bonhoeffer, *Discipleship*, 59.
15. Bonhoeffer is no fan of ideology. In his *Ethics* he makes strong statements
against any form of ideology. This is based in equal parts in both his historical locale
in ideology-soaked Nazi Germany and also his personalist theology. All forms of
theological and philosophical personalism (in which I locate myself) are uneasy with
ideology, for it obscures the concrete person and covers his or her ideological layers.

and programs can be finalized. When youth ministry sweats in fear
that it has failed if its kids don't believe in the idea of Jesus before
they are eighteen, it has lost the living Christ that calls, and has made
itself into a program of principles serving only the *idea of Christian
faith* and not the *reality of the living Jesus.*

Relationships of persons, especially those of love and participation,
always exist in openness and the mystery of our day-to-day encounter
with each other's world.[16] Youth ministry, then, has no task of locking
young people down into some idea of faith. Rather, youth ministry
seeks only to open free spaces where young people are affirmed and
loved as persons, and through person-to-person encounter are asked
to listen for the *call* of the living Christ, who, as person, calls out to
their own person to come and follow. Youth ministry should concern
itself with these questions of Bonhoeffer: "What did Jesus want to
say to us? What does he want from us today? How does he help us
to be faithful Christians today? It is not ultimately important to us
what this or that church leader wants. Rather, we want to know what
Jesus wants."[17]

Youth ministry, I believe, has ironically fallen short in faith formation because it has gripped young people too tightly. And, gripping
them too tightly, it has seen the idea as more efficient than the biblical
reality of personhood. For it appears that ideas can be finalized and
foreclosed on, but personhood needs to always be tended, embraced,
and cared for. Youth ministry has been tempted to want young people
to foreclose on the idea of Jesus as proof of a formed faith, rather than
to live day-to-day in communities of *Stellvertretung* who encounter
the living personhood of Christ as they share in each other's person.
Bonhoeffer says helpfully:

> What should the disciples do in the face of hardened hearts? When
> their approach to others is unsuccessful? They should recognize that
> they have no right or power over others at all, and that they have no
> sort of immediate access to others. The only way open to them is the
> way to the one in whose hand they themselves are kept, just like those

16. Which is a closedness that echoes a point from Bonhoeffer's in *Sanctorum
Communio.*

17. Bonhoeffer, *Discipleship,* 37.

others. . . . The disciples are called to prayer. They are told that no other way leads to their neighbor except prayer to God.[18]

Faith formation in the idea is evaluated by what young people are committed to, shown through what they are willing to affiliate with. But this is cheap because it gives young people only the idea of Jesus, and not the living Lord himself. Faith formation through personhood is the cost of the church continuing to share in its young people's lives through *Stellvertretung* (place-sharing), to embrace their person through prayer, testimony, and friendship, seeking together, up against our distinct concrete lives, to follow the Jesus who calls us to himself through one another—through ministering one to another (*Stellvertretung*).

So What's So Costly?

Grace is costly, then, not because it is an idea; it is no principle, program, or doctrine. Grace is costly because it is a person; it is the very Christ who calls us. Jesus's person is the living reality of grace itself. And because it is a person who calls us to come and follow, it is not based in our own works, it is not based in the power of the human will to create for itself. Grace is based solely on the encounter with the person who lives and calls us to himself through love and life.

Christian faith is no "idea"; it is, at its core, first and finally, a person. Christian faith exists not through its ideas, institutional programs, principles, and doctrines, but only because the person of Jesus Christ lives and continues to call us, even today, Bonhoeffer would say, beckoning our young people to come and *Nachfolgen*, to come and follow. Christian faith is not believing the ideas of Christianity, but following the person of the living Christ. Personhood and Christian faith cannot be separated, for grace can only be free and yet costly when it is bound in the personhood of Jesus Christ who comes to our own person through his Word that, even today, calls our person to come to him, to *Nachfolgen*, to follow him into the world, to be his disciple by sharing in the life of our neighbor (Matt. 25).

18. Ibid., 174.

So for Bonhoeffer what makes grace costly is the call to follow Jesus's person by joining his person with our own. Grace is costly because Jesus ministers to the world through his person, and to follow Jesus's person is for us to be moved through our own person into ministry, into action.

The story of the rich young ruler is paradigmatic for Bonhoeffer in *Discipleship*. The young man comes to Jesus seeking an idea; he wants the moral principle that will make him good. But Christian faith has no conception of the good as idea; it knows the good only in and through God the Father who is known to us through the personhood of Jesus the Son. Jesus says as much to the young man, denying his very way of thinking, asking him why he calls Jesus good, for only God is good (as a pure idea). Jesus is denying the category of the good as a principle, redirecting him away from the idea. Yet the young man pushes for the idea. And Jesus can only tell him to go and sell all he has and *follow* him.

The young man leaves because he wanted the idea, he sought the program and principle, but Jesus offered him something much more, something that in the end he could not do. Jesus offered him his very person through *Nachfolge*. Jesus called him to come and follow, to rid himself of all that stands in the way of his person following Jesus's person and to come.

The young man is not willing, and Jesus's heart breaks for the young man, because in giving his Word (come and follow) he opens his person to the personhood of the young man. And when persons share, there is no longer law but the heat of love that melts the law into the purified gold of the gospel. Jesus loves the young man's person, even though the young man hits the wall and will not follow Jesus. Jesus would hate the young man if he was calling him to an idea, he would see the young man's inability as an offense. But because he calls the young man not to the work of an idea but to the grace of his person, the young man's inability is no hateful offense to Jesus. Jesus loves him even in his failure to follow.

Grace is costly, then, not because it is a work but because when we hear the call of Jesus to join his person, we must follow. Our person is called to follow his person and to do so at such a depth that Jesus's ministry of bearing the suffering of the world in love becomes our own, for our person is bound to his through the Spirit. It is costly because Jesus's call to *follow* is to join his person in ministering to the concrete personhood of others in the world. Each of us leaves behind riches to follow Jesus's person, experiencing his own *Stellvertretung* as a calling ourself to be a *Stellvertreter* to others by seeing and acting for their personhood. Grace is costly because it calls us through our person to the person of Jesus Christ. And when we follow the person of Jesus Christ, when we follow his call through our person, we're sent to act for the concrete person of our neighbor in the world.

Following Ideas

There is no discipleship, no following-ship, without personhood. In a sense we can follow Apple, we can follow their Twitter feed, and their advertising beckons us to follow them into the Apple Store and get a new iPhone. The idea of Apple can produce a form of following, but it is cheap. Because it is an idea, we can commit to it without it costing us our person (just our money, just our loyalty for now). We can follow the idea of Apple, but because it is not a person, it does not draw us into being our neighbor's *Stellvertreter* (place-sharer). It doesn't cost us our person because it gives us no other person to share in. Apple beckons us to follow from the level of sensation and desire—not person. Following the idea through sensation and desire, we can, at any time and with little friction, turn to a different idea we desire more.[19] Ideas are easy to leave; that is their advantage.

But departure from persons (which is always a possibility) is costly. For persons who encounter each other wrap their life together. The person who follows Jesus joins his person; they are disciples because they indwell him as he them (John 15). Sharing in personhood is

---

19. Bonhoeffer says some powerful things about desire, which to develop would take us far afield. So a small taste will have to do. Bonhoeffer says, "But those who create their own god and their own world, those who allow their own desire to become their god, must inevitably hate other human beings who stand in their way and impede their designs. Strife, hatred, envy, and murder all have the same source: they spring from our own selfish desire" (ibid., 265).

transformational—which is why the rich young ruler wishes only for the idea and balks at Jesus's invitation to follow him. Ideas leave him in his autonomy, but personhood binds him to another.

If, when following Apple, we desire something different, like to get a Samsung Galaxy, we can turn to a new idea with ease. Faith is easy for our young people to drift from when it has become only an idea. Because it is cheap, it can be discarded for new ideas that promise new sensations. And when a popularized (lazy) postmodern deconstruction makes all ideas equal and my own feelings and sensations the proprietor of their value, then we are free to move in and out of ideas as they serve our desires. The irony in North American youth ministry is that we continue to work to find the right idea to make faith stick, but it will never be possible until we shift from idea to person, for only then do we move from cheap to costly grace.

We can see this in our very language in youth ministry. We say things like, "I'm just concerned my kids don't believe enough; I'm just really trying to get them to believe." So often what we mean by "believe" is believe in an idea. And what we mean by "obey" is something similar. We want them to believe in the idea and show this by obeying the principle. Bonhoeffer, too, links belief and obedience, but does so outside the category of idea and principle. "Only believers obey," Bonhoeffer says.[20] Most of us in youth ministry would agree, and this is what stresses us out; we need youth to believe the ideas of Christianity so that they will obey its principles and be good, sober virgins. Yet Bonhoeffer continues this statement, saying not only do "believers obey" but, just as importantly, "only the obedient believe."[21] This statement is obscured if we have failed to follow Bonhoeffer out of the swamp of the idea and onto the firm ground of the person. Obedience to ideas, principles, programs, and doctrines as the measure

20. See ibid., 63.
21. Bonhoeffer says further, "Only the obedient believe. A concrete command-ment has to be obeyed, in order to come to believe. A first step of obedience has to be taken, so that faith does not become pious self-deception, cheap grace. The first step is crucial. It is qualitatively different from all others that follow. The first step of obedience has to lead Peter away from his nets and out of the boat; it has to lead the young man away from his wealth. Faith is possible only in this new state of existence created by obedience" (ibid., 64).

of our belief is work; it is to turn the gospel into law. But when it is a concrete person who calls us, when it is *Jesus* who calls, and obedience is the direct response to his Word to *Nachfolge*, to follow, then what Bonhoeffer is saying is that only those who follow Jesus out into the ministry of *Stellvertretung* truly believe something (the truth of the gospel). Our belief is bound not in our intellectual consent to ideas but in our willingness to follow Jesus into the life of our neighbor. Only the obedient—only the ones who risk and follow—believe, because Christian life is lived in the world; it is experienced in the encounter with personhood.[22]

Young people will continue to wrestle with Christian faith only if we move away from the idea (especially in our popularized postmodern ethos) and make space for young people to articulate their experiences with the living Christ that call them out into ministry. Youth ministry's job is *not* to get youth to believe an idea, fighting to convince young people why the idea of Christianity is better than other ideas. Rather, youth ministry seeks, through *Stellvertretung*, to invite young people to join in the ministry of Jesus's own person, to *Nachfloge* (follow) Jesus out into the world, to minister to the world as Jesus does, through the personal act of *Stellvertretung* (place-sharing). Faith is not young people assimilating to the moral, participatory, religious idea but is the testimony that they themselves have experienced Jesus's person come to them with a Word to leave all behind and follow Jesus's person.

22. It is interesting that in making this point Bonhoeffer turns again to the analogy of the child. I think this shows further the consistency of Bonhoeffer's focus on children.

> How is such a reversal possible? What has happened that the word of Jesus has to endure this game? That it is so vulnerable to the scorn of the world? Anywhere else in the world where commands are given, the situation is clear. A father says to his child: go to bed! The child knows exactly what to do. But a child drilled in pseudo theology would have to argue thus: Father says go to bed. He means you are tired; he does not want me to be tired. But I can also overcome my tiredness by going to play. So, although father says go to bed, what he really means is go play. With this kind of argumentation, a child with its father or a citizen with the authorities would run into an unmistakable response, namely, punishment. The situation is supposed to be different only with respect to Jesus' command. In that case simple obedience is supposed to be wrong, or even to constitute disobedience, How is this possible? (ibid., 80)

The Call

Bonhoeffer has shifted our focus from the *idea* of cheap grace to the *personhood* of costly grace. A youth ministry that journeys with Bonhoeffer into costly grace is molded by one driving commitment; it is driven by the call. The youth worker expects, and continues to remind both young people and adult leaders, that Jesus has come to them and comes with a call. If there is any direct content to the ministry itself, it is only to always be reminding, reviewing, and reexamining the call of Jesus that has come or is coming to them, to follow. It is the work of the whole church-community to continue to remind, review, and reexamine with young people the call of Jesus that has come to them, the very beckoning that they have experienced.

Bonhoeffer says directly, "Faith has no content"; it is from beginning to end the continued *call* to follow, to seek Jesus's person.[23] Bonhoeffer says, "No further content is possible because Jesus is the only content. There is no other content besides Jesus. He himself is it."[24] Our youth ministries may be simply spaces that draw the whole church-community to dwell with young people on what this call means. The church-community continues to remind young people in love that Jesus has come to them and is calling their person to his. Youth ministry might be little more than helping young people give language to their experience of the event of Jesus coming to them, and then discerning with them what the call that this event put upon them may be leading them into. This would be inviting us to share our stories, listening for

23. I don't think with this statement Bonhoeffer means that tradition does not matter to ministry and faith. Rather, I think he would see, in some sense, that tradition is the trusted testimony of others' following of Jesus's call.

24. Ibid., 59. Bonhoeffer says further,

What is said about the content of discipleship? Follow me, walk behind me! That is all. Going after him is something without specific content. It is truly not a program for one's life which would be sensible to implement. It is neither a goal nor an ideal to be sought. It is not even a matter for which, according to human inclination, it would be worth investing anything at all, much less oneself. And what happens? Those called leave everything they have, not in order to do something valuable. Instead, they do it simply for the sake of the call itself, because otherwise they could not walk behind Jesus. Nothing of importance is attached to this action in itself. It remains something completely insignificant, unworthy of notice. (ibid., 58)

significant moments, and wondering together how God may be leading us within them. And this sharing of stories could happen inside the youth ministry itself, or the youth ministry could work to create spaces for young people to hear the stories of others in the church-community.

Faith has no content, but this does not mean that there is no reason to care, read, or understand the Christian theological, creedal, or confessional tradition. Rather, we need these very materials to find the language for our experience of Jesus's call and to continue to discern what Jesus is calling us to as we hear the stories of those who have followed the call of Jesus before us. The Christian tradition is transformed, then, from ideas to the personal testimony of those before us who have obeyed by following.

The biblical text—and most profoundly for Bonhoeffer, the Sermon on the Mount (Matt. 5–7)—is the articulation of the shape of *Nachfolge*. The Sermon on the Mount is not law for Bonhoeffer but the concrete and lived shape of discipleship. It is the testimony of what the action of following Jesus looks like in the world. We read it not as iron-heavy law dropped on our heads to concuss us into submission but as a picture painted of what following Jesus's person looks like in the world. We are called to do the Sermon on the Mount, but this doing should not be confused as content (as idea), but only as the amplification of the personal Word of Jesus to come and follow—following that takes the shape of the Sermon on the Mount.

The Cross

But just so this won't be confused, and cheap grace turned into the law of the Sermon on the Mount and we forget Jesus's person, Bonhoeffer ups the ante. He writes one of his boldest statements in a book of bold statements. Bonhoeffer drops the line, "When Jesus Christ calls a person, he calls him [or her] to come and die." Bonhoeffer says further, "The cross is not the terrible end of a pious, happy life. Instead, it stands at the beginning of community with Jesus Christ. Whenever Christ calls us, his call leads us to death."[25]

25. Ibid., 87.

For Bonhoeffer, the call of Jesus takes the shape of the *crucis*, the cross. The Sermon on the Mount can only be the shape of following Jesus into the world if it, too, passes through death. The Sermon on the Mount is no law that can save us; it is, rather, the texture of the life of those who have died with Christ and are now made alive with him through resurrection (e.g., blessed are those who mourn, who hunger and thirst for righteousness, who turn the other cheek, etc.). The disciple is called to the cross, to come and follow Jesus into death. And this is not because Jesus's call seeks masochism, but rather because Jesus's call is the gift of giving us new life through the *Stellvertretung* (the place-sharing) of Jesus's very person. The disciple is called to the cross because it is from the cross that Jesus calls us, calling us to carry our cross, calling us to love the person of our neighbor in and through suffering of the cross that they bear.[26] Bonhoeffer states, "Suffering passes when it is borne."[27] Jesus is present, still today, in the world, near those persons who suffer. To hear Jesus's call we must turn our ear in the direction of his beckoning. And this beckoning to follow comes from the cross.

To hear Jesus's call, to step out and follow him, is to see and respond to the suffering of the world; it is to feed the hungry, clothe the naked, and visit the prisoner (Matt. 25). It is not simply to do something good—to look for the good is to fall into the trap of the idea that the rich young ruler could not escape. Rather, we feed the hungry, clothe the naked, and visit the prisoner because it is the following of Jesus into death, into the suffering of real persons; in so doing, Jesus is there.

The call of Jesus to come and follow is the call to embrace the suffering of our neighbor for the sake of new life. When Jesus calls us, he calls us to come and die, for he calls us to find his own person suffering with and for the concrete personhood of our neighbor. He calls us to find, in the death of our own person, the new possibility of his own person; he calls us to die with him, so that we might live with him, following him into love of neighbor. Bonhoeffer says, "As

26. This is a profound christological statement: "Suffering must be borne in order for it to pass. Either the world must bear it and be crushed by it, or it falls on Christ and is overcome in him. That is how Christ suffers as vicarious representative for the world" (ibid., 90).

27. Ibid., 133.

Christ bears our burdens, so we are to bear the burdens of our sisters and brothers. The law of Christ, which must be fulfilled, is to bear the cross."[28] He calls us to come and die in *Stellvertretung* with our neighbor, so that in our communion the Spirit might move us from death into the new life. We are his disciples because we have followed Jesus, and we know it is Jesus we follow because he has called us to himself through our suffering, through our deaths, giving us new resurrected life through them. Jesus has given life to our suffering person through his own suffering person, making us alive so we might be sent into the world to embrace our neighbors' deaths, witnessing to life. By following Jesus's steps, we are then molded in the shape of the Sermon on the Mount.

Youth ministry invites young people to listen for Jesus's call not next to their strength, to hear his calling not in all their possibilities. We have made this mistake, turning God into the charm that gives young people all they want, that helps them achieve the strength they desire. Rather, following Bonhoeffer, we invite young people to listen for the call of Jesus up against their nothingness, next to their yearnings for new life. Faith formation in youth ministry is nothing more than following the call of Christ, and this call of Christ is heard next to young people's own dead places, next to their crosses. Discipleship in youth ministry is young people hearing and responding to Jesus's call next to their suffering person. For it is to their suffering person that the person of Jesus comes near and calls, speaking a word of grace to come and follow him from the death of their suffering to a new life of *Stellvertretung* (place-sharing).

So to help young people be reminded of, review, and reexamine the call of Jesus that comes to them is to help them seek for Jesus where he can be found—at the cross, bearing the world's death so that all might live through his person. Youth ministry invites young people to put their ear to their deepest questions of fear and death and listen intently for the Word of Jesus to come to them, to call them forth, from this fear and death to *follow* and find life in his person!

---

28. Ibid., 88.

---

(16)

The Youth Worker and
Life Together

There were about thirty of them, most in matching T-shirts and shorts, all but two under the age of twenty-five. They had been together long enough for both strong and stressed connections to form among them. They began their gathering with announcements and safety updates, discussing undertows, missing basketballs, and ripped screens. As the announcements concluded, the young adults sat quietly, covered by the fatigue of the early morning meeting and the long days that had preceded it. They were stirred into motion, moved from trance to action, as they were asked to pull out their copies of the thin volume that bore the name *Life Together*.

The leader (one of the two over age twenty-five) explained that a summer working at camp, a summer away from college life and family to live together with others doing Christian ministry, is a deep experience of community. It would be an experience of community that many of these young adults had tasted before, choosing to spend their summer as counselor because of their own camper experience of *communio*.

But now that it was week three and the honeymoon of camp community was giving way to the chafed rub of life together, it was time to reflect. And there seemed to be little better than Bonhoeffer's *Life Together* with which to frame their reflection.

It seems like almost two different universes to imagine young, first-time ministers at camp, sitting on rocks and nursing lattés in travel mugs as they page through *Life Together* and Bonhoeffer's own locale as he moved thoughts to paper and typed each word with the rhythmic mechanical notes of his typewriter.

Life Together is, arguably, the most direct and important book written about Christian communal life in the twentieth century. But each of its crafted sentences was formed in a hauntingly quiet house as Bonhoeffer stood among the loss of the two most significant communities of his life. Finkenwalde had been closed; the experiment that brought the coalescing of Bonhoeffer's pastoral and academic commitments was upended. But it was not only Finkenwalde on his mind as he worked on *Life Together*. Bonhoeffer retreated with Bethge to his twin sister Sabine's house to craft this little book. Little time had passed since Sabine, Gerhard, and their children had, with the help of Bonhoeffer, escaped to London via Switzerland. So not only was the community of Finkenwalde upended but so too was Bonhoeffer's family, as his very own twin was exiled. It adds to the depth of this little book to know the heartbreak of lost community Bonhoeffer must have been feeling as he quickly produced *Life Together* in a house haunted by his sister's and her children's absence. All in the house remained as it had been before, furniture and full cupboards still left as if they would be home by noon; but they were gone. Bonhoeffer quickly pounded finger to key as he sat in the absence of his sister.

And he wrote *Life Together* quickly, moving it from head to paper in just a handful of weeks. The objective was simple; Bonhoeffer wanted to articulate as directly and practically as possible what he had been up to in Finkenwalde, presenting the plan he had used to train and prepare these Confessing Church pastors confronting the cataclysmic challenges before them.

It actually then makes good sense that camp directors and others would choose this little practical book for assistance as they, too, seek to train and prepare young people for some of their first ministry experiences, inviting them into the legacy of Finkenwalde, to join in a life together as the very way to do ministry in the world.

Community

Life Together is constructed in five short parts. The final four ("The Day Together," "The Day Alone," "Service," and "Confessing/The Lord's Supper") are highly practical and explore direct actions and practices of a life together. But for these four parts to make sense and not slide into theological problems, they must rest on part 1, "Community." Without a handle on this part, *Life Together* may be as dangerous as *Discipleship* in leading the imprecise reader into problems.

Community is a central theme of Bonhoeffer's theology from the beginning. *Life Together* took shape eleven years after *Sanctorum Communio* sought to articulate the revelation of God in Jesus Christ in the church-community. Even pieces we explored in part 1, like the "Eight Theses on Youth Work," reveal the centrality of the church-community for Bonhoeffer. Yet as Bonhoeffer begins his practical guide to life together, with its theological roots in *Sanctorum Communio* and *Act and Being*, he must exorcise the demons of "communal idealism."

If there is ever going to be life together, Bonhoeffer believes, then the community can never become anything other than the actual existence of broken people. The community itself has no power to save, heal, or reconcile; that power exists only in the Christ of the cross who comes to us bearing our brokenness with the Word to *Nachfolge*, to follow him.

But when we follow him, we are led into community; for, like Peter, to follow Jesus is to be led to his body. And post-Pentecost, this body of the living Christ is concretely the church-community. Bonhoeffer states boldly that there is no Christian life outside of community, for there is no Christian faith outside of Christ; and Christ, because he is the incarnate one, can only be where his body is found. And this body is the church-community.

The Word to follow must individually confront the disciple, encountering her own body. But encountering this Word through her

body, she is led into community, into the body of Christ,[1] and given
the great joy of living with others, of being held by others and cared
for by them bodily. And because this is a bodily community, Bonhoeffer believes, it is never constituted as an idea, psychological longing,
or solely as institutional form, but only as an embodied actuality, as
a communion of embodied persons. The Christian community is a
community of physical presence; it is an embrace of your concrete
life. Bonhoeffer says, "Whether it be a brief, single encounter or the
daily community of many years, Christian community is solely this:
We belong to one another only through and in Jesus Christ."[2] He
also says, "The physical presence of other Christians is a source of
incomparable joy and strength to the believer."[3]

It is a source of great joy because it is a lived, concrete, and practical reality. In the midst of suffering, fear, and sin, the community of
faith, as an actual physical community, embraces the fullness of us.
It gives us food, shelter, hospitality, and friendship at the core of our
humanity. The church-community cannot hide from the embodied
realities of its people by escaping into the "idea" of its communal
life, into even its institutional form or function. For the church-community *may be* an institutional reality societally, but theologically,
even ontologically, it is an embodied *communio* of sharing persons.
Bonhoeffer says poignantly in *Discipleship*, "While we are used to
thinking of the church as an institution, we ought instead to think
of it as person with a body."[4] The church can then never avoid the

---

1. In *Discipleship* Bonhoeffer points directly to the communal life he unpacks
practically in *Life Together*.

> A truth, a doctrine, or a religion needs no space of its own. Such entities are
> bodiless. They do not go beyond being heard, learned, and understood. But
> the incarnate Son of God needs not only ears or even hearts; he needs actual,
> living human beings who follow him. That is why he called his disciples into
> following him bodily. His community with them was something everyone could
> see. It was founded and held together by none other than Jesus Christ, the
> incarnate one himself. It was the Word made flesh who had called them, who
> had created the visible, bodily community. Those who had been called could
> no longer remain hidden; they were the light which has to shine, the city on a
> hill which is bound to be seen. (Bonhoeffer, *Discipleship*, 226)

2. Dietrich Bonhoeffer, *Life Together*, Dietrich Bonhoeffer Works (Minneapolis:
Fortress, 1996), 5:31.

3. Ibid., 29.

4. Bonhoeffer, *Discipleship*, 218.

embodied and concrete life of its people, to maintain its ideal. The church-community is a physical community in the world, loving people concretely and practically. It is bound to the concrete personhood of Christ and embodied in the practical life of its people.

Away from the Devious Ideal

But since the church-community is a physical community that is made up of, and therefore seeks, the concrete life of others, and because it is not simply an institutional ideal or disembodied spiritual idea, the church-community is always open and inevitably confronts discord within itself. *Life Together* is a deeply realistic book. Bonhoeffer asserts that, because the church-community is a physical embodied reality that has its being only in the concrete and lived, it cannot escape discord. Bonhoeffer says boldly in this little book that idealists love to complain about their churches, complaining that they are far from what they should ideally be. But Bonhoeffer states boldly that there is no ideal church, that there is no ideal church-community, but only the embodied actual physical communities in which we live. And actual living communities, made up of physical, embodied persons, always wrestle with discord, walking the precarious wire above the pit of dysfunction. This, Bonhoeffer says, is normal and necessary.

The fact that some churches become dysfunctional should be grieved but is not a surprise to those who truly live in community. True community is always messy, for it seeks life in the friendship of embodied living persons. A church with no discord, a church that has climbed to the mount beyond the possibility of dysfunction, is no longer a community but an ideal facade where preaching becomes only principles and worship just Muzak. There is *no way* to avoid discord, and the Christian leader that wants community without discord wants not true community but to drug himself with a needle of the ideal to the vein. The leader who wants the ideal community does not want community at all, for the ideal community is community without the humanity of physical bodies in relationship. The leader who wants the ideal community has turned community into an idol.

Bonhoeffer makes this point in *Life Together* by turning to Luke 9. He reminds the reader that even in the community where Jesus was present in the bodily form of beard and bones, the disciples still argued about who was the greatest among them. Bonhoeffer opines, "But perhaps we do not think enough about the fact that no Christian community *ever* comes together without this argument appearing as a seed of discord."[5] Bonhoeffer pushes further, telling us again that true community is bound in physical persons, and such persons always have the possibility of becoming a burden. Bonhoeffer says, "The other person never becomes a burden at all for the pagans. They simply stay clear of every burden the other person may create for them. However, Christians must bear the burden of one another. They must suffer and endure one another. Only as a burden is the other really a brother or sister and not just an object to be controlled."[6]

It is interesting that Bonhoeffer turns to brothers and sisters. Of course, this is biblical language. But writing these words in his exiled sister's house, entering deeply into her burden, hiding and lying for her, Bonhoeffer was quite aware that to be there for her concrete physical person, he had to leave all idealism behind and enter her actual messy life. And even for us, no family is without the bearing of burdens, without confronting and living, often through discord. The family always lives in discord between siblings, parents, and spouses, for the family can never escape into idealism. It must be with the concrete and physical actualities of each person, building its life together through its burdens and around its discord. The great enemy of life together is communal idealism that cannot stomach discord and therefore avoids all burdens, for to avoid the burden is to avoid the concrete embodied reality of the persons who make community a possibility.

The Youth Worker and Communal Idealism

It is not infrequent for youth workers (and actually quite common with my own students) to be bitten by the bug of communal idealism. They enter churches and find themselves frustrated that the church is

5. Bonhoeffer, *Life Together*, 93; my italics.
6. Ibid., 100.

not perfect, that it is always coming in and out of discord. They often cannot stomach the discord because they see it as a threat or blockage to their ministry. And they see their ministry as implementing initiatives or programs that bring vitality to the institution.

We would rarely say it like this, but discord becomes maddening, and we become embittered when we are more committed to some ideal called "community" that is somehow disconnected from the concrete, embodied persons in it.

The frustration and burnout most youth workers confront has much to do with idealist dreams of what the church should be. In this space the actual community of persons of burden only leads to annoyance at best and hatred at worst. The church becomes hated because it is an actual community, for actual communities of physical bodies, of persons, always exist in and through burdens and discord. There can be no community, then, where "community" is held as some idea and not embraced as the actual broken lives of physical people. Bonhoeffer says colorfully, "The bright day of Christian community dawns wherever the early morning mists of dreamy visions are lifting."[7]

The fresh young adult youth workers at camp reading *Life Together* in the introduction of this chapter run a great risk about which they are rarely informed. When they read the pages of *Life Together* they must be told directly that the emotional ideal of camp cannot be transformed completely to the church. They will be tempted to believe the enclosed emotional experiences of camp can be transferred directly to the day-to-day life of the church-community. But so often they cannot. And this is not because of the church-community's impotence but because of its strength.

The camp experience tempts young people and young youth workers because it is self-enclosed, and as self-enclosed it exists for its short time by forgetting the messy realities of our day-to-day lives. It can be a retreat from them—and a positive one at that. But too often young people and young youth workers take these experiences in so deeply that they are tempted to grab the ideal with both hands. And with the ideal in grip they use it like a bat to bash the church for being an actual community of bodies, which, because it is, is moving in and

7. Ibid., 37.

out of embracing burdens and confronting discord. For these young people and young youth workers, Bonhoeffer says boldly, "Those who love their dream of a Christian community more than the Christian community itself become destroyers of that Christian community even though their personal intentions may be ever so honest, earnest, and sacrificial."[8]

As mentors and ministers to young youth workers (and young people) we must encourage them to put away the idol of "their dream of Christian community" and to instead enter its actual real life.[9] Asking them to put down their gripes of frustration that the church is "messed up," we need to instead invite them to enter the mess with the gratitude that even in its messiness (and maybe because of it) there is the possibility of encountering the living Christ there. If Bonhoeffer was their mentor, the encouragement to give up the idea for the actual community would come with thunder. Bonhoeffer's words crackle with their directness.

> God hates this wishful dreaming because it makes the dreamer proud and pretentious. Those who dream of this idealized community demand that it be fulfilled by God, by others, and by themselves. They enter the community of Christians with their demands, set up their own law, and judge one another and even God accordingly. They stand adamant, a living reproach to all others in the circle of the community. They act as if they have to create the Christian community, as if their visionary ideal binds the people together.[10]

He continues:

> If we do not give thanks daily for the Christian community in which we have been placed, even when there are no great experiences, no noticeable riches, but much weakness, difficulty, and little faith—and if, on the contrary, we only keep complaining to God that everything

8. Ibid., 36.
9. Bonhoeffer says some powerful and important words about emotional conversation, which I unfortunately simply do not have the space to unpack. Bonhoeffer's discourse on emotional conversation describes how it leads into self-love, which has significant correlations for youth ministry. For Bonhoeffer's discussion of this, see ibid., 44.
10. Ibid., 36.

is so miserable and so insignificant and does not at all live up to our expectations—then we hinder God from letting our community grow according to the measure and riches that are there for us all in Jesus Christ. That also applies in a special way to the complaints, often heard from pastors and zealous parishioners about their congregations. Pastors should not complain about their congregation, certainly never to other people, but also not to God. Congregations have not been entrusted to them in order that they should become accusers of their congregations before God and their fellow human beings. When pastors lose faith in a Christian community in which they have been placed and begin to make accusations against it, they had better examine themselves first to see whether the underlying problem is not their own idealized image, which should be shattered by God.[11]

And maybe the reason youth workers (and young people) fall so deeply into the trap of the ideal community is because they place the legitimacy of community on the feeling of community. Community is only real if it *feels* like something; so it is not the Holy Spirit that holds the community together, filling the temple that is our very bodies in communion, but it is some feeling that, when examined, is very similar to the feeling we get when we buy Gucci or Apple. We belong not through the act of God who brings union through the sharing of burdens and discord but through the emotional connection to a brand.

Bonhoeffer is actually not opposed to the emotion; feelings are important and a gift. But the church-community is based on the work of the Spirit, not psychic emotions of feeling like you're at camp. Bonhoeffer says it this way:

> There is probably no Christian to whom God has not given the uplifting and blissful experience of genuine Christian community at least once in her or his life. But in this world such experiences remain nothing but a gracious extra beyond the daily bread of Christian community life. We have no claim to such experiences, and we do not live with other Christians for the sake of gaining such experiences. It is not the experience of Christian community, but firm and certain faith within Christian community that holds us together. We hold fast in faith to God's greatest gift, that God has acted for us all and wants to act for

11. Ibid., 37.

us all. This makes us joyful and happy, but it also makes us ready to forgo all such experiences if at times God does not grant them. We are bound together by faith, not by experience.[12]

The Day Together

After the rich articulation of community in the first part of *Life Together*, Bonhoeffer is ready to move more fully into the practical. In the four parts that follow, starting with "The Day Together," Bonhoeffer seeks to explain what the community at Finkenwalde did and why these practices were significant.

The "day together" consists of (morning) worship, prayer, and Scripture reading. The community must gather to sing *together*, to pray *together*, and to read Scripture *together*.

Bonhoeffer believes that there is no Christian life without this all-important *togetherness*. In singing, our voices come together, and together we direct ourselves toward God. In praying together we tell each other our needs, narrating together our gratitude and suffering. And together Jesus comes to us, to pray for us. Bonhoeffer even goes so far as to say, "There must always be a second person, another, a member of the church, the body of Christ, indeed Jesus Christ himself, praying with the Christian in order that the prayer of the individual may be true prayer."[13]

Bonhoeffer encourages the Finkenwalde community to pray the Psalter (the Psalms), seeing it as the prayer book of the Bible, as Jesus's own prayers.[14] Praying the Psalms, we pray with Jesus, and as we bring our needs through intercession (as we pray the Psalms), Jesus prays with us.

Bonhoeffer even organized Finkenwalde's morning worship to conclude with intercessory prayer, asking all his students to pray out loud together their needs and joys.[15] Intercessory prayer heard one to

---

12. Ibid., 47.
13. Ibid., 57.
14. "The Psalter is the prayer book of Jesus Christ in the truest sense of the word. He prayed the Psalter, and now it has become his prayer for all time" (ibid., 55).
15. Kelly explains Bonhoeffer's commitment to prayer at Finkenwalde:
    At the closing of the service Bonhoeffer strongly recommended that the members of the community bring up their requests, their expressions of gratitude,

another places the community in the Spirit as they bring forth their burdens and discord in the embodied act of praying together aloud. Prayer together, Bonhoeffer believed, shakes us free from the idealism of community and moves us into its actual physical life.

Scripture reading is the final component that should shape the community, Bonhoeffer believes. We read the text together, to listen with each other, for the very call of Jesus to come and *Nachfolgen*. We each individually hear this Word of call, directing and sending us through our own person to Jesus's person. But to hear this call and not be overtaken by our own subjective emotionalism, we must hear this Word to *Nachfolge* with our brothers and sisters; we must recognize how our call to action in the world, as a response to the living Word of Jesus, is connected to the Word of Scripture. For Bonhoeffer we read the Scripture *together* to discern *together* in community where it is that the Spirit is calling each of us to *Nachfolge*. Bonhoeffer would encourage youth workers today, like he did with his own students at Finkenwalde, not to read Scripture to find the point to teach or preach, but to read it instead for the Word the living Christ brings to you. It may be that we can only teach the Bible to young people when we have ourselves sought for the word that comes to us from the living Christ through the Scripture.

All three of the movements of the day together—worship, prayer, and reading—are deeply embodied physical realities for Bonhoeffer. They are spiritual because they are done in the Spirit, but they are not disembodied, for they are done in the community of gathered bodies. It is bodies that share in songs and prayer. It is bodies that read the Scripture seeking the action that will move bodies to follow the resurrected body of Jesus.

It is interesting that in youth and children's ministry we have focused a great deal of energy on making space for young people in worship.

---

and intercessions in a common prayer. He believed this practice had the power to break down one's fears of the reactions of others and the inhibitions one feels against praying freely and publicly in the presence of others. For Bonhoeffer, this common intercessory prayer in the name of Jesus Christ was "the most normal thing in our common Christian life." Bonhoeffer would cap the common worship service with extemporaneous prayer led by an individual in the community, often the head of the house or director of the group. (*Reading Bonhoeffer*, 116)

We desire for our worship services to be more friendly to the young and for young children, particularly, not to be ushered out of worship as a break in our life together. This has been important and often difficult because we have not remembered that we are bodies in worship and that our bodies sing and pray together. We imagine that we need quiet to get the information or experience that we individually need, not recognizing it is only together that we are the community of Christ. And this togetherness includes all the baptized, Bonhoeffer would assert. It is in and through the togetherness that we are the community of Christ; it is in and through participating with other bodies (even loud, wiggly ones) that we are taken into communion with the living Christ.

But what is more curious is that while we have rightly fought for the space for the young in our times of worship, we have spent less time thinking about how the young and not so young might pray and read the Bible together. It is not hard in our churches to find people that will pray *for* young people, but it is much more difficult, and shows the breakdown of our communion, that so few young people have the experience of other adults verbally praying *with* them, interceding for them in their presence. It may be that a major objective of youth ministry is to create these spaces in which adults and young people pray with one another, as one body speaks her needs to another body that responds with compassion and the words of intercession.[16] The discord between young and old will never be evaporated—it will always exist—but through praying together, discord can be transformed to a bond of understanding and love. It may be that the only way to move our communities beyond the generation gap, as Bonhoeffer pled in his "Eight Theses on Youth Work," is to invite the young and not so young to pray together in shared intercession.

In the same way that it is odd that the younger and older do not pray together, it is just as odd how often we exhort young people to read their Bibles, but how rarely adults in the church-community read

16. This is a powerful line by Bonhoeffer: "A Christian community either lives by the intercessory prayers of its members for one another, or the community will be destroyed. I can no longer condemn or hate other Christians for whom I pray, no matter how much trouble they cause me. In intercessory prayer the face that may have been strange and intolerable to me is transformed into the face of one for whom Christ died, the face of a pardoned sinner" (*Life Together*, 90).

Scripture with them. If we truly want young people to follow the living Christ, then why would we send them away from us to read their Bibles alone? It is most often together, in the discernment of bodies in communion, that the Word to follow comes directly to us. If we yearn for our young people to be disciples of Christ, then it will be through our life together as young people are invited to pray and be prayed for, to interpret and hear interpretation of Scripture, that they will hear the call to *Nachfolge*.

The Day Alone

The community is to live life together. But this togetherness does not come without boundaries and can never promote enmeshment. Because the community is made up of physical bodies, we need each other; but we also, as physical bodies, need to be alone. Community moves us in ways both of being together and being alone. Bonhoeffer says it this way: "We recognize, then, that only as we stand within the community can we be alone, and only those who are alone can live in the community. Both belong together. Only in the community do we learn to be properly alone; and only in being alone do we learn to live properly in the community."[17]

Community is not a possibility, Bonhoeffer believes, without the boundaries of closedness. If we are to truly see a brother we must respect the boundary of his embodied self that places a barrier between us. The community needs time together but also—so it might be together—times when its persons are alone. It is the time alone that keeps the community—which is always moving in and out of discord—from dysfunction. Discord turns into the cancer of dysfunction when persons in the community cannot, for fear or pride, be alone. When they cannot differentiate themselves from the community, they will demand the community be ideal by meeting all their emotional needs, forcing the community to serve them so that they need not fear or so they might have the power they seek. Such people who cannot be alone will swallow the community, blurring the line between their

17. Ibid., 83.

own personal life and the community's life in the day together. It is only by upholding the day apart, holding to the boundary of being alone, that the community can have a life together. Bonhoeffer heralds:

> Many persons seek community because they are afraid of loneliness. Because they can no longer endure being alone, such people are driven to seek the company of others. Christians, too, who cannot cope on their own, and who in their own lives have had some bad experiences, hope to experience help with this in the company of other people. More often than not, they are disappointed. They then blame the community for what is really their own fault. The Christian community is not a spiritual sanatorium. Those who take refuge in community while fleeing from themselves are misusing it to indulge in empty talk and distraction, no matter how spiritual this idle talk and distraction may appear. In reality they are not seeking community at all, but only a thrill that will allow them to forget their isolation for a short time.[18]

If the church-community were an idea, and not a physical community of bodies, then it would need no time alone. But because it is just such a physical community of embodied persons, time alone is essential to it. Bodies need rest, quiet, and the calm to be. Bodies are together through the freedom given to them by being alone.

The pressure of the ideal that young youth workers receive at places like camps, retreats, and conferences often drown out the need for being alone. In the fun and engagement of constant action, swimming deeply in the electricity of the collective experience, youth workers are rarely alone enough to cool the buzz of their cacophonous ministry experiences. They then believe that the church-community should give them the same hit of all-encompassing collective experience as camp, for instance.

Rather, it may be more important for us to use these camp experiences (and some no doubt already do) to give youth workers and youth opportunities to be alone, to sink into silence and listen for the voice of God. Being alone is not antithetical to life together but rather the very path that makes it possible, leading youth workers beyond the ideal community to the actual community of physical bodies in relation.

18. Ibid., 82.

Youth ministry people are often known for being extroverted energy junkies. There is no problem with an extroverted personality type; it may be of great help in youth ministry. But what *is* a problem is when the extroverted youth worker cannot take on the discipline of being alone, challenging herself to depart from her young people so that she might have the time alone that will allow her to truly be with them, seeing them as embodied persons and not as ideals that can be possessed. For as Bonhoeffer says, "After a period of silence, we encounter others in a different and fresh way."[19]

Service and Confession

The final two parts of *Life Together* possess a number of rich ideas and practices. For instance, Bonhoeffer talks about listening and giving help, placing these actions of the community within its need to preach.[20] Yet the two most interesting discussions in these final two parts, in my opinion, concern secrets and confession. By "secret," Bonhoeffer does not mean that people in community are not allowed to have their secrets. This would be to evaporate the day alone and the boundary that embodied persons possess. People are actually free to have secrets, to possess experiences or personal information they wish not to disclose. This is no threat to the community. What is a threat, Bonhoeffer says boldly, is the secretive nature of talking about

19. Ibid., 86.
20. Bonhoeffer says,
> The first service one owes to others in the community involves listening to them. . . . So often Christians, especially preachers, think that their only service is always to have to "offer" something when they are together with other people. They forget that listening can be a greater service than speaking. Many people seek a sympathetic ear and do not find it among Christians because these Christians are talking even when they should be listening. But Christians who can no longer listen to one another will soon no longer be listening to God either; they will always be talking even in the presence of God. The death of the spiritual life starts here, and in the end there is nothing left but empty spiritual chatter and clerical condescension which chokes on pious words. Those who cannot listen long and patiently will always be talking past others, and finally no longer will even notice it. Those who think their time is too precious to spend listening will never really have time for God and others, but only for themselves and for their own words and plans. (ibid., 98)

another member of the community without him or her being present. The core practice of the Finkenwalde community, as we discussed above, was the rule to never talk about another brother when he was not present. Bonhoeffer explains, "Thus it must be a decisive rule of all Christian community life that each individual is prohibited from talking about another Christian in secret. . . . Talking about others in secret is not allowed even under the pretense of help and goodwill. For it is precisely in this guise that the spirit of hatred between believers always creeps in, seeking to cause trouble."[21]

This rule is one that youth ministers could practice during a trip or retreat, telling the young people that no adult will talk about a young person without him or her being present. And if it becomes necessary because of circumstances to do so, soon afterward the young person will be told about the conversation. We could then challenge young people to do the same as an act of community. While it is sport in their schools and social media hubs to talk behind people's backs, here on this summer trip, here in this cabin at camp, we will seek to have no secret conversations. Bonhoeffer tells us what will happen when this rule is kept; against the backdrop of the teenage world, it will have a prophetic, countercultural impact. Bonhoeffer says, "Where this discipline of the tongue is practiced right from the start, individuals will make an amazing discovery. They will be able to stop constantly keeping an eye on others, judging them, condemning them, and putting them in their places and thus doing violence to them."[22] A youth ministry that could create an ethos where young people did not need to keep an eye on others, judging them before they get judged, would be a prophetically distinct community indeed.

Maybe the most challenging piece of the whole of *Life Together* for the church-community today is Bonhoeffer's discussion of confession. In Finkenwalde Bonhoeffer sought to make confession a deep part of the community. Each student had his confessor (Bonhoeffer's was Bethge). Almost all students resisted this personal verbal confession, wishing instead to confess their sin alone, for, after all, sins were most often between the student and God. Yet here in *Life Together* Bonhoeffer takes

21. Ibid., 94.
22. Ibid., 95.

apart such logic. He asks the profound question to the reader: why is it easy to confess our sins to a holy and righteous God who is without sin, but to our own sinful brother or sister we wish not to speak a word of confession? Bonhoeffer asserts that maybe, just maybe, this reveals that when we confess our sin alone, we are actually not confessing our sins to God but to ourselves, giving ourselves easy and cheap absolution.[23] To avoid this trap of self-confession, Bonhoeffer pleads that we must take on the courage to confess our sin to another sister or brother.[24]

I know of many lovers of *Life Together*, but none (myself included) who have been bold enough to follow Bonhoeffer's words. But the need to follow these words may be mounting in youth ministry. One of the most significant findings of phase two of a longitudinal national study of youth and religion, according to Christian Smith and his research team, was that nearly all the young adults interviewed refused to regret.[25] They told many stories to the interviewer, tales of

23. Here are Bonhoeffer's bold words:

Why is it often easier for us to acknowledge our sins before God than before another believer? God is holy and without sin, a just judge of evil, and an enemy of all disobedience. But another Christian is sinful, as are we, knowing from personal experience the night of secret sin. Should we not find it easier to go to one another than to the holy God? But if that is not the case, we must ask ourselves whether we often have not been deluding ourselves about our confession of sin to God—whether we have not instead been confessing our sins to ourselves and also forgiving ourselves. (ibid., 113)

24. Geffrey Kelly adds texture. He says, "Bonhoeffer did set two conditions to the practice. First, only those who themselves practice confession of sins should act as confessors of another. Second, those engaged in the practice should not regard it as part of a pious act or routine. The essence of the confession of sins lay in the promise of forgiveness in Christ" (editor's introduction to ibid., 17).

25. Christian Smith explains,

Despite often smarting from hard lessons learned, most of the emerging adults who were interviewed explicitly denied feeling any regrets about any of their past decisions, behaviors, or problems. Reinforcing their widespread feeling of optimism about the future, most of the survey respondents—including many of those with miserably depressing current problems, as well as those who seem to take full responsibility for their own mistakes and stupidities—insisted that the past was the past, that they learned their lessons well, that they would not change a thing even if they could, that what's happened is part of who they have become, and that they have no regrets about anything at all. . . . It is almost as if they feel that admitting having regrets would somehow be capitulating to a self-doubt or compromise or nascent despondency against which they are holding out at all costs through the power of positive thinking. (*Souls in*

incidents and episodes that led to brokenness, pain, and devastation. But as Smith says, they refused to say they regret these happenings, espousing the popular cultural acronym YOLO (you only live once). It seems this generation, for cultural reasons, has chosen to regret nothing, saying things like, "Yeah, I got pregnant, had an abortion, became addicted to alcohol, and lost a good job before moving in with a guy that was totally bad for me, and all this hurt my relationship with my mom. But honestly, I don't regret it; it just is what it is." This very mentality shows that there are significant events to regret but that the young person has chosen not to. But choosing not to, and continuing to swim deeper into the cultural waters, takes her farther and farther away from community. It may be that one of the most significant practices we can help young people with in our cultural time is to learn to confess. Joining the practice of confession one to another may be a significant gift we can offer our young people (young adults particularly). Starting this by constructing youth group time around weekly confession would be a bold and beautiful start.[26] And it would be one small but profound step on the path Bonhoeffer lays for us as the forefather of the theological turn in youth ministry.

Transition: The Religious and Spiritual Lives of Emerging Adults [New York: Oxford University Press, 2009], 41)

26. If you're brave enough to move confession into your youth group, Bonhoeffer has some other words of direction.

A Christian community that practices confession must guard against two dangers. The first concerns the one who hears confessions. It is not a good thing for one person to be the confessor for all the others. All too easily this individual will become overburdened, one for whom confession becomes an empty routine, giving rise to the unholy misuse of confession for the exercise of spiritual tyranny over souls. Those who do not practice confession themselves should be careful not to hear the confessions of other Christians, lest they succumb to this most frightening danger for confession. Only those who have been humbled themselves can hear the confession of another without detriment to themselves. The second danger concerns those who confess. For the well-being of their soul they must guard against ever making their confession into a work of piety. If they do so, it will become the worst, most abominable, unholy, and unchaste betrayal of the heart. Confession then becomes sensual prattle. Confession understood as a pious work is the devil's idea. We can dare to enter the abyss of confession only on the basis of God's offer of grace, help, and forgiveness; only for the sake of the promise of absolution can we confess. Confession as a work is spiritual death; confession in answer to God's promise is life. The forgiveness of sins is alone the ground and goal of confession. (*Life Together*, 116)

Index